Timber Decay in Buildings

Timber Decay in Buildings

The conservation approach to treatment

Brian Ridout

ENGLISH HERITAGE

HISTORIC SCOTLAND

London and New York

First published 2000
by E & FN Spon, an imprint of Routledge
11 New Fetter Lane, London EC4P 4EE

Simultaneously published in the USA and Canada
by Routledge
29 West 35th Street, New York, NY 10001

Commissioning Editors: John Fidler (English Heritage), Ingval Maxwell
(Historic Scotland); Consultant Editor: Kit Wedd

Typeset in Plantin by Keystroke, Jacaranda Lodge, Wolverhampton
Printed and bound in Great Britain by St Edmundsbury Press, Bury St Edmunds, Suffolk

British Library Cataloguing in Publication Data
A catalogue record for this book is available from the British Library

Library of Congress Cataloguing in Publication Data
Ridout, Brian, 1946–
    Timber decay in buildings: the conservation approach to treatment
  / Brian Ridout.
        p.   cm.
    Includes bibliographical references and index.
    1. Wood-Deterioration. 2. Wooden-frame buildings—Conservation
  and restoration. I. Title.
  TA422.R54   1999
  691¢1—dc21   99–20873
                                                          CIP

ISBN 0–419–18820–7

Contents

CONTENTS

CONTENTS

Foreword

Study of the historical development of conservation shows that, in terms of ethics and practice, we are becoming much more sensitive and refined in our approaches to the treatment of timber decay in historic buildings. There are analogies with medicine here.

At the turn of the nineteenth century, many illnesses were poorly understood and injured limbs were simply cut off to prevent infection. If diseases spread, noxious potions were used in vast quantities – some so strong as to cause further injuries as part of the 'cure'. Today, non-invasive diagnostic technology, keyhole surgery and therapeutic medicines are available, which target diseases without excessive collateral damage. And the emphasis is moving still further towards preventative medicine – healthy living engendered by hygiene, diet and exercise.

Until fairly recently, specifiers, contractors and specialists from the wood preservation industry had a similarly simplistic and damaging approach to the treatment of insect and fungal infestations in older property. Perfectly healthy decorative plasterwork was damaged in vain hunts for the dreaded dry rot. Viable roofing timbers were cut out and destroyed for fear of death watch beetle. Masonry walls were pockmarked with bore holes for injecting fungicides and insecticides, sometimes applied in such high concentrations that blistering and exfoliation occurred due to the mobilization and crystallization of salts. In many cases, costly and time-consuming treatments were deployed where historic outbreaks of decay posed no further threat. Prime examples of our built heritage were being disfigured and dismembered in the name of conservation.

Times are changing. This book, prepared for English Heritage and Historic Scotland by Dr Brian Ridout, describes the development of a true conservation-based approach to timber decay in historic buildings. It is the long-awaited product of many years of consulting and research for both organizations and the first joint publication from the United Kingdom's leading heritage bodies.

Dr Ridout has pioneered, along with an international consortium of researchers led by English Heritage in the European Commission-sponsored Woodcare project, the more refined concept, principles and practice of integrated pest management for controlling death watch beetle. He has also, along with one or two other private consulting mycologists in the field, been at the forefront of reintroducing the concept of what we now call the environmental control of timber decay.

The scientific background and practical applications of environmental control are described here. This straightforward approach, as applied in the field, leads to less physical disruption during remedial works, more targeted and therefore restricted use of potentially hazardous materials, and better risk management (based on preventative maintenance and cyclical monitoring rather than simplistic treatment guarantees). More historic fabric should thereby be saved from destruction so that more of the physical, archaeological and architectural integrity of the original building is preserved. The quality and standards of conservation practice in our respective countries should be raised by the adoption of this approach to timber decay treatment.

Complementary publications in English Heritage's Practical Building Conservation, Research Transactions and Technical Advice Notes series, and among current and future publications in Historic Scotland's Technical Advice Notes series, give appropriate guidance and comprehensive advice on non-destructive diagnostics or on structural carpentry and other engineering repairs to historic timberwork damaged by fungus and insects.

Happily, the trade association for, and the most responsible members of, the remedial treatment and wood preservation industries are already moving towards the adoption of many of Dr Ridout's most important recommendations. Those charged with the ownership, maintenance, repair and planning control of statutorily listed buildings of special architectural or historic interest and the rest of the United Kingdom's construction sector should also pay heed to the sound technical advice provided here by an acknowledged expert in the field. The information provided in this book is the foundation on which the technical policies of both English Heritage and of Historic Scotland are built.

John Fidler RIBA IHBC FRSA
Head of Building Conservation and Research
English Heritage

Ingval Maxwell DA (Dun) FRIAS RIBA FSA Scot.
Director of Technical Conservation, Research and Education
Historic Scotland

Preface

The remedial treatment of timber decay in British buildings with chemical formulations is predominantly a recent activity. In earlier times, if any action at all was deemed necessary, infected or infested timber was cut out and replaced. Then, in 1914, death watch beetle damage was found in the medieval roof of Westminster Hall in London. A method of destroying the beetles was sought: if their activity could be stopped, then more of the timbers could be retained. The lethal formulation devised for use in Westminster Hall, and subsequent variations on the same recipe, were marketed as a new method of eradicating death watch beetle and furniture beetle, and remained in widespread use until contact insecticides became commercially available.

There would have been but a small market for wood-boring beetle treatments if the quality of available softwoods had not deteriorated and there had not been two World Wars. The combination of inferior construction materials and wartime neglect created conditions in which decay organisms could flourish, and formulations for the *in situ* treatment of fungi were added to the treatment repertoire. The development of a remedial industry that not only supplied biocides, but also the technicians and equipment to apply them, was the inevitable result.

The 1950s and 60s witnessed huge expansion of the timber treatment industry, but at the close of the twentieth century, awareness of environmental issues challenged our faith in the power of technology to solve all problems. Many people now consider the methods and treatments evolved by the remedial industry unnecessary, and find the destruction of original fabric, use of hazardous chemicals and cost unjustifiable. The result is confusion: one eminent timber decay consultant informs me that 'dry rot treatment only fails if it has not been thorough enough', whereas another believes that dry rot treatment is never necessary and that the fungus can be treated by drying the building alone. Defenders of the remedial industry argue that it has done much to save the nation's heritage of historic buildings, while its detractors claim that it is a clan of charlatans preying on the unwary and misinformed. The truth, as usual, lies somewhere in between the two views.

The epithet 'preservative', although doubtless a powerful marketing device, is an unfortunate generic name to apply to biocides for use on timber, because it implies that decay will inevitably occur unless the timber is given some form of treatment. Yet timber is easily preserved by a dry environment, as a visit to any major museum collection of furniture or woodwork will confirm. This dry environment need not be a desert; a well-maintained building will suffice. But the term 'preservative' is persuasive, and timber treatment has become so integrated into the concept of conservation that those who advocate the environmental control of timber decay (see Chapter 14) now appear to be taking an entirely new approach. In fact, the first book on the environmental control of dry rot was written in the eighteenth century (Johnson, 1795).

The problem with environmental control alone, however, is that the building fabric must be dried before decay will cease, and this may present considerable difficulties. In some building environments it may be difficult to achieve timber moisture contents that are too low for wood-boring beetles. Appropriate biocide treatment may therefore be necessary in order to stabilize the decay or infestation. Timber durability is also an important consideration, because organisms which require biocides to control their proliferation in modern softwoods may struggle to damage the mature heartwood of historical timbers.

The environmental approach to timber decay is also hampered by the guarantee, a sales gimmick of the 1950s and 60s, which has become a desirable commodity in itself. At a recent site meeting the question arose of a guarantee for biocide treatment of an eighteenth-century roof in which there were no signs of decay or infestation. The area manager of a treatment company agreed that no treatment was necessary, but the client's agent required a guarantee. If one company would not spray the timber, then the agent would find another company that would, because he wanted a document to say that the roof had been treated. He had no interest in evaluating the chances of decay or defining what the roof was to be treated against. Current legislation requires that these precautionary treatments be justified, and how likely is it that eighteenth-century pine will suddenly become vulnerable to beetle attack, or that a spray coat of biocide will protect against decay if there is water penetration at some future date?

Honest justification of treatments and intervention will reduce the loss of original material and protect the environment from the unnecessary use of biocides. Honest justification of treatment, however, requires a great deal of basic knowledge. Much has already been achieved. The excellent publications of the Building Research Establishment provide guidance on the identification and treatment of decay organisms, and stress caution against unnecessary treatments. The British Wood Preserving and Damp Proofing Association keeps its members informed on relevant topics and promotes appropriate qualifications. There remains, however, a great deal of information that has not been readily available.

The desire to share and interpret that information is the reason for writing this book. The text is an attempt to draw together disparate threads of knowledge from diverse relevant areas, and thus to synthesize a holistic approach to timber decay in historic buildings. The scope of the book is ambitious; many topics merit whole books to themselves, but cannot be explored as fully as they deserve without making the whole task impracticable. Other subjects have already been exhaustively described by better authors; thus there is very little on architectural or building history, or on carpentry and other timber repair systems in the text. I have felt justified in providing more information where it is required for a full understanding of my argument – an account of the history of dry rot treatments is provided, for example, because experience suggests that it is difficult to counter misconceived ideas and prejudices unless it is explained how they have developed.

Thanks are owed to many people for their help. The following people read the manuscript and made helpful comments: Dr Dorothy Bell, Dr Walter Blaney, Mike Bromley of the BWPDA, Dr John Palfreyman at the University of Abertay Dundee, and Arnold Root. Individual chapters were checked by Richard Harris of the Weald and Downland Museum and by Gillian Smith and her colleagues at the Health and Safety Executive. I would also like to thank the BWPDA for permission to quote various extracts from their publications, including their guide to CDM Regulations; James Simpson for permission to quote the letter in Section 14.3; Dr D. Bebbington for permission to quote the formula given in Section 4.4.3; and Chris Cullen, Emma Clarke and Karen Holyoake for drawing the figures.

I am particularly grateful to John Fidler of English Heritage and Ingval Maxwell of Historic Scotland for commissioning this book as a joint undertaking between their respective organizations, to Chris Wood of English Heritage for co-ordinating the project, and to my editor, Kit Wedd. Finally, I would like to thank my wife Elizabeth for her patience and encouragement during the years this book has taken to compile, and for many important amendments to the manuscript.

Brian Ridout
1999

Illustration acknowledgements

We would like to thank the following individuals for permission to reproduce illustration:

Dr Maurice Anderson, School of Biological Sciences, University of Birmingham: 4.1, 4.2, 4.4, 4.6, 5.2, 6.2, 6.3, 6.4, 6.5, 6.7, 14.2, 14.4

Dr Stephen Belmain, Natural Resources Institute, University of Greenwich: 1.10, 4.9, 4.10, 5.5, 14.3

Greg Hastings, Office of Public Works, Dublin: Colour Plate 12

Country Life: B.1

John Bustin, 1 Philips Close, Headley, Hants: Colour Plate 1, Colour Plate 2

Neil Greave, Duncan of Jordanston College of Art, Dundee: B.14

John Fletcher, 24 Pelham Road, Cowes, Isle of Wight: 1.6, 1.7, 1.8, 3.3, 3.4, 3.6, 3.7, 3.8, 3.9, 4.17, 5.4, 7.3, 7.4, 8.2, 8.4, 8.5, 8.6, 8.7, 10.1, 11.1, 11.2, 11.3, 11.4, 11.5, 11.6, 11.15, 11.17, 11.19, 11.20

David Pinniger, 83 Westwood Green, Cookham, Berks: 5.1

Christine Cullen, 58 Hawkesworth Road, Bagshot, Surrey: 1.4, 1.5, 1.9, 3.2, 4.13, 8.1, 11.13, 11.14, 14.5, B.6, B.11, B.12, B.13

Emma Clarke, Ridout Associates, Hagley, West Midlands: 1.3, 6.1, 11.11

Karen Holyoake, Ridout Associates, Hagley, West Midlands: 1.11, 3.1

PART ONE

Nature of Wood

CHAPTER ONE

Origins and durability of building timber

1.1 Introduction

If I discover a few beetle emergence holes in the rafters of my roof, then I have 'woodworm' damage in my house. But what are the implications? The beetle grubs (larvae) eat wood, and the roof is mostly wood. Will the beetles spread until all the timbers have been destroyed? The answer to this question is usually no, but if we are to understand why, we must unravel the story of how wood is constructed, and how the woody material is organized to form a tree.

If we do this then we will find that wood is not the uniform material it appears to be. A plank of European redwood, for example, will contain a variety of substances distributed in a variety of microscopic cells. It is these variations that initially define the potential damage that decay organisms could cause, and thus give the wood whatever natural durability it might possess.

1.2 Structural polymers

The natural durability of building timber is determined by the properties and age of the tree from which it originally came. Healthy trees are living structures in harmony with their environment, and every element of that harmony, whether structural or chemical, affects the quality and durability of the converted timber.

A tree, like all living plant material, is largely a factory for the production of structural and consumable sugars. The bulk of the tree ultimately derives from the reaction of carbon dioxide in the air with water from the air and soil to produce sugar (carbohydrate). This process is fuelled by the radiant energy in sunlight together with agents in the plant that capture light energy, and is called photosynthesis. The sugar-producing reactions may be summarized by the simple equation:

carbon dioxide + water = carbohydrate + water + oxygen

Glucose, a simple sugar, is a the end product, as shown in Figure 1.1. This interesting molecule forms the basic building block for a variety of useful substances. If glucose molecules are assembled all in the same plane, starch is produced:

glucose + glucose + glucose + glucose = starch

Starch is readily broken down again for energy, and forms an easily consumable storage product for plants. If glucose molecules are assembled so that alternate units are inverted, cellulose is formed:

glucose + ǝsoɔnlɓ + glucose + ǝsoɔnlɓ = cellulose

Although constructed from precisely the same molecules as starch, cellulose has entirely different properties. It is very stable and forms straight chains which average between 8000 and 10 000 glucose molecules in length (Siau, 1995). Cellulose

STRUCTURAL POLYMERS

The production of sugars from air, water and sunlight is called photosynthesis:

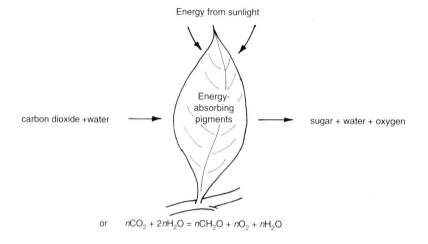

Energy from sunlight

Energy-absorbing pigments

carbon dioxide + water ⟶   ⟶ sugar + water + oxygen

or $nCO_2 + 2nH_2O = nCH_2O + nO_2 + nH_2O$

The end product, nCH_2O, is usually given as glucose, which is a simple sugar with the structural formula

Glucose

Glucose molecules join together to form polymers.
If all molecules are the same way up then starch is produced:

Starch

If alternate molecules are inverted then cellulose is produced:

Cellulose

Figure 1.1 The production of sugars as building blocks, and the construction of starch and cellulose.

forms about 40–50% of wood and is largely responsible for the strength within the cell wall (Goring and Timell, 1962).

Once the plant has managed to incorporate carbon from the atmosphere then the formation of a wide range of sugars (carbohydrates) and other organic products becomes possible. A second structural polymer, hemicellulose, which differs somewhat between hardwoods and softwoods, is also formed from sugars. The molecular chains of hemicellulose are shorter than those of cellulose, and are frequently branched. Hemicellulose, which commonly forms about 20–30% of softwoods and 25–40% of hardwoods, is responsible for elasticity (Siau, 1984).

Sugars also start the formation of an immensely complex series of molecules known as lignin. Lignin, which is very stable and crucial to durability, is the third structural component in wood. Fengel and Wegener (1989) believe that it was the incorporation of lignin into and around cell walls that gave plants the mechanical strength to colonize the earth's surface. Hardwoods tend to have less lignin (20–25%) than softwoods (25–30%); (Siau, 1995).

Lignin is constructed from different combinations of three phenolic molecules (Figure 1.2) which occur in different proportions in hardwoods and softwoods (Adler, 1977). Their relative proportions affect the properties of the lignin, and in general lignins from hardwoods are weaker and more easily degraded than those from softwoods. This feature, as will be discussed later, influences timber's vulnerability to different kinds of fungi.

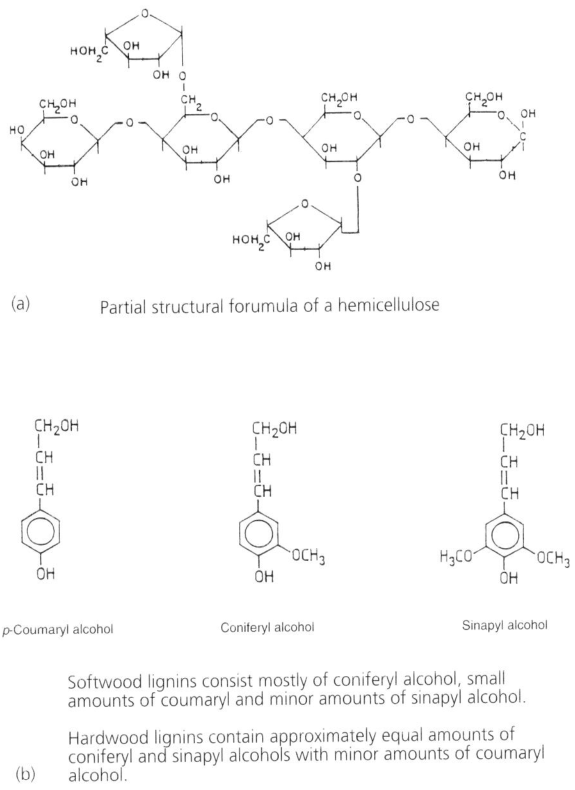

1.3 Cell wall

We have seen that wood is mainly composed of three complex molecules: cellulose, hemicellulose and lignin. These three components together form the wall of the cell, the fundamental unit of the tree. It is the arrangement and orientation of these three components that give wood the ability to support tall trees.

The basic cellulose component of a cell wall at the molecular level is usually called a microfibril,

(a)   Partial structural forumula of a hemicellulose

p-Coumaryl alcohol   Coniferyl alcohol   Sinapyl alcohol

Softwood lignins consist mostly of coniferyl alcohol, small amounts of coumaryl and minor amounts of sinapyl alcohol.

Hardwood lignins contain approximately equal amounts of coniferyl and sinapyl alcohols with minor amounts of coumaryl alcohol.

(b)

Figure 1.2 (a) Mixed sugars produce branched chain polymers called hemicelluloses. (b) Photosynthesis also commences the production of three phenoliz building blocks that form complex polymers called lignin.

although smaller, elementary fibrils have been described (Mühlethaler, 1960). Microfibrils are about 10–30 nm in diameter (1 nm = 1 nanometre = one millionth of a millimetre). Each consists of bundles of cellulose chains arranged at various angles along the long axis of the microfibril. Some regions of the microfibril are known to be crystalline, and some amorphous, but there is no generally accepted theory regarding internal molecular organization. It is usually considered that the hemicellulose encrusts the cellulose microfibrils (Tsoumis, 1991), but no doubt the exact arrangements will prove to be variable and complex when they are finally unravelled.

The generalized manner in which the three complex structural substances are arranged to

5

construct the cells has a significant bearing on decay. Each decay organism attacks celluloses and lignin in its own way, and the final results of decay will depend on the way in which the cell structure is organized.

An array of powerful modern laboratory techniques has allowed this organization to be assessed. The cell wall, which is largely composed of cellulose microfibrils, is constructed from two, or sometimes three, distinct layers (Figure 1.3): the outside or primary wall, the secondary wall and sometimes an innermost tertiary wall or wart layer, which is next to the lumen or hollow interior of the cell. The thickness and arrangement of these layers has been investigated in several coniferous woods (Saiki, 1970).

Primary wall (P)
A very thin wall constructed from a loose weave of microfibrils with limited organized orientation.

This is the first wall produced, and its organization controls the expansion of the juvenile cell. It is bounded on its outer side by the middle lamella, a lignin-rich matrix between the cells.

Secondary wall (S)
This layer forms the bulk of the cell wall, and close investigation reveals two to three groups of laminations that differ in the orientation of their closely packed microfibrils.

S1 layer
This thin layer is usually indistinguishable under a microscope from the primary wall, with which it is closely associated. It consists of 4–6 laminations (lamellae), each of which possesses an alternating left-hand and right-hand spiral arrangement of microfibrils across the transverse axis of the cell. The result produces a crossed texture. This layer usually becomes encrusted with lignin.

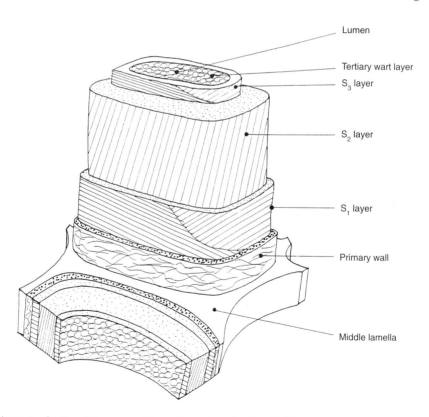

Lumen

Tertiary wart layer

S_3 layer

S_2 layer

S_1 layer

Primary wall

Middle lamella

Figure 1.3 Diagram of cell-wall layers and the orientation of microfibrils.

S2 layer

The S2 layer is the thickest within the cell wall, and may consist of 30–150 lamellae. Microfibrils are densely packed and run approximately parallel to the cell axis in mature wood.

S3 layer

Usually thinner than the S1 layer and frequently absent altogether, this layer consists of about six lamellae with microfibrils alternating in their direction of orientation, which mostly approaches the transverse axis of the cell.

Tertiary/wart layer

Microfibrils are arranged in a gentle slope as in S1 and S3, but the microfibrils are not strictly parallel. The interior surface of this wall becomes covered with warts in many types of timber. Warts are mostly formed from lignin.

Between the cells lies a layer of material called the middle lamella (Figure 1.3). Analysis has shown that it is composed mostly of lignin.

A considerable proportion of the lignin in wood therefore forms a matrix between the cells, whereas most of the cellulose is within the thick secondary walls. Hemicellulose encrusts the microfibrils, and tends to replace cellulose in the thinner walls. The proportions of the three structural polymers in each element of the cell wall will vary considerably from tree to tree, across the thickness of the tree, and in earlywood and latewood.

The strength of timber is a function of all three components, but cellulose mostly confers strength in axial tension because of the orientation of microfibrils in the thick S2 layer, whereas the other layers, hemicellulose and lignin provide elasticity and strength in compression.

The arrangement of microfibrils within the secondary wall layers also affects the swelling properties of wet timber. The predominance of microfibrils oriented parallel to the long axis in the S2 layer restricts longitudinal swelling in mature wood, whereas transverse dimensional change, though substantially greater than longitudinal, is ultimately restrained by the transverse orientation of microfibrils in the S1, S3 and tertiary layers. These relationships are discussed further in Section 2.1 and Chapter 11.

Trees react to strain forces acting on stems, boughs and branches by forming reaction wood in the zones of compression or tension. These tissues differ chemically, physically and anatomically from each other, and from normal wood. Reaction wood forms only a small fraction of building timbers and will not be discussed further here.

1.4 Structure of wood

We have now seen how water and carbon dioxide react, using the energy from sunlight and energy-capturing molecules within the tree to form simple sugars, the building blocks that are assembled and modified to form the three structural polymers (cellulose, hemicellulose and lignin) which together constitute 97–99% of temperate zone woods and about 90% of tropical woods. The remaining few per cent are a wide variety of substances known collectively as extractives. These are of considerable significance and will be discussed further in Sections 1.5.2. and 11.12.

The three structural polymers are not randomly deployed, but are assembled into cells in a manner that maximizes tensile and compression strength for the tree, and restrains excessive swelling as a consequence of water absorption. Strength and the efficient conduction of liquids are of paramount importance in the organization of cells into a large and vigorously growing tree.

The tree must support its own weight, withstand adverse conditions, and convey water and nutrients to the highest branches. These exacting requirements cannot be satisfied at cell level alone, and specialized structures within the wood are required in order to maximize efficiency.

1.4.1 Softwoods and hardwoods

The terms 'softwood' and 'hardwood' are used extensively within the timber trade, and frequently lead to confusion. Softwood refers to the conifers, the needle-leafed or cone-bearing trees (for example pine and cedar), some of which provide quite hard timber. Hardwood is used to describe timber from the so-called broad-leafed trees (for example oak and mahogany) and includes species whose wood is in fact very soft. Nonetheless, the distinction between softwood from cone-bearing trees and hardwood from broad-leafed trees remains extremely useful.

The softwood trees are botanically known as gymnosperms (from the Greek: naked-seeded) because the seeds develop exposed on the surface of a cone scale. The gymnosperms living today are the representatives of a group that extends back in time for more than 300 million years (Sporne, 1965). Modern softwood trees are mostly restricted to regions where the climate is harsh and the soil is poor in nutrients. Their ability to survive in these areas derives to a large extent from an ability to restrict water loss, by the possession of a water-conducting system controlled by valves, and by narrow waxy needles that restrict vapour loss.

The hardwood trees are known botanically as angiosperms, or hidden-seeded plants, because the seeds develop enclosed in an ovary which eventually becomes a seed capsule. They are a more recent addition to the flora, and do not appear in the fossil record until about 100 million years ago (Sporne, 1974). The majority of the hardwoods have broad leaves to maximize light absorption, and an open water conducting system. They tend to favour environments where conditions are suitable for prolonged vigorous growth, although many are able to tolerate poor soils and harsh weather.

These differences in efficiency of water transportation and habitat have a considerable effect on the structure of their timbers.

1.4.2 Structure of softwoods

Softwoods have a uniform structure (Figure 1.4). About 90–95% of the wood consists of slender cells orientated along the stem axis with closed flattened or tapered ends. These cells, known as tracheids, average about 3–5 mm in length and 0.02–0.04 mm in diameter. Tracheids are the only cells that can supply most of the necessary strength to the tree while allowing water (sap) conduction. Strength is supplied by seasonal thickening of the cell wall (Section 1.5) and, in Douglas fir, yew and

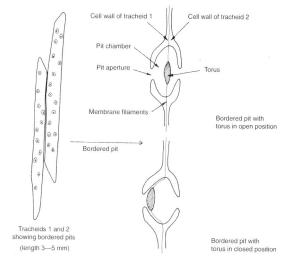

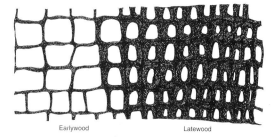

Tracheids produced in the spring have thin walls and a wide lumen to maximize water conduction. Those produced during the second half of the year have thick walls and narrow lumens to maximize strength.

Figure 1.4 Tracheids and the softwood water conducting system.

sometimes spruce, by spiral thickenings of the S3 layer (Jane, 1970).

Water conduction is possible because of apertures in the cell walls called pits (Figure 1.4), which form passages of communication between the cells. Typically, softwood pits, known as bordered pits, are formed from two apertures in adjacent cell walls (Panshin and DeZeew, 1980). These apertures together form a chamber with rather narrower entrances in the walls between the cells. The middle lamella between the two cells and the two primary membranes remains, forming a circular valve structure known as a torus. Surrounding the torus is a suspensory mechanism of radial filaments known as the margo. This type of pit is capable of closure if the cells start to dry out because the torus moves from its central position to block one or other of the chamber entrances. The irreversible closure of the valves when the cells dry makes some types of wood, for example spruce, very difficult to impregnate with preservatives (Liese and Bauch, 1967).

The majority of living material in the wood of both hardwoods and softwoods is organized into rays, consisting of narrow ribbons of cells with cellulose walls, which penetrate radially from the surface through the sapwood. Above and below these cells in some softwoods are small oblong ray tracheids. Ray tissue and some longitudinally orientated tissue (ray and axial parenchyma) function as a store – primarily for starch – and for the lateral conduction of water. Communication between rays and tracheids is via simple apertures (pits) without valves.

1.4.3 Structure of hardwoods

Hardwoods exhibit a more complex structure (Figure 1.5), and the functions of strength and water conduction are largely undertaken by different types of cells.

Strength appears to be mainly supplied by long narrow cells with closed pointed ends called fibres. These fibres average about 1.2 mm long and 0.01–0.05 mm in diameter (Tsoumis, 1991).

Water (sap) movement probably takes place to a limited extent in fibres and is the main function of hardwood tracheids (the latter are rather different from softwood tracheids), but most of the water transport is carried out in a direct fashion by elongate units known as vessels (Panshin and DeZeew, 1980). Vessels are constructed from individual cells joined end-to-end over a considerable distance. End walls disappear to a greater or lesser extent and may form a perforation or sieve plate. This water transportation system is far more direct than the tracheid system of the softwoods. Bordered pits occur in the vessel walls, but these do not possess the torus that is characteristic of most softwoods.

Ray cells form a far greater proportion of hardwoods, amounting to perhaps 30% of the volume. Wide bands of cells produce conspicuous rays in some types of wood. Ray tissue in hard-

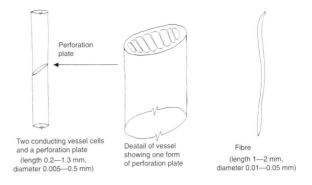

Two conducting vessel cells and a perforation plate (length 0.2—1.3 mm, diameter 0.005—0.5 mm)

Deatail of vessel showing one form of perforation plate

Fibre (length 1—2 mm, diameter 0.01—0.05 mm)

Liquid conduction and strength are mainly achieved by two different cell types in hardwoods

Earlywood   Latewood   Earlywood

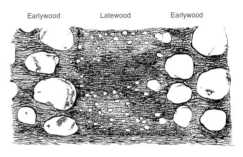

Some hardwoods, including oak and elm, increase moisture conduction in earlywood by the production of large vessels. Latewood vessels are small and fibres are numerous to increase strength.

Figure 1.5 Fibres, vessels and the hardwood water-conducting system.

woods, unlike some softwood ray tissue, is not associated with ray tracheids. Other groups of living cells in hardwoods are found as columns or aggregations of parenchyma.

One last, important feature found in both softwoods and tropical hardwoods cannot really be classed as a structure. Resin/gum canals are tubular cavities that produce resin in softwoods (Section 1.5.2) and gums in some tropical hardwoods. They are lined with secreting cells.

1.5 Functional tree: differences between softwood and hardwood species

At the molecular level, softwood trees and hardwood trees are similar, even though the exact make-up of the lignin and hemicellulose components may differ. At the structural level, however, there are differences that relate to environment and growth form. Softwood trees have leaves and wood structure that reduce water loss in harsh environments (Rundel and Yoder, 1998). But these environments, particularly the colder environments, impose restraints on form. Damage from high winds and snowfall is easier to avoid if the tree has a straight trunk and an open-branched structure (Figure 1.6): wind resistance is reduced and snow falls off as the branches bend down under its weight. The tree can maintain sufficient growth by maximizing conduction within the tracheids during the early vigorous growing season, when the tracheid walls are thin (earlywood cells), and maximizing strength by thickening the tracheid walls during the latter part of the year (latewood cells). The two types of tissue together produce a more or less distinctive annual ring. Storage requirements are low because the tree can maintain a longer growing period by minimizing water loss, and the soil is of poor quality. The ray tissue is therefore very narrow.

Hardwood trees have a rather different lifestyle. They favour milder climates where water and nutrients are more plentiful. These conditions mean that the tree can sustain a bulky growth form if competition will allow, producing a wide crown of leaves for photosynthesis. If growth is affected by direct competition from other trees, as in an oak woodland, then long straight trunks will be produced, pushing the leafy head towards the light (Figure 1.7). In contrast, parkland growth allows plenty of space, and produces oaks with a lower and more spreading form because light is readily available (Figure 1.8). In economic terms, the forest growth produces a greater volume of better quality timber. Modern forestry techniques aim to maximize growth by giving space, while providing enough competition to maintain quality. A thicker stem and wider crown require stronger wood, and the larger species tend to have denser timber and a high volume of structural fibres.

Tree roots cannot function at soil temperatures below 4°C so water vapour lost from the leaves during cold periods cannot be replaced from the

Figure 1.6 Pine trees grow long straight trunks and 'self-prune' their lower branches.

soil. Hardwood trees, with thin-cuticled broad leaves that maximize photosynthesis, must either drop their leaves when the ground is cold, and become dormant, or risk desiccation and the loss of leaves (and the nutrients they contain) as a result of frost damage. If leaf fall is part of the tree's natural strategy then nutrients can be withdrawn, and the leaf sealed from the stem. The leaf then dies, changes colour, and falls off. Loss of leaves in winter also reduces wind resistance and snow deposition, thus reducing mechanical stress to the tree during adverse weather.

Substantial storage facilities are required, and many hardwood trees have wide rays which add considerably to the decorative qualities of timber

10

Figure 1.7 Plantation oaks grow tall as they compete for light with their neighbours.

Figure 1.8 A park oak, growing without competition from other trees, develops a low trunk and a wide crown.

such as oak by producing a patterned grain. When the favourable season returns the stored material must be rapidly mobilized and photosynthesis maximized. This is aided by an open and direct water-conducting system.

The woody tissue, which contains storage products in living cells and is capable of conducting liquids, is called sapwood (Figure 1.9). Sapwood is produced by a narrow band of cells called the cambium, which in temperate trees is only active during the spring and summer months. The inner half of the cambium produces sapwood cells, whereas the outer half produces phloem or inner bark cells. Phloem is responsible for the conduction of sugars and the metabolites around the tree. Inner bark cells die and increase the outer bark in a manner analogous to heartwood formation. The bark protects the tree, and is gradually shed as excess is formed.

Wood cells in the inner margin of the sapwood eventually die from oxygen depletion as the trunk diameter increases. Death of the ray cells is accompanied by the total metabolization of stored food reserves (notably starch), by pit aspiration (closure) and by the deposition of lignin in the cell

membranes. These processes take place abruptly or in a transition zone that forms the inner margin of the sapwood. Sometimes outgrowths from the ray cells grow through the pits in their walls to form foam-like structures called tyloses, as found in oak (Figure 1.10). These, together with deposited fungicidal products, block the adjoining vessels and are useful to the tree in that they will restrict the spread of fungal decay (Chattaway, 1949). This physiologically inactive tissue is called heartwood, and it forms an increasing percentage of the tree's bulk as the trunk expands. Sometimes the heartwood is differentiated from the sapwood by colour due to the extractives it contains. In many types of low-durability timber, however, the two types of tissue are indistinguishable.

The start of heartwood production varies. In European redwood in southern Norway it has been shown to commence around the pith after 20 years (Uusvaara, 1974) but the starting point apparently depends upon latitude. Bruun and Wilberg (1964) demonstrated heartwood production after 30–40 years in Finnish redwood, whereas Hägglund (1935) showed that it commenced after about 25 years in southern Sweden and 70 years in northern Sweden.

Living trees are vulnerable to infection and destruction by pathogenic fungi if the latter can breach the tree's natural defences. These pathogenic fungi cause disease in living trees and may be contrasted with the different assemblages of fungi that attack dead timber and are classed as saprophytes. It is the saprophytes that mostly concern us in our work on building timbers, but the pathogens are of interest because they complete the picture of the living tree, and because some forms of pathogenic brown rot decay may continue for a limited period after the timber has been converted. Oak beams cut from trees containing pathogenic heart rots may be hollowed before the beam eventually dries, and this form of decay greatly facilitates death watch beetle attack (Chapter 4).

The woody tissue of the tree is protected from attack by the living sapwood, which is mostly too wet to be susceptible to colonization by pathogens (Hudson, 1986), and is also able to respond in a variety of ways to infection. Sap rots do sometimes

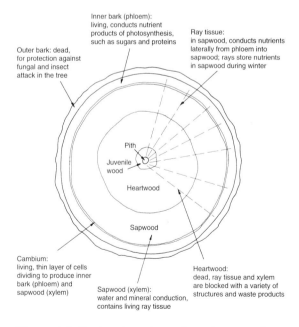

Figure 1.9 Section through a softwood tree trunk.

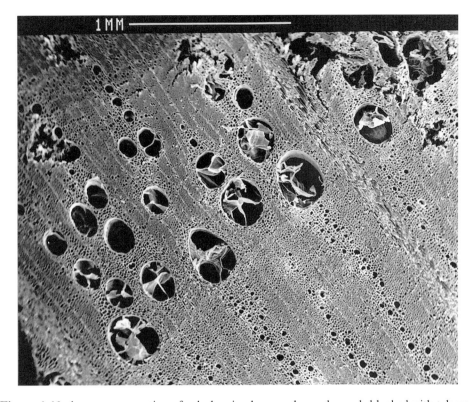

Figure 1.10 A transverse section of oak showing large earlywood vessels blocked with tyloses.

occur in living trees if the sapwood is damaged, but the decay is usually localized.

If a wound occurs in the sapwood zone of a living tree then the tissue can respond by compartmentalizing the damage and any consequent infection (Shigo, 1983). The wound is healed by the stimulation of growth hormone production, which in turn stimulates the production of callus tissue over the surface. Damaged and diseased sapwood is isolated by the production and deposition of tyloses, gums, resins and other toxic materials in wall-like zones which box in the injury (Shain, 1979). If the wound penetrates to the inert heartwood, then the barrier will be incomplete and decay may occur.

It is the dead heartwood in the living tree which is vulnerable to a greater or lesser degree, depending on its natural durability. This difference in durability between the sapwood and heartwood is, as described presently, reversed when the tree dies.

Most fungi appear to enter the heartwood zone via small dead branches, sapwood wounds, broken tops and roots. Decay may be categorized as a butt rot if it is at the base of the tree, or a heart rot if it is further up the stem.

The molecular and structural organization of wood is not the only influence on durability. Age and extractives also have a bearing on durability and resistance to decay.

1.5.1 Juvenile or core wood

The centre of a young tree consists of unspecialized, thin-walled cells (parenchyma) and is known as pith. The first few growth rings nearest to the pith in any tree comprise the juvenile core, which starts as juvenile sapwood and becomes juvenile heartwood (Krahmer, 1986). The cells of this juvenile wood are usually rather shorter than those of mature wood and contain less cellulose.

The microfibrils in the S2 layer are less crystalline and at a greater angle to the longitudinal axis (Figure 1.11). These differences are usually substantially greater in softwoods than in hardwoods. The microfibrils gradually straighten as successive years produce longer cells. Juvenile timber is therefore weaker than mature wood of the same density, and may break under load with a brash type of tension failure (Krahmer, 1986). It is also more susceptible to longitudinal shrinkage (Harris and Meylan, 1965) and will be less resistant to decay. This is because the concentration of extractives

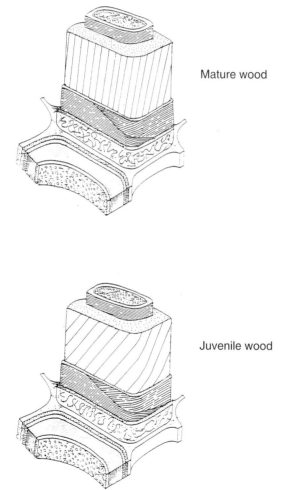

Mature wood

Juvenile wood

Figure 1.11 Angle of cellulose fibres in wood cell walls.

(Section 1.5.2) that have biocidal properties is substantially lower in the core than in the mature heartwood (see Section 11.12).

1.5.2 Mature wood

The period of juvenile growth varies in length and the density/strength of the timber increases away from the centre. Eventually, the cells reach a maximum length with nearly vertical microfibrils in the S2 layer, and the tree may be considered to be mature. At about this time (usually about 10–20 growth rings from the centre) the cycle of earlywood and latewood is fully established in those species where this occurs (Krahmer, 1986). Earlywood in softwoods, as discussed in Section 1.4.2, is constructed from thin-walled conducting tracheids to maximize water transport, whereas latewood consists of thick-walled tracheids to maximize strength. Raczkowski (1963) has shown that the latewood of Polish-grown Douglas fir is about four times denser than the earlywood, and Tsoumis (1991) quotes densities for redwood of 0.67–0.92 g cm^{-3} for latewood and 0.30–0.34 g cm^{-3} in earlywood.

The variety of metabolic products deposited in the heartwood increases considerably in mature wood, particularly in the resin canals and ray parenchyma cells. These products, which as noted earlier are collectively known as extractives, may alter the colour and significantly increase the natural durability of the wood.

The term 'wood extractive' is used because the majority of these products may be removed from the wood with organic solvents. A wide variety of substances may be involved, depending on the tree species and the geographical site (Simonsen, 1954). Many of the extractives found in wood are collectively classed as resins, a group of substances that together are resistant to crystallization. Resins contain terpenes, lignans, stilbeans, flavonoids and other aromatics together with fats, waxes, fatty acids, alcohols, steroids and higher hydrocarbons. Another grouping of compounds is named after their effects upon the proteins found in hides; these phenolic-based compounds are collectively known as tannins.

The protective properties of extractives may be illustrated by some early work on teak (Rudman and Da Costa, 1959). These researchers found that resistance to two test fungi did not normally begin until between five and ten growth rings from the pith had been formed. In other words, the juvenile wood was susceptible to the fungus although less so than the sapwood, which contained few extractives. The resistance to decay in all the timber was drastically reduced if the extractives were removed by solvent treatment. These extractives were then added to sawdust from mountain ash, and the resistance of that normally susceptible species was found to be significantly enhanced in most of the samples. Variation in extractive content between trees was sometimes considerable and appeared to be genetically, rather than environmentally, controlled.

1.5.3 Over-mature wood

A tree may live for a very long time, but eventually vigorous growth slows and the tree becomes senile. Increase in trunk height ceases first; increase in diameter may continue for many years. Growth rings become narrow, and latewood production declines as lignin production decreases, so that the timber produced is brittle. Accompanying these changes are changes within the heartwood, which progress outwards from the pith. These changes, which frequently include the breakdown of extractives and the formation of minute compression fractures, increase the timber's susceptibility to decay. The centre of the tree is usually invaded by fungi which slowly destroy the core, leaving a hollowed trunk.

CHAPTER TWO

Sorption of water by timber

2.1 Natural hygroscopicity

Timber is a hygroscopic material, which responds to changes in air moisture content. Water molecules become attached by hydrogen bonds to the OH groups of the cell wall components, particularly cellulose (Figure 1.1); (Spalt, 1958). The quantity of water vapour absorbed by a piece of timber will depend to a large extent on the amount of OH groups which are exposed. Access to the groups may be blocked by extractives within the timber (Skaar, 1988), and it has been demonstrated that the removal of these increases hygroscopicity (Wangaard and Granados, 1967). Thus timber with a high extractive content will tend to have a low equilibrium moisture content (see Section 11.4). Water which is held by molecular forces within the wood is called 'bound water'. Adsorption of water vapour onto the cell wall components continues until they can accept no more and this point, which is generally accepted for timber species which concern us to be at a moisture content of 28–30%, is known as 'fibre saturation' (Tiemann, 1906). Fibre saturation point is actually rather variable, and may range over 20–40%, depending on timber species. Once this moisture level is exceeded then 'free water' will commence to fill the cell cavities. Total saturation rarely occurs in most situations because of trapped air bubbles in the cell cavities.

The incorporation of water into the cell wall fills any cell wall cavities that are present and pushes the cellulose microfibrils apart so that dimensional changes occur. These changes will be at right angles to the long axis of the microfibrils and, as these are nearly parallel to the long axis of the tree, longitudinal changes in mature wood will be minimal. Published figures for European softwoods and hardwoods suggest that radial and tangential swellings average 10 and 20 times greater, respectively, than longitudinal swelling. If, however, the microfibrils are less upright, as in juvenile wood, then significant longitudinal swelling may occur (Harris and Meylan, 1965). The difference in swelling between radial and tangential directions (anisotropy) may result in distortion rather than simple expansion and contraction of the cross-sectional area (Barber and Meylan, 1964; Barber, 1968). It is important to remember that swelling occurs within the cell walls and is therefore a consequence of an increase in bound water. Free water within the cell cavities has no further effect, so that neither swelling nor shrinkage occurs above fibre saturation point.

Because shrinkage and swelling are associated with the cell wall, and with exposed OH groups on the cellulose/hemicellulose molecules, timber is rather variable in its response. Hardwoods tend to have higher cellulose and a lower lignin content than softwoods and are therefore more prone to dimensional change. This may be offset in some species of hardwood by a high extractive content which will block water movement (Skaar, 1988), and many tropical hardwoods are therefore dimensionally rather stable.

There is no general agreement as to why

tangential shrinkage should exceed radial, and there are probably several reasons. Two are cited here, from Tsoumis (1991), as examples of how the structural model of wood may be used to explain observed phenomena.

2.1.1 Ray cell orientation

Most of the cellulose microfibrils in mature heartwood are orientated at an angle nearly parallel to the long axis of the cell and thus the perpendicular axis of the tree (see Figure 1.11). Shrinkage and swelling (caused by water molecules between the microfibrils) are therefore minimal in that direction. Cells within ray tissue are, however, set at right angles to the perpendicular (see Figure 1.9). Thus radial sections are also afforded a degree of lateral restraint which tangentially cut samples would not possess.

2.1.2 Latewood/earlywood orientation

Latewood cell walls in soft wood are much thicker than earlywood cell walls and therefore absorb up to about 3.5 times more water. The swelling and contraction of the latewood will tend to be more even in radially cut timber than in tangential because of the orientation of latewood tissue.

Distortion caused by shrinkage and swelling is generally recoverable to a large extent, provided that no plastic deformation of the cell walls has occurred. Permanent distortion may, however, arise if there is lateral restraint, perhaps caused by panel surrounds or floorboard fixings.

The shrinkage of timber from green to air dry was important in traditional timber-framed construction. Joint pegs provide an interesting example. Oak was usually worked more or less green and would therefore shrink. If the joint pegs behaved in a similar fashion then the joints would loosen, but if the pegs were made from dry timber, which would expand as it absorbed moisture, the joints would be tightened.

Dimensional changes which are a response to diurnal or seasonal humidity fluctuations are generally called 'movement', and are of importance in good quality joinery and carpentry. If timber

with a high movement value is used, or timbers with different movement values are mixed, or timber is worked at a substantially higher moisture content than it will achieve in its intended environment, then loose joints and undesirable gaps are likely to occur. Tables that group commercially available timbers by their movement values are published by the Building Research Establishment and other similar organizations. Values are usually quoted for dimensional change from fibre saturation down to 12% moisture content.

Sometimes changes in the building environment make undesirable movement inevitable. This type of damage frequently occurs when central heating is installed in rooms with window linings and dado panelling. Heat from radiators placed in front of the windows may cause localized lowering of humidities to 25–35% and timber moisture contents to 6–8%. The resulting movement of the timber will be readily visible, and is frequently mistaken for decay. If some concealed decay is present, perhaps as a result of water penetration 200 years earlier, substantial buckling and distortion may occur. This is a major reason why active dry rot is sometimes reported from dry buildings after restoration works.

2.2 Age-related changes

Most observations on structure and properties that are recorded are made on good specimens of recently felled timber. There are no reasons, however, to suppose that wood in most practical environments is entirely stable over time. Nilsson and Daniel (1990) have stated that few physical changes are observable in historical timber if it remains dry, but changes in property may be discernible. Figure 2.1 compares surface moisture readings, as taken with resistance type moisture probes, with variations in relative humidity. These data were obtained with a remote sensing system installed in the nave roof of Lincoln Cathedral during 1994. All timbers of different ages respond similarly in this experiment, but the response of the medieval timbers is far more exaggerated.

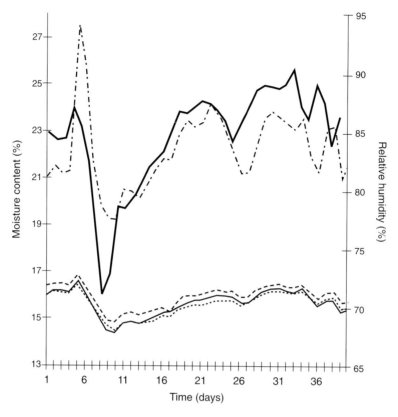

Figure 2.1 Relationship between relative humidity and surface timber moisture contents at 1 cm depth in oak heartwood: (---) new oak; (—) 17C oak; (- - -) 15C oak; (—·—) 13C oak; (—) relative humidity.

This difference in response has been observed in many buildings, but the cause remains unclear and is probably a combination of factors. These will include surface degradation by fungi, photo-degradation of lignin, or perhaps the exposure of more OH groups by the loss of volatile extractives. It is not normally possible to elucidate the history of building timbers over a 600–700-year period. The result is, however, that the equilibrium moisture content at the surface of some ancient oak timbers becomes erratic and may be surprisingly high at elevated humidities.

If the relationships between equilibrium moisture content and relative humidity variation are investigated at a greater depth within the timber (Figure 2.2), the same response is found. It is, however, far more muted. The modern oak used in the Lincoln Cathedral study has a large cross-sectional area, and hence has a high moisture content because it has not become air dry and will not be so for many decades. The other timbers are all grouped together in a moisture content range that approximates to the expected value as calculated from the average ambient humidity. The practical implication of this is that unusually high moisture meter readings in an old roof cannot automatically be taken to mean that there is a damp problem unless these reading are localized. High readings may be due to the age of the timber.

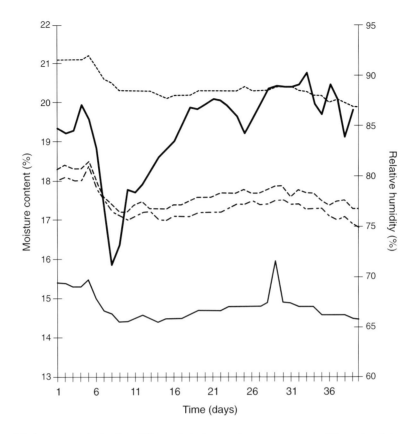

Figure 2.2 Relationship between relative humidity and timber moisture contents at 10 cm depth in oak heartwood:
(----) new oak; (——) 17C oak; (- - -) 15C oak; (—·—) 13C oak; (——) relative humidity.

2.3 Effects of decay on moisture sorption

Decay commences in softwood timber by the breakdown of pit membranes, thus increasing porosity. This process is sometimes encouraged, particularly for species which are difficult to treat with preservatives, by storage in water. Increased porosity can, however, lead to excessive and uneven uptake of preservative, which may cause surface bleeding, and to difficulties with the application of glues and coatings.

Decay by brown and white rot fungi will substantially alter moisture uptake. It will be remembered that water molecules are held by the cellulose/hemicellulose within the timber and that it is these structural polymers that are destroyed by brown rots. Brown rots therefore cause a sharp drop in equilibrium moisture contents, particularly during the early stages of decay.

White rots remove lignin and the proportion of cellulose exposed increases. Timber decayed by white rots therefore tends to have a higher equilibrium moisture content once about 60% weight loss has been exceeded. Moisture meter readings should not normally be taken from decayed sections of timber.

PART TWO

Agents of Decay and Traditional Treatments

CHAPTER THREE

Post-harvest changes and decay

3.1 Effects of moisture content

It has been shown that it is difficult for most decay organisms to exploit the living tree (see Section 1.5). The nutrient-rich sapwood, the most vulnerable part of the actively growing tree, is too wet for colonization by most organisms, and the living tissue can produce growths that check the spread of pathogens. Decay fungi therefore mostly enter via dead or damaged tissue, particularly branch wounds and roots. The fungus still has to overcome the natural resistance of the tree, and also any gums, resins or phenolic compounds produced at the site of wounds, which inhibit spore germination and compartmentalize fungal growth. It is easier for fungi to attack the juvenile wood at the centre, where the concentration of antiseptic extractives and the moisture content are lower. The most common forms of decay in standing trees are therefore butt or heart rots.

Because of its moisture content, sapwood may weigh twice as much when green as it does after oven drying. Heartwood is usually drier in softwoods (and in some hardwoods); in some pines, for example, moisture levels are about 120% of the dry weight in the sapwood and 35% in the heartwood. This situation changes when the tree is felled. The moisture content is slowly reduced as the timber dries, to about 17–20% in the wood yard and perhaps about 15% in a cool building. In a heated building the moisture content may drop to less than 9%. As the water content drops and the air content increases, a variety of changes, including decay, may occur. Decay remains a possibility until the timber moisture content is too low for the relevant organisms to survive.

The progressive moisture loss, from living tree through felled log, conversion and finally incorporation into a building, presents a wide range of conditions which different decay organisms may exploit, although the extractives may remain an insurmountable obstacle in some timber species. Sapwood, which was a resistant material in the living tree, becomes highly susceptible to decay as it dries, because of its elevated nutrient content.

Wood decay fungi and insects vary widely in the moisture contents they can tolerate. Most require relatively high timber moisture levels in order to thrive. Some groups can cope with drier conditions, but as moisture content decreases, so does the variety of decay organisms. Moisture levels below about 18% provide a harsh environment for all except a few specialized insects, which probably derive a proportion of their water requirements from the breakdown of cellulose. In temperate climates, most of these specialists are beetles; in warmer regions termites have a major economic impact. In general, fungi in buildings will not damage timber with a moisture content below about 22%, whereas colonies of most wood-boring beetles will not thrive at moisture levels below about 12%. A few may continue their attack at moisture levels as low as 8%. These differences enable the classification of biological hazards (see Section 3.5).

23

It is important to remember that damp timber provides an environment which will ultimately be colonized and decayed by a succession of organisms. The types of organisms that take part in this progression and the speed of attack depend on parameters which include moisture content, temperature and the different chemicals present in the wood. Preservative treatments may inhibit or destroy some organisms, but preservatives are really only changing the environment, and sooner or later a suitably tolerant sequence of colonizers will reach the damp timber and commence its destruction. These colonizers need not themselves be decay organisms. Benign microfungi, for example, may modify the toxins so that decay fungi may develop. Wood is only immune from decay if it is kept dry.

Decay organisms may be classified by their ability to degrade the components of the timber, and they will range from cell content feeders in sapwood, to those capable of destroying the entire cell wall of sapwood and heartwood.

3.2 Nutrient availability after conversion: the potential for decay

Oak building timbers frequently become more porous as they age, although the effect is not particularly significant until the timbers are many centuries old, and then only at high humidities. Few softwood timbers available for examination are older than about 250 years, and age-related changes in porosity are not apparent. It has been suggested, however, that the composition of amino acids present in softwoods changes during ageing, and Becker (1976) believes that this may be a factor which restricts house longhorn beetle activity to fresh timber (see Section 6.1).

Wood is not an easy food source for decay organisms to exploit. Timber conversion may increase the problem for decay organisms because soluble nutrients tend to be carried to the surface as the timber dries and large amounts of this surface zone are lost when the timber is planed and worked.

Lack of nutrients, together with other factors, which include the preservative action of extractives and acidity, restrict insect damage to the sapwood of most traditional construction timbers. Mature heartwood is only attacked if it has already been modified by fungal decay, or if it was derived from a species of tree in which there are few or no preservative extractives. Heartwood becomes rather more susceptible to attack by many decay fungi if it remains wet enough for long enough. The susceptibility of juvenile timber has not yet been adequately evaluated, but preliminary results suggest that it has a lower resistance than mature heartwood (see Section 11.12).

The breakdown of the structural and storage polymers will produce a carbon source that decay organisms require for growth and respiration. Life cannot, however, exist on carbon alone, and organisms also require nitrogen (in order to form proteins) and a variety of other substances, ranging from trace elements to vitamins. Available nitrogen in wood is found mostly in the form of proteins that participate in the cell wall structure (Fengel and Wegener, 1989). Nitrogen levels are low in timber, and there is considerable variation both between trees (even of the same species) and within trees.

Bletchley and Farmer (1959) provided the figures given in Table 3.1 for total nitrogen content. Figures are expressed as a percentage of the sample dry weight.

In general there is more available nitrogen (in the form of free amino acids and proteins) within the outer part of the sapwood than within the inner, and levels are higher at the base of the tree than at the crown. Usable nitrogen levels are very low in the heartwoods of traditional building timbers, but there may be large amounts in the pith (Zabel and Morrell, 1992). Nitrogen levels also vary with the season in which the tree was felled. Bletchley (1969) found that levels were highest in early spring and lowest in midsummer. He noted, however, that variation between samples was greater than between seasons, so that controlling the time of felling would probably have little effect on decay potential. Some samples of sapwood may thus be more suitable for wood-boring insects to attack than others.

Table 3.1 The distribution of nitrogen in felled timber (Data from Bletchley and Farmer, 1959)

Type of timber	Location of sample	Total nitrogen (percentage of dry wt)
Scots pine sapwood	butt end, outer zone	0.086
Scots pine sapwood	butt end, middle zone	0.080
Scots pine sapwood	butt end, inner zone	0.079
Scots pine sapwood	crown end, outer zone	0.052
European oak	butt end, sapwood	0.128
European oak	butt end, heartwood	0.088

The amount of nitrogen present in dead woody tissue amounts to at best 1% (dry weight) of the cells that make up the cambium and the bark. The nitrogen contained within wood after the bark and cambium have been stripped is far lower (0.03–0.13%; Hudson, 1986) and decay organisms have had to evolve methods of overcoming this limitation.

Fungi survive by extensive growth, and by efficient metabolization and re-use of nitrogen. Nitrogen is reabsorbed from parts of the fungus no longer required as the decay fronts advance (Cowling and Merrill, 1966). Nutrients are also removed from other fungi encountered as the decay proceeds.

Insect larvae have to bore extensively, frequently for many years, in order to obtain sufficient nitrogen to become adult and reproduce. It has been suggested that some larvae rely on nitrogen sinks formed by fungal decay, and these, in some species, may increase the speed of larval growth (Fisher, 1941). However, recent investigations provide no evidence to support this theory (Ridout, 1999).

Some wood-decaying insects are dependent on yeasts contained within their gut. The yeasts are picked up from the surface of the eggshell by the young larva as it hatches, and are passed on from generation to generation. They appear to play an important part in nutrition, perhaps connected with nitrogen processing or vitamin production, but their exact role appears to be unknown. If these yeasts are removed from the furniture beetle (*Anobium*), the larvae can no longer mature in timber (Behrenz and Technau, 1959).

3.3 Damage caused by insects

Insects are six-legged members of a diverse group of animals collectively known as the arthropods. All arthropods have a horny segmented outer covering of cuticle and jointed limbs. The hard outer covering (exoskeleton) gives protection against predators and, for terrestrial forms, against desiccation. It does not, however, allow for growth, so that it has to be shed periodically, allowing the new elastic covering (which has formed underneath) to expand and harden. Arthropods are particularly vulnerable to predators and to desiccation at this time.

Insects as a subgroup comprise about 70% of the known species of living animals. The weevil family (Curculionidae) alone, for example, comprises about 60 000 species, many of which attack timber. Insects have been able to exploit most ecological niches, both natural and man-made, and are therefore a highly diverse and successful group.

The majority of insects lay eggs and these hatch into larvae which follow one of two main types of development (Chapman, 1971).

The first (hemimetabolous) is associated with those insects, for example locusts and dragonflies, in which the larval stage usually differs from the adult only by the lack of wings and perhaps the presence or absence of other specialized organs (for example gills). The larva, which is the growing phase, simply enlarges, aided by periodical moults which culminate in the adult. The adult represents the dispersal/reproductive phase, but the adults of hemimetabolous insects continue to feed on the same food as the larvae, and there is thus direct competition between phases within the population if all phases live in the same environment.

It is those insects that follow the second (holometabolous) type of development (for example beetles and wasps) that attack timbers in the UK (Figure 3.1). In holometabolous development, the division of roles is more or less complete: the larva represents the feeding/growing stage and the adult does not need to feed (except perhaps for a high-energy source to aid dispersal, or occasionally a high-nitrogen source – for example blood – to permit egg production if the larval food source is deficient in proteins). There is thus no competition between phases. A further refinement is the insertion of a quiescent or pupal phase between the larva and the adult stages. This means that a total redesign (metamorphosis) is possible so that the larva need not resemble the adult at all. The larva

is thus freed to develop whatever body shape is necessary to become an efficient eating machine in the exploited habitat.

Moisture contents of converted timber, timber nutrient content and insect temperature tolerance are important restricting factors, and only a few insect families contain species that are capable of damaging air-dry building timbers. This capability must be seen in perspective: these insects are part of the natural progression of organisms that reduce dead trees to soil. Their natural habitat is dead sections of trees and they have not adapted to life in buildings; a building is just another environment containing dead wood, and wood-destroying insects will cope with different humidities and moisture contents etc., depending on their niche in nature. A dead branch of an oak tree, for example, might be dry for long periods, and will certainly contain fungus. Death watch beetles which live in

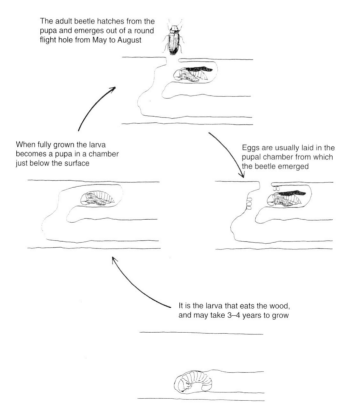

The adult beetle hatches from the pupa and emerges out of a round flight hole from May to August

When fully grown the larva becomes a pupa in a chamber just below the surface

Eggs are usually laid in the pupal chamber from which the beetle emerged

It is the larva that eats the wood, and may take 3–4 years to grow

Figure 3.1 Life cycle of the furniture beetle.

this natural environment are likely to prefer similar conditions in buildings. Beetles which attack decomposing logs (e.g. weevils) will be adapted to higher timber moisture level contents and greater levels of decay. The ability to degrade the cells of air-dry timber and thrive in buildings to the extent that these activities have any economic significance has been achieved in the UK by just three beetles. Two of these, the furniture beetle and the death watch beetle, are closely related members of the family Anobiidae, whereas the third, the house longhorn beetle, belongs to a group known as the Cerambycidae. Most other members of the Cerambycidae live in timber, and some may emerge in buildings (see Section 6.1), but none is able to reproduce and maintain an infestation under normal building conditions. Other beetles decay timber within buildings (see Chapter 6), but all are restricted either to fresh wood with a high starch content, or to wood where there is significant fungal decay. All of these wood-boring beetles may be grouped as follows (Parkin, 1940).

3.3.1 Cell-content feeders

Cell-content feeders live mostly on starch and free sugars. They are therefore restricted to fresh sapwood and their colonization will cease as the carbohydrate level drops with time. They do not possess the enzymes required to attack hemicelluloses or cellulose. Carbohydrates as well as nitrogen may therefore limit growth, and the larvae have to burrow extensively in order to obtain sufficient. Examples are powder post beetles (Lyctidae and Bostrychidae; Section 6.2).

3.3.2 Cell-content and partial cell-wall feeders

These live on starch and are also able to attack the hemicellulose within the cell wall. Examples are pinhole borer beetles (Scolytidae, Platypodidae; Section 6.5).

3.3.3 Cell-content and cell-wall feeders

These are also able to produce enzymes capable of degrading cellulose (Serdjukova, 1993). Examples

include furniture beetle, death watch beetle and house longhorn beetle (Anobiidae, Cerambycidae; Chapters 4 and 5, and Section 6.1).

A further group of insects, which are not important in Britain at present, contain bacteria or micro-organisms capable of breaking down cellulose as a gut fauna (Slaytor, 1992). This group includes the termites (see Section 6.6).

3.4 Decay caused by fungi

Fungi are curious organisms that are not easy to fit into the classical categorization of the plant kingdom. Unlike plants, they do not synthesize organic molecules from carbon dioxide and water by photosynthesis; they must obtain these molecules from a food source. They do not have the ability to ingest solids, however, and so they must live by secreting digestive juices (enzymes) onto the food source and then reabsorbing the nutrient liquids that are produced.

Most of the fungi that affect timber consist of a fine network of tubes (hyphae) which ramify extensively within the substrate. Like plants, these tubes are mostly constructed from a form of cellulose, but they also frequently contain chitin, another glucose-based polymer, which also forms the basis of insect cuticle.

Hyphae, which are individually fine enough to grow within the wood cells, and are therefore microscopic, frequently grow together and produce a visible loose mass of strands called a mycelium. The relatively simple hyphal organization of most fungi gives them the plasticity to exploit a wide range of ecological niches.

Fungi develop from a variety of microscopic spore types, and their life cycles are varied and often rather complex. For the purposes of this discussion, however, it is only necessary to differentiate between a sexual phase, when spores formed from the fusion of two nuclei are produced within or on fruit bodies (sporophores), and an asexual phase when spores are produced by simple division of special cells. The life cycle is shown diagrammatically in Figure 3.2. The fungi that produce a sexual phase and are associated with

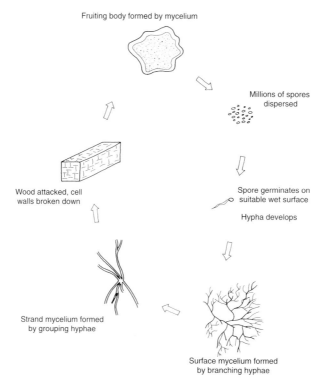

Fruiting body formed by mycelium

Millions of spores dispersed

Wood attacked, cell walls broken down

Spore germinates on suitable wet surface

Hypha develops

Strand mycelium formed by grouping hyphae

Surface mycelium formed by branching hyphae

Figure 3.2 Life cycle of a fungus.

damp damage and timber decay belong to the Basidiomycetes and Ascomycetes. Those that produce asexual spores (conidia) are loosely grouped as moulds (fungi imperfecti) and are mostly asexual forms of Ascomycete fungi. As most fungi are classified by characteristics exhibited by their fruit bodies or sexual spores, the fungi imperfecti produce a different grouping. A fungus that is capable of both forms of reproduction may therefore have two scientific names, depending on whether it is found in its sexual (perfect) or asexual (imperfect) state. Some of these associations are known, but others have yet to be made. The types of decay that fungi cause are described below.

3.4.1 Moulds and stains

Mould and stain fungi (fungi imperfecti) are mostly cell-content feeders that exploit the nutrients in sapwood. They usually do little significant damage (Viitanen and Ritschkoff, 1991b), although the bulk of pigmented hyphae produced by stain fungi may cause the discoloration of damp timber. They do, however, have a primary part to play in the natural cycle of decay by increasing porosity and detoxifying some natural fungicides. Colonization by moulds is facilitated by some types of bacteria that break down the pit membranes within the sapwood (Blanchette *et al.*, 1990). Stain fungi are more independent than other moulds, and travel from cell to cell by boring fine holes in the walls. Viitanen and Ritschkoff (1991b) grew a range of common moulds on redwood and spruce. They concluded that the lowest air relative humidity for growth on sapwood was 80%, and that growth was very slow at this humidity level.

3.4.2 Soft rot

The term 'soft rot' was proposed by Savory (1954) to describe a form of decay caused by some moulds and smaller ascomycete fungi. These organisms cause distinctive conical-ended cavities parallel to the cellulose microfibrils in the wood cell walls (Blanchette *et al.*, 1990). Savory found that the fungi principally attacked cellulose and hemicellulose, although lignin could be substantially modified. Damage was more common in hardwoods than in softwoods, and even rather durable timbers were susceptible to attack.

Soft rot damage progresses slowly as a surface decay in wet timber, and the wood has a fine surface checking, similar in appearance to brown rot damage, when it dries. The fungi can, however, tolerate a wide range of environmental conditions, and dry timber which is intermittently wetted may eventually be destroyed (Savory, 1955). Savory also showed that the brash surface frequently found on timbers where there were no other indications of fungal decay, could usually be attributed to soft rot fungi. Significant rot damage is more common in timber exposed in soil or aquatic environments than it is in buildings. This restriction has been ascribed to a lack of additional nutrients, particularly nitrogen (Blanchette *et al.*, 1990). It would be interesting to see whether bird or animal droppings could supply these requirements in derelict buildings or roofs. Soft rot fungi are also able to detoxify some fungicides, for example creosote and copper/ chromium/ arsenic formulations (Savory, 1955; Zabel and Morrell, 1992).

3.4.3 *White rot*

The primary division of decay into white rots and brown rots, according to the colour of the visible damage, was proposed by Hartig in 1874. The fungi that cause white rot (Basidiomycete; Figure 3.3) grow within cell cavities and attack all constituents of the cell wall from the lumen inwards. Some white rot fungi commence by attacking hemicelluloses and lignin, whereas others utilize all cell-wall components at the same rate. Decay commences with the depolymerization of the hemicellulose. The resulting decay appears as a mass of white fibres, and weight loss may eventually exceed 95% (Zabel and Morrell, 1992). White rot decay is predominantly associated with

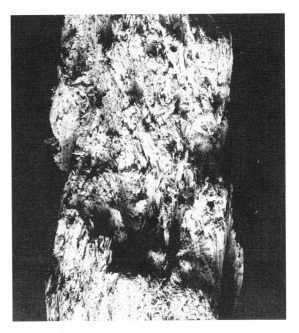

Figure 3.3 White rot fungi also destroy lignin. A partially decayed mass of fibres and vessels remains.

hardwoods (Hudson, 1986). The reason seems to be that most of the white rot fungi have difficulty in attacking the lignin unit which predominates in softwood lignin (see Figure 1.2). White rot fungi in buildings tend to thrive in wetter sites than brown rot fungi; thus they are frequently found in external window sills and below substantial roof leaks. This view is perhaps supported by laboratory decay tests, which showed that white rots required more water than brown rots to achieve an optimal wood-weight loss (Highley and Scheffer, 1970). Examples are oak rot (see Section 8.5.2) and some others of the 'pore' fungi (Polyporaceae).

3.4.4 *Brown rot*

Brown rots are caused by fungi (Basidiomycete) which may penetrate deep within the timber to produce decay. In many cases a relatively sound outer surface is maintained. This is probably the commonest form of timber decay found in buildings. Brown rot fungi attack cellulose and hemicelluloses but, like soft rot fungi, are unable to

Figure 3.4 Brown rot fungi remove cellulose and hemicellulose from the timber. The remaining matrix of lignin cracks into cubes as it dries.

break down lignin, although it might be modified (reduced methoxyl content and increased solubility). A fragile brown lignin matrix is left, which cracks into cubes as it dries (Figure 3.4). The fungi grow within cell cavities and the digestive enzymes spread outwards, causing a rapid depolymerization of the secondary cell wall (S2 layer) and therefore an early and drastic reduction in wood strength. Timber weight loss may approach 70% (Zabel and Morrell, 1992). In order to attack the cell walls the fungi must have a method of penetrating the enshrouding lignin. It has been postulated that this is achieved by some unknown non-enzymatic co-factor (Koenigs, 1974). Brown rot fungi are more commonly associated with softwoods (Hudson, 1986); the reason for this preference is at present unknown, but it may simply be that it gives a competitive advantage because white rot fungi have difficulty in colonizing softwoods. Examples are dry rot (see Chapter 7) and cellar rot (Coniophoraceae; Section 8.4.1).

3.5 European hazard classification for building timbers

In 1987 the Technical Board of the European Committee for Standardization (CEN) established a Technical Committee (CEN/TC38) to prepare harmonized standards on the durability of wood and wood-based products. It was considered that a primary requirement was to define the end use of timber according to the biological hazard to which it was exposed. The five classes of hazard defined in European Standard EN 335–1 make a useful framework within which to summarize biological decay potential.

Class 5: Salt water, moisture content greater than 20%
This class encompasses a wide range of marine environments. Timbers frequently wetted with salt water are attacked by a variety of specialist fungi and invertebrates.

Class 4: In ground or fresh water, moisture content greater than 20%
The predominant decay organisms are microfungi that cause soft rots. Other decay fungi may occur at the soil/air interface.

Class 3: Above ground, uncovered, moisture content sometimes greater than 20%
This class is probably nearest to the forest-floor situation. Timbers may be decayed by insects, brown rots and white rots. Stain fungi may also be a problem. White rots are commoner than brown rots.

Class 2: Above ground, covered, risk of wetting, moisture content sometimes greater than 18%
Insect attack predominates. Fungal decay may occur if high moisture contents (actually in excess of 20%) are sustained because of prolonged faults or condensation. Brown rots are commoner than white rots in this class because the latter seem to need a higher timber moisture content.

Figure 3.5 Fire damage causes a surface checking of the timber which resembles brown rot damage. This may be because the cellulose is destroyed before the lignin.

Class 1: Above ground, covered, moisture content less than 18%
Only insect attack is likely to occur.

3.6 Physical/chemical decay

Physical forms of degradation (those not caused by organisms) may be divided into the following categories:

3.6.1 Thermal damage

The commonest thermal damage to building timbers is caused by fire. The temperature at which ignition will occur depends on many things. The wood cell-wall components start to break down at about 200 °C and the flammable gases methane and carbon monoxide are released. Spontaneous ignition of these gases seems to require a surface temperature above about 500 °C (Jackman, 1981) but ignition will occur above about 250 °C if background radiation levels are high, as in the case of a fire that is already established. The timber chars and checks, producing an effect not dissimilar in appearance to brown rot damage (Figure 3.5), perhaps because lignin is the last component to be completely consumed. Wood, however, is not a good conductor of heat, and the charred surfaces may serve to insulate the interior of the timber if direct exposure to the flames is not prolonged. A common consequence is that fire-damaged beams, which at first glance appear to be irretrievably damaged, are found to be substantially sound when the surface charring is removed. However, joints may have suffered more significant damage, and will require close investigation.

Heat insufficient to char may eventually damage timber because there is a near-linear reduction in strength with increase in temperature. This is usually considered to be reversible below 100 °C, although the long-term effect may be to cause degradation. As the temperature exceeds 100 °C the wood becomes brown and brittle at the surface with a concomitant loss in weight and strength. Damage will depend on several factors, including temperature, length of exposure, moisture content, heating medium, density and dimension (Moore, 1983; Beall, 1982). Changes in property seem to be increased by thermal softening of the lignin and hemicelluloses, and ultimately cellulose depolymerization at 200 °C. Increase in moisture content exacerbates the effects.

The classic example of heat damage was the ceiling of the House of Lords. This yellow pine (*Pinus strobus*) ceiling, completed in 1847, survived intact until 1980, when a carved pendant boss became detached. Close examination revealed that the colour of the wood had darkened, the timber was brash, there was a strong smell of caramel, the pH had dropped to between 2 and 3 (strongly acid) and the loss in density was about 40–50% (Orsler, 1983). Slow thermal degrade, accelerated by iron contamination from the roof structure and acid pollution from the atmosphere, was diagnosed. (Phenols and organic acids liberated by the degrade would also tend to make the wood acidic.) It was discovered that the room had been subjected to a wide range of heating regimes, some of which, during the nineteenth century, had been criticized because they produced too much heat and presented a fire risk. These included gas burners and gasoliers suspended a few feet below the ceiling; it was the heat from these that had caused the damage. Unfortunately, the ceiling had to be replaced, and only the fragile carvings were retained after vacuum impregnation with a low-viscosity epoxy resin.

3.6.2 Visible and ultraviolet (UV) light

The primary change shown by timber exposed to sunlight is one of colour: light woods tend to turn brown whereas dark woods first bleach before changing to a similar brown colour. Degradation, primarily of lignin which releases the discolouring materials, is caused by UV light (Hon *et al.*, 1986) but, because the depth of penetration is small (0.05–0.5 mm), this is strictly a surface effect (Figure 3.6). Lignin suffers the greatest photo-degradation, and the solubilized products are washed away, leaving a loose matrix of partially modified cellulose fibres (Feist, 1982). The timber surface takes on a silvery appearance and is resistant to further UV degradation. Shrinkage and swelling by water sorption may, however, lead to slow surface delamination, thus exposing fresh surfaces (see Section 3.6.3). The application of coatings which absorb or reflect the ultraviolet light and prevent moisture content changes, is the usual method of dealing with this problem.

The silvery appearance of a timber surface is not necessarily caused by UV light alone; under damper conditions it may occur as a result of the stain mould *Aureobasidium pullulans* and similar fungi which feed on the breakdown products. These will also cause a very slow surface erosion (Schmidt and French, 1976).

3.6.3 Surface degradation caused by mechanical damage

The combined effects of light, wind and water movement produce stresses which result in small surface checks and cracks. Surface material loosened in this fashion is eventually lost and erosion takes place. This process is mostly very slow, published estimates ranging from 1 to 7 mm per century (Kühne *et al.*, 1972; Browne, 1960). Erosion varies with the type of tissue: the softer earlywood is likely to be preferentially removed, leaving behind ridges of latewood (Feist and Mraz, 1978). A severe artificial form of this type of damage will occur when softwood is cleaned by grit blasting (see Section 12.3).

3.6.4 Chemical decay

Timber, particularly hardwoods, may be subject to chemical decay because of a hostile acid or alkaline environment (Thompson, 1982), or because of electrochemical reactions within the timber.

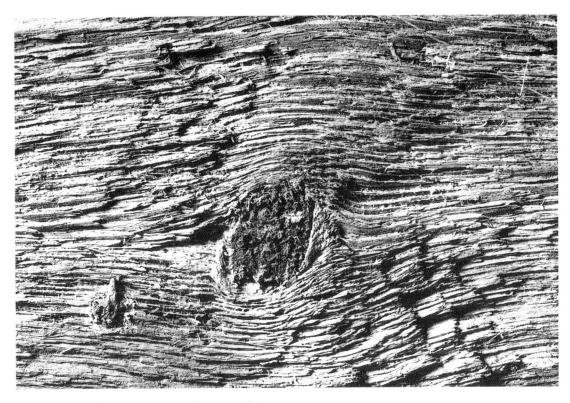

Figure 3.6 Surface erosion caused by light, wind and water.

Acid and alkaline environments affect timber in different ways. Acids break the carbon bonds (hydrolysis) between sugars (McBurney, 1954). This seems to be easier to achieve with five-carbon-ring sugars than with six and, as hardwoods tend to have more of the former (in their hemicellulose) than softwoods, they are usually more susceptible to acid degradation. Once the hemicellulose sheath has been degraded then the cellulose molecules are broken into short lengths. The extent to which damage will occur depends on the concentration of the acid, the duration of exposure and temperature.

Acids make the wood brittle (Wise and John, 1952), and the tracheids and fibres become disassociated. The end result is a mass of sharp-ended filaments which may be mistaken for a white rot. Surface damage of this type is frequently found in softwood roof timbers, particularly in industrial cities, and may be ascribed to airborne pollution.

As air pollution has been drastically reduced in the last few decades, most, if not all, of this damage in the UK will be old. An interesting example is St Pancras Chambers (formerly the Great Midland Hotel) in London. Roof timbers here have suffered more severe surface degradation than normally noted, and it is interesting to speculate on how steam train emissions might have contributed to this.

Chemical damage from historical pollution is usually stable, and does not require any form of preservative treatment. Localized repairs may be needed if damage is severe.

Alkaline environments produce a rather different and more severe result. Whereas acids attack cellulose but, even at high concentrations, have little effect on lignins, the reverse is true for alkalis. Lignins and hemicelluloses are degraded, and the timber loses strength and is softened. This process has little practical relevance in the normal building

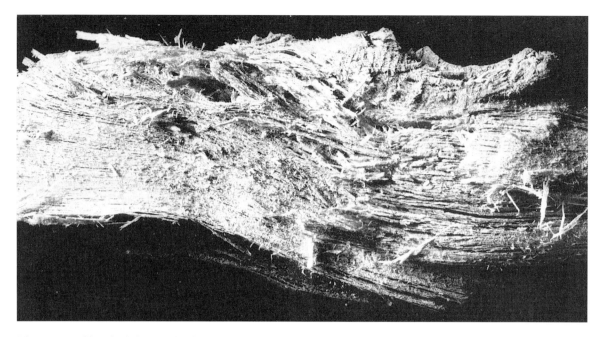

Figure 3.7 Chemical damage in the base of a wall stud that was embedded in a basement wall with a high salt concentration. The damage superficially resembles a white rot.

environment but is central to the wood pulp industry for the manufacture of paper.

The direct effects of salts depends on their acidity or alkalinity and the duration of exposure (Figure 3.7). Lead salt deposition under lead sheeting for example will eventually produce a surface degrade in softwood boarding and wood with a fluffy appearance is frequently found when lead is lifted (Figure 3.8). Exposure to acidic conditions also occurs when timber is pretreated with water-soluble salts of copper, chromium and arsenic (CCA treatment; Section 9.2). These salts do not seem to have a deleterious effect, however, even though the treatment solution is fairly strongly acidic (pH 2.0), probably because the period of wetting is fairly short.

Both alkaline and acid attack may occur in damp timber if there are partially embedded iron fastenings (Figure 3.9). The resulting electrochemical reaction is driven by differential oxygen availability (Baker, 1974). In essence, the exposed portion of the fastening acts as a cathode while the

Figure 3.8 Surface damage caused by an acid environment under lead. This type of fibrous surface damage has historically been caused by atmospheric pollution.

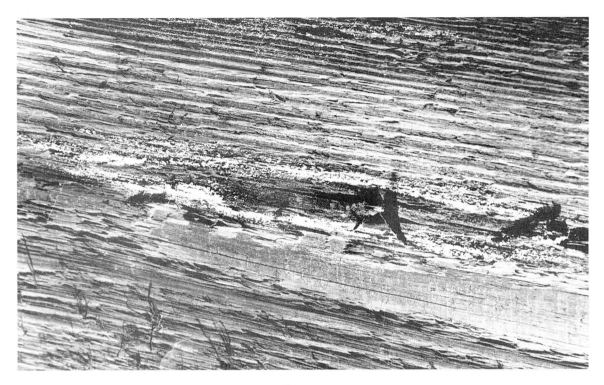

Figure 3.9 Corrosion products forming around a nail.

concealed section acts as an anode. Electron flow from the anode to the cathode produces corrosion products at the anode which may be hydrolyzed to free acid. A progressive and concomitant increase in alkalinity at the cathode produces an increasingly alkaline environment so that surface degradation also occurs. Blue/black staining frequently spreads from the cathode, particularly in oak, as soluble iron salts react with tannins to form iron tannate.

3.7 Acidity and corrosion of metals by timber

Most, though certainly not all, timbers are acidic (Fengel and Wegener, 1989). This property is produced by free acid, predominantly acetic acid, and by acidic chemical groups (predominantly acetyl groups). Acetyl groups, which derive from hemicellulose, are easily hydrolyzed and therefore produce more acetic acid in humid conditions.

There is considerable variation in acidity between tree species and sometimes between trees of the same species, but in any one tree the acidity of the sapwood is likely to vary little from that of the heartwood (Fengel and Wegener, 1989), although small differences do occur (Gray, 1958).

Acidity/alkalinity is measured on a scale of pH, with most solutions falling in the range 1–14. Neutral is 7 on the scale; lower figures denote acidity and higher figures alkalinity. Because the scale is logarithmic there is a tenfold change between each reading. Thus a solution with a pH of 5 is 10 times more acidic than one with a pH of 6 and 100 times more acidic than a solution that is neutral.

The measurement of pH is of practical importance because acidity/alkalinity may affect the corrosion of metals, the adhesive properties of glues or the fixing of preservatives. Our traditional building timbers, European redwood and European oak, have pH values of about 5 and 4 respectively, and oak is therefore about 10 times more acidic than pine. Acidity is not normally a problem unless timber is damp, but some timbers, and oak or chestnut are important examples, will readily emit acetic acid under drier conditions (Bordass, 1997).

Fresh oak tends to contain particularly high levels of acetic acid. This can often cause metal corrosion, so fixings in oak must be corrosion resistant. Acid vapours from oak can also corrode objects considerable distances away, as is well understood by museums, who would not specify oak for use in this environment. Lead roofing sometimes suffers from underside corrosion and, where this is particularly severe, acids from oak roof structures are often implicated (Bordass, 1997). Oak (and other woods) that have been in service for many years have often lost the free acid initially present, reducing the corrosion risk. However, if the timber becomes damper or more subject to cyclical wetting and drying – for example owing to changes in heating, ventilation, insulation or occupancy – more acid can be produced by hydrolysis.

It is worth noting that kiln drying tends to raise acidity, as during the process hydrolysis tends to occur more rapidly than the acids generated can disperse. Air drying, however, will produce a steady loss of volatile acid.

It is generally accepted that the rate of metal corrosion increases markedly in timbers with a pH below 4; these include Douglas fir, Caribbean pine and western red cedar (Thompson, 1982).

CHAPTER FOUR

Death watch beetle
(*Xestobium rufovillosum*)

4.1 Brief history of the beetle and the development of insecticides

This insect (Figure 4.1), which is closely related to the furniture beetle, has been known as the death watch beetle (*Xestobium rufovillosum*) for several centuries because the noise made by both sexes tapping with their heads on timber during court-ship was believed to presage a death.

Figure 4.1 The death watch beetle, showing the cowl-shaped thorax that protects the head.

The beetle occurs throughout Europe and the north-eastern states of North America, although it is frequently not recognized. In the British Isles it rarely occurs in Scotland, and has so far only been recorded in four buildings in Ireland. This may, however, particularly in the case of Ireland, reflect a scarcity of suitable building timbers, rather than a geographical distribution.

The insect's natural habitat is decayed hard-wood trees, commonly oak and willow. Oak is the timber usually attacked in buildings, although a variety of other temperate hardwood species may also be colonized. Softwood is sometimes also attacked if active infestation in hardwood is present within the building. Occasionally beetle attack is reported in buildings where no oak is apparent (McCoy-Hill, 1967); further investigation usually reveals that there are concealed oak lintels, or that the building once contained oak timbers.

The beetle does not seem to have attracted much attention as a decay insect before the beginning of the present century. The noise it makes, however, did, as correspondence in *The Queen* for 17 April 1875 makes clear:

Death watch. No real misfortune need be apprehended from the presence of the death watch in a house, but a very simple method will effectually rid your correspondent of this insect. Place a loud ticking watch in close proximity to the prophetic sounds, and the insect will soon kill itself in its efforts to out-tick the watch.

In 1914 Sir Frank Baines, Director of His Majesty's Office of Works, produced a report on the condition of Westminster Hall roof in London. It was found that substantial death watch beetle damage had occurred, particularly to the rafters. There had clearly been a history of past repairs, but permanent measures were now thought to be required. H. Maxwell Lefroy, Professor of Entomology at Imperial College, London, was eventually asked to investigate the problem and to evolve some method of chemical treatment (Ridout, 1999). His treatment represents probably the first attempt at a scientifically formulated preservative treatment for the wood rather than a straightforward poison to kill the beetle. The principles, once established, were commercially adopted.

Use of the first mixture had to be discontinued because the toxic effects on the workmen were too pronounced (a frequent problem with early preservatives), and a rather safer recipe was substituted. This mixture was applied as a spray in two liberal coats. The formulation contained cedar wood oil as a carrier fluid and metallic soap as a poison; dichlorobenzine acted as a fumigant, and paraffin wax held the mix in the timber (Blake, 1925). The formulation was elegant, but in fact there is no evidence that it was particularly successful, despite the highest expectations. This is also true of most of the other surface treatments that have been tried. Over many years, Westminster Hall timbers have been treated with a variety of sprays and smokes, but the beetles continue to emerge. Maxwell Lefroy's formula was later marketed, and remained popular until the development of contact insecticides.

Several other treatment formulations were used to control death watch beetle prior to the Second World War. Notable were mercuric chloride, which is highly poisonous, and an intriguing mixture marketed as the 'Kenford Death-watch Beetle Fluid', which, according to Ealand (1916), contained a slowly vaporizing radioactive mineral compound to act as a fumigant. The author has not been able to confirm this, and it is to be hoped that Ealand was mistaken.

One account (Richardson, 1977) of the origin of the *in situ* timber treatment industry traces it to the pharmacy of Stanley Richardson in Winchester. In 1932 Richardson was asked to dispense large quantities of a mixture of soft soap, paradichlorobenzene and cedar wood oil to an individual engaged in treating the cathedral roof timbers. Unfortunately this variation on Maxwell Lefroy's mixture proved as harmful to the operative as it was to the beetles and the treatment was never completed. Richardson, however, became interested in the problem of death watch beetle. His subsequent investigation led to the marketing of a safer product, known as Anobol, which contained rotenone (a root extract of the derris plant) dissolved in trichloroethylene (Richardson, 1977). The mixture was applied with a fine spray. The main product of Richardson's company, Richardson & Starling, subsequently became known as Wykamol.

Intensive wartime research produced a series of organochlorine and organophosphate contact insecticides, particularly one whose long name (dichlorodiphenyltrichloroethane) became abbreviated to DDT. Insecticide formulations prior to 1945 (when DDT became commercially available in the UK) had contained volatile respiratory poisons as noted above, and a range of 'stomach' poisons which had to be ingested by the insects. The new range of contact insecticides were stable and able to penetrate the insects' cuticle; their addition to formulations therefore made surface treatments theoretically far more effective.

DDT had been first synthesized by Zeidler in 1874 but its insecticidal properties were not discovered until 1939. Its simple structure made it easy to manufacture, and its broad spectrum of insecticidal properties, with prolonged stability and long-term residual activity, seemed to make it an ideal active ingredient. It was, however, these latter characteristics, and the problem of its accumulation in animal fats that led to its decline in popularity. Some insects were also becoming resistant to the insecticide.

Many formulators replaced DDT with dieldrin, a cyclodiene insecticide produced as a result of research undertaken in 1945. Dieldrin also had excellent residual properties, and unlike many other insecticides it was odourless at the concentrations used. Some preservative manufacturers therefore considered that dieldrin, and for similar reasons the fungicide pentachlorophenol with which it was frequently formulated, were particularly suited for use in areas where food was stored, because there was no risk from tainting. Both chemicals are now perceived to be unacceptably hazardous to human health, and their use is either banned or highly restricted.

In the decades that followed, dieldrin began to be displaced by lindane, the gamma isomer of hexachlorocyclohexane. Lindane (named after van der Linden, who first isolated the isomer in 1912) was less toxic but also less persistent. In recent years the properties of lindane have also been perceived to be environmentally unacceptable, and it has now been largely displaced by the pyrethroids.

In the 1970s the pyrethroids, a new group of contact insecticides, began to attract attention. The group comprised six insecticidal constituents isolated from extracts of a chrysanthemum (*Chrysanthemum cinerariaefolium*). Together they were known as pyrethrins, and several, including permethrin and cypermethrin, have become more acceptable alternatives to lindane in wood preservation.

Permethrin in particular has a low mammalian toxicity while remaining highly toxic to beetles at low concentrations. The chemical is also persistent in the subsurface of the timber.

It must be remembered, however, that today's panacea has a nasty habit of becoming tomorrow's poison. It seems unlikely that any insecticide can ever be considered to be absolutely safe. Volatile chemicals are slowly released into the atmosphere, whereas non-volatile chemicals may remain within the timber but may eventually enter the environment if the timber is discarded.

It was not until the 1930s that the biology of death watch beetle was studied in any great detail. In 1937 Ronald Fisher of the Forest Products Research Laboratory produced the first of four papers that examined the biology and behaviour of the insect in some depth. These papers provide the basis of our current knowledge, and little has been

added or disputed over the intervening years. Some at least of Fisher's work, however, suffers from the flaw that he could not obtain larvae in oak. He therefore collected his larvae from decayed willow branches and inserted them into holes drilled into his oak test blocks. Unfortunately, we do not know how physiologically similar wild willow-dwelling populations of beetles are compared to domestic oak-dwelling populations . It is therefore difficult to distinguish between fatalities caused by the factors that Fisher measured, and those caused by a change in the density and type of wood as a food material.

4.2 Biology of the death watch beetle

A considerable quantity of new information has been obtained by an international research group, co-ordinated by English Heritage and part-funded under the European Environment Programme DGX11. The results from this research have not yet been published, but unattributed information included in this chapter derives from that study.

Two forms of death watch beetle attack, which frequently overlap, may be distinguished. The first (Figure 4.2) occurs in the sapwood, which has a higher nutrient content than heartwood and is therefore more susceptible to beetle attack. Damage will tend to occur anywhere on the surface of the beam where there is sapwood (Figure 4.3). Close observation suggests that beetle larvae do not normally penetrate far below the sapwood band into heartwood by this route unless fungal decay is present (Figure 4.4).

The second mode of attack, which is ultimately controlled by the level of fungal decay present, destroys the heartwood of the timber. The requirement for fungus in heartwood can be understood by considering the beetle's natural habitat. Death watch beetles live in the dead parts of trees, and fungus will always be present as an additional organism breaking down the materials which gave the wood resistance to attack. Recent research indicates that fungi alter the chemistry of the wood, rather than just depleting some

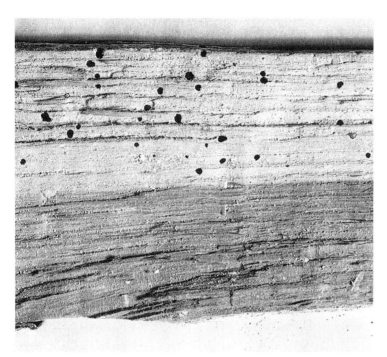

Figure 4.2 Death watch beetles may attack sapwood without the presence of a fungus.

Figure 4.3 (below) Emergence holes occur all over the surface of sapwood and active infestation is shown by bore dust the colour of freshly cut timber.

Figure 4.4 Sapwood destroyed by death watch beetle falls away to reveal the rounded heartwood surface, which is usually immune from attack unless fungus is also present.

components (Esser and Tas, 1999). The beetles never normally encounter undecayed heartwood, and they have not developed any additional ability to deal with it in buildings. Destruction frequently commences in the juvenile heartwood (pith) where the young larvae burrow along the vessels between the rays. The products of metabolism, which are deposited in the rays when they become part of the heartwood, seem to make this tissue unpalatable or too hard for the insects to attack. Ray tissue, however, is eventually broken down mechanically as the tunnels coalesce to form a cavity.

The mature female beetle lays between 40 and 60 eggs in cracks and perhaps old emergence holes, so that the eggs are placed just below the surface (Figure 4.5; Simmonds *et al.*, 1999). Observation suggest that joints and shakes are favoured sites for egg laying, and this probably reflects access to a more stable and humid microclimate deeper within the timber. The eggs and newly emerged larvae are liable to desiccate, so that maximizing and stabilizing the humidity will be an advantage. Eggs laid below the surface are also more protected from predation by other insects.

Eggs hatch in about 20 days, depending to some extent on temperature and humidity. Fisher (1938) found that no hatching took place at a relative humidity (RH) of 23% (his next batch were kept at 41% RH, therefore the minimum humidity necessary for hatching is between 23% and 41%) nor at temperatures above 30 °C. He concluded that warm, moist conditions were the most favourable, and that condensation might produce suitable conditions where ventilation was inadequate.

In laboratory cultures where eggs have been laid on the surface of timber blocks, the newly hatched larva walks actively over the surface before

41

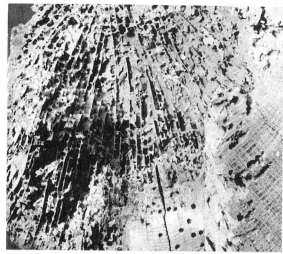

Figure 4.6 The young larvae burrow between the rays of the oak, perhaps because the rays are too hard or contain unpalatable substances.

Figure 4.5 Each beetle lays between 40 and 60 eggs below the surface of the timber, and these hatch in about 20 days.

burrowing. Hickin (1975) concluded from this that the eggs do not necessarily have to be laid where conditions are suitable for the larvae, but the rapid dispersal observed may have been the larvae's response to exposure. When offered the choice between smooth or fissured egg-laying sites, the female beetles always prefer the fissured (Belmain *et al.*, 1999).

The newly hatched larva is probably the only stage during which the legs are important. The larva becomes less mobile as it grows, and pulls itself along by means of 'spines' on its skin (which also act as anchors to aid in gnawing) and by muscular contractions of the body wall. The young larvae tend to burrow between the rays of the timber (Figure 4.6), perhaps because the rays are too hard or contain unpalatable substances. They may thrive in the core of the timber where there are few extractives (Figure 4.7), and eventually a large cavity will be formed if an undetected heart rot was present when the timber was installed (Figure 4.8).

The beetle larvae gnaw through substantial quantities of wood in order to obtain the nutrients they require. This activity produces large volumes of fine dust and bun-shaped frass pellets (Figure 4.9). Preliminary analysis (pyrolysis mass spectroscopy and discriminant analysis) suggests that the pellets are very similar chemically to, but may be distinguished from, the dust (Ridout, 1999). The function of the pellets may not be simply, as Becker suggests (1977), to package the dust and thus reduce its volume. Both the furniture beetle and the house longhorn beetle produce pellets, each with its own distinctive shape. The powder post beetle (*Lyctus* sp.) does not. Powder post beetle damage may sometimes be identified by the exploded surface of the timber, which is the result of the increase in dust volume caused by the beetles' activities.

The larval stage of the death watch beetle may take over 10 years to complete, depending on the nutrient content of the timber, temperature, moisture content and the presence of fungal decay (Figure 4.10). Larvae kept under identical conditions, however, do not all emerge after the same number of years. Blocks of oak sapwood which have been partially decayed by a white rot

Figure 4.7 The core of the timber contains far fewer toxic extractives than the mature heartwood, and may also contain heart rots that originated in the standing tree. This zone provides a good environment for the death watch beetle.

(*Coriolus versicolor*) before sterilization and used as an egg-laying substrate, produced most beetles in 6 years under constant conditions with an artificial winter cycle. Some beetles, however, emerged after 2 years, and X-ray investigation shows that some blocks still contain larvae after 13 years.

The effects of temperature and moisture content may be similar to the effects of these parameters recorded for furniture beetle (see Section 5.2). Elevated moisture levels certainly seem to be favourable, and it seems probable that infestations will die back if moisture contents within the timber remain below about 12% throughout the year. The effects of fungal decay were examined over several years by Fisher, and his results, published in two papers (1940, 1941), are the basis for the statement, often quoted, that death watch beetles need the presence of fungal decay before they can attack oak (Figure 4.11). In fact his data suggest that the situation is rather more complex. Moreover, as his experimental method was potentially flawed, the larvae may have more ability to attack timber than his results suggest.

The following conclusions may be drawn from Fisher's work.

- The length of the larval stage is inversely proportional to the extent of fungal decay, although recent observations suggest that severe decay provides a less suitable environment.
- Larvae are sometimes capable of attacking both sapwood and heartwood in the absence of fungus, although the larval stage may be greatly prolonged in the heartwood.
- Recently grown oak is not usually attacked unless fungal decay is present.

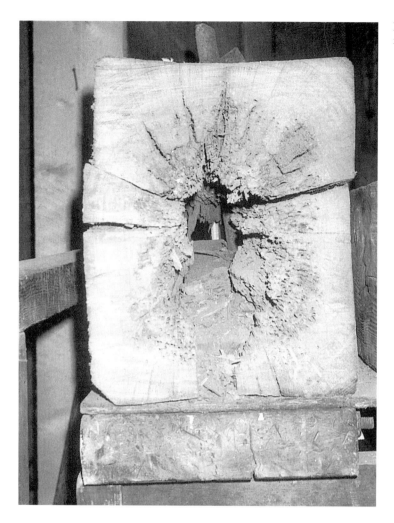

Figure 4.8 Eventually a large cavity may be found in the centre of the timber.

The final conclusion is interesting because it supports Hickin's (1975) contention that European oak does not become susceptible to insect attack for about 60 years. American oak appears to be rather more susceptible to decay than European oak, but egg-laying females, when given a choice between modern and medieval heartwood samples, will normally select the medieval.

Frass was collected and subjected to chemical analysis, from which it was concluded that the fungus exerted a softening effect rather than supplying nutrients to the beetle (Campbell and Bryant, 1940). Fisher (1941) later modified this conclusion by suggesting that it might also accelerate growth by concentrating nitrogen. It now seems likely that the fungus assists the beetle by changing the chemistry of the timber.

Available information suggests that the beetles pupate in summer, and that the adults emerge from the pupal case some 3 weeks later. The beetles are not reproductively mature until the following spring, when those that are going to emerge from the timber do so during the period mid-April to mid-June (Figure 4.12). Harris (1969) recorded the numbers and sexes of beetles found on the floors of several churches. He found that males predominated during the first half of the emergence season and that their numbers reached a peak during about the third week of April and declined almost to zero by the first or second week

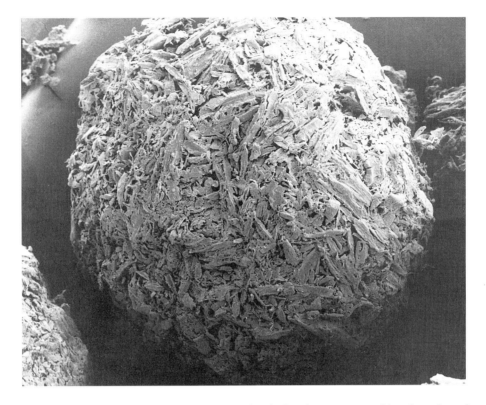

Figure 4.9 The fine timber fragments eaten by the beetle are processed into bun-shaped pellets within the insect's gut (· 250).

of May. Emergence of females peaked rather later in the season and numbers did not decline to nearly zero until the first weeks of June in laboratory colonies. Recent observations with beetles in culture suggest that the sex ratio of beetles found on the floor does not reflect staggered emergence. Both sexes emerge together and the males die first. Unmated females live a little longer than males, and mated females live the longest.

Harris believed that the emergence pattern he recorded reflected a dispersal mechanism because the females that dropped during the first few weeks mated and dispersed, whereas females that emerged later laid their eggs in the roof timbers, dropped to the floor and died shortly after. Harris also observed that the females were not sexually mature when they emerged, and that although mating might take place shortly after emergence, maturity and egg laying did not occur for some

time. The early emerging females tended to wander for at least 3 weeks before laying eggs, whereas for the later-emerging females this period diminished to 1 week. Long periods of wandering, rather than a short emergence period, increase the potential for natural predation (see Section 14.5.1).

Females, unlike the males, have not reached full sexual maturity when they emerge. They mate shortly after emergence, but eggs (oocytes) are not produced for several weeks. The male passes spermatophores to the female during copulation. These are sacs of sperm embedded in a gelatinous protein capsule. The capsule is ruptured after transfer and the sperm is stored by the female in a spermatheca until required. A few sperm are released from the spermatheca as each egg passes down the oviduct during egg laying.

Goulson *et al.* (1993) showed that the male beetles donated an average of 13.5% of their body

Figure 4.10 The larvae may take 10 or more years to grow, depending on the environment and the presence of fungus within the timber.

Figure 4.11 Death watch beetle and fungi act together where timbers remain damp for many years. The damaged timbers shown in this photograph were under a faulty valley gutter at Queen Elizabeth's Hunting Lodge, Epping Forest.

weight to the females in the spermatophores. Nutritional materials are included within the sperm, and the female will select the males she mates with on the basis of body weight when they mount her. Goulson found that light males could be made acceptable by loading their backs with Blu-Tac.

Maxwell Lefroy (1924) noted that it might be possible for the beetles to reproduce in cavities within the timber without ever appearing at the surface. No data has been found to support this suggestion, but it would certainly help to explain the limited efficacy of preservative treatments. Clearly, if the preservative cannot reach the insect then it will not kill it. Cavities might be formed by rot pockets or, as discussed above, eroded by the beetles themselves where infestations are advanced.

Emergence onto some form of surface, either inside timber or outside it, would certainly seem to be necessary for mating to occur. Furniture beetle mate end-to-end, and may therefore copulate in the entrances to tunnels, but the male death watch beetle mounts the female so that more space is required. Furniture beetle communicate with volatile chemical signals (pheromones) which, while of limited use in tunnels, suit an actively dispersive population. Death watch beetles communicate by sound (Birch and Keenlyside, 1991) and their mode of dispersal is not understood. Sound propagation suits a population which stays closely assembled, but is ineffective in a maze of tunnels.

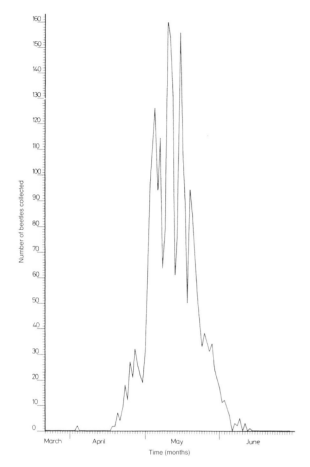

Figure 4.12 Death watch beetles found on the floor of Westminster Hall during the 1970 emergence period.

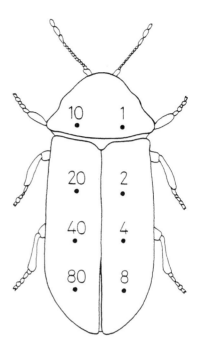

Figure 4.13 Painted numbering code for individual death watch beetle identification.

Ridout Associates acting as English Heritage consultants have investigated beetle behaviour by a variety of techniques including the labelling of live beetles with a dot code to identify individuals (Figure 4.13) at the beginning of the emergence season, lightly dusting them with a luminous powder and then releasing them. They were relocated at the end of the season with an ultra-violet lamp. One important discovery was that the beetles would emerge and re-enter the timber via very old emergence holes and shakes (Colour Plates 1 and 2). This behaviour suggests oviposition within the timber. If this behaviour is typical, neither the larva nor the beetle would have much contact with the treated timber surface.

Monitoring beetle emergence (Section 4.3) at the Tide Mill, Beaulieu, Hampshire, during 1997 showed that five out of 18 beetles emerged from pre-existing holes. This may explain the frequently observed phenomenon that many beetles may be found where there are few emergence holes.

Both death watch beetles and furniture beetles are a distinctive shape. Both insects have a large cowl-like expansion of the thorax, which protects the head and is presumably used for burrowing in tunnels blocked with frass, and during emergence.

Birch and Keenlyside (1991) have shown that both sexes of the death watch beetle tap the timber with the front part of the head (frons). This appears to be sexual communication via substrate vibrations. The females usually remain stationary while the males move towards them.

Little is known for certain about the way in which infestations commence, and it has been generally accepted that the beetles cannot fly. This is certainly untrue. Baker (1964) investigated death watch beetle flight and found that the beetles would fly if they fell from a surface warmed to 30–40 °C in an ambient temperature above 22 °C. He suggested that 22 °C was the threshold for free flight. Recent investigations at Kew Palace and Winchester Cathedral have demonstrated that the beetles are active fliers, and that they fly at a threshold temperature of about 17 °C. It seems likely that many of the beetle populations found in buildings could have been brought in during construction, within second-hand replacement timbers, or introduced in firewood; they may even have flown in. Introduction via firewood may have been an important means of dispersal because beetles remain within the timber during the winter months. They might perhaps emerge and fly if the log in which they resided was placed on a fire or was stored in a warm room at the appropriate time of the year.

4.3 Monitoring current activity and population

Death watch beetle populations seem to decline naturally and much of the beetle attack found in buildings is inactive (Maxwell Lefroy, 1924). Presumably populations wax or wane depending on the suitability of the environment, and this will change in accordance with the condition of the building. For example, moisture contents and humidities might rise as leadwork fails, and fall again when it is replaced (Ridout, 1999).

Active infestation is sometimes denoted by clean, sharp-edged holes approximately 2–3 mm in diameter, and the presence of bore dust the colour of the freshly cut timber. In practice, however, these indications may be restricted to sapwood or not be so easy to detect if a population

Figure 4.14 Current activity can be detected by closely fastening tissue paper over groups of flight holes. Emerging beetles will punch holes through the paper.

Figure 4.15 The paper around an exit hole has been pulled back to show that the beetle emerged from an old flight hole (compare with Figure 4.3).

Figure 4.16 A flight hole (ringed) from which a beetle has just emerged. Current activity cannot necessarily be determined by the appearance of the flight holes.

is at a low level, and few beetles are emerging. Emergence from old flight holes may also disguise current activity. Care must be taken to distinguish between dust which pours from holes due to insect activity and dust produced by vibration, for example during building works. Ambiguity can be resolved by pasting or otherwise securely fastening acid-free tissue paper to the timber, through which beetles will punch holes as they emerge (Figures 4.14–4.16).

4.4 Methods of treatment

Any effective preservative treatment must achieve the following:

- Bring a sufficient quantity of the active ingredient into contact with one or more stages in the insect's life cycle.
- Penetrate the insect cuticle or be ingested by the insect, or make the timbers unusable as a food source.
- Remain in sufficient quantity for a sufficient period of time to severely deplete or destroy the target insect population.
- Conform to the relevant legislation by being relatively harmless to non-target organisms, primarily mammals.

Clearly the fulfilment of these requirements will depend substantially on the biology of the targeted pest. Methods which may be successful against one species may have little effect on others.

Insecticides may be either contact poisons or stomach poisons. Contact poisons, as discussed in Section 4.1, include lindane and the pyrethrins (permethrin, cypermethrin, tetramethrin etc.) and have the ability to penetrate the insect's cuticle. Cuticle protects the insect from desiccation chiefly by means of a thin layer of surface wax, which contact insecticides have to be able to penetrate. Contact insecticides may have a limited persistence in the timber and must be formulated in an organic solvent or in an emulsion.

Stomach poisons, which include boron, are far more stable, and may be formulated in water.

They must, however, be ingested by the insects. This presents a problem with surface treatments intended to kill emerging beetles, because although they may bite exit holes, they do not consume the timber. It is possible that their main effect is to make the timber unacceptable to the larvae, so that they starve.

4.4.1 Defrassing

The term 'defrassing', as defined by Locke (1986), 'describes the removal of material from timber – usually its surface layer – which has been so degraded by beetle attack that it is no longer structurally useful'. In practice, any aggregation of holes, usually death watch beetle holes, along the sapwood edges of the timber, tends to be used as an excuse for defrassing.

Locke mentions three uses for this technique:

1. To evaluate how much real strength and physical integrity is left in timber reduced by attack.
2. To enable chemical treatment to reach underlying sections which retain strength but have live infestation.
3. In repair, to mate new timber to old or to reinforce upon relatively sound hard surfaces.

Modern techniques, such as the use of microbore drills, have removed the necessity for defrassing as a means of structural investigation, and defrassing for repair is never acceptable (there may be occasions when a timber has to be cut back to a sound point to provide a strong joint in repair, but this is not the same as cutting off all the sapwood in a consistent manner). Once timber has been defrassed, its value as historical evidence – and the possibility of accurate dating from growth rings – is significantly reduced. In the author's experience the second reason is the most frequently offered justification for defrassing. In practice, what is mostly removed is damaged sapwood; as discussed earlier, death watch beetle does not usually pass from the sapwood into the heartwood. Even where it does, the treatment concept is flawed. The freshly exposed heartwood does not readily accept the preservative, and the little that does penetrate

will soon be lost. Frassy timber, however, is porous and will readily absorb preservative. The active ingredient remains more stable because penetration is far deeper, and the preservative will therefore be retained within the surface layers of timber for a significant period of time. Defrassing is therefore frequently ineffective, always unsightly (Figure 4.17), and should only be used where absolutely necessary.

4.4.2 Spraying

Traditionally, roof timbers are spray treated as a protection against all wood decay organisms, but it is doubtful whether spray treatment alone is ever particularly effective against death watch beetle. This is not a new observation, and the British Wood Preserving and Damp-proofing Association has always recognized that spray treatments are inadequate and untargeted for this purpose. Comparative field trials undertaken by the Princes Risborough Laboratory (now part of the Building Research Establishment) are discussed in Coleman, 1999. Surface treatments with contact insecticides may kill beetles if they emerge, or destroy eggs and newly hatched larvae if they are in the surface layer. They are unlikely to reach the growing larvae deep within the timber because the depth of chemical penetration achieved by the preservative will be small, probably only 1–2 mm, and will certainly not reach beetles reproducing in cavities.

Formulations based on organic solvents generally penetrate further into dry timber (i.e. with a moisture content of less than 20%) than water-based preservatives can, and the solvent provides additional fumigant action. They do, however, render the timber more flammable until the carrier solvent has evaporated. Environmental concerns are also rendering organic solvents increasingly unpopular. The use of organic solvents as carrier fluids has been reduced by the formulation of emulsions, which, in a sprayable form, consist of the preservative dissolved in an organic solvent with a variety of emulsifying chemicals. The concentrate is then diluted with water to produce an emulsion. There was considerable disagreement between the manufacturers and independent assessors regarding the effectiveness of the early sprayable emulsions, and research by the Building Research Establishment (1983) suggested that their usefulness was limited in dry timber. Results from the use of synthetic pyrethrins were rather more encouraging than those from lindane-based formulations, probably because lower volatility allowed greater stability of the pyrethrins in the surface layers of the wood. Microemulsion formulations have recently appeared on the market. It is claimed that these have the same penetrative qualities as organic solvent formulations without the disadvantages (Dawson and Czipri, 1991).

Water-based preservatives do not penetrate well in dry timber and should generally only be used where timber is damp. The addition of further water into a damp situation may be highly un-desirable, for example in enclosed spaces with limited potential for evaporation. In these situations a solution of borate in a water-miscible glycol carrier may be useful. Formulations at a range of concentrations are now marketed. Boron, though an effective fungicide and insecticide in sufficient concentration, has no contact insecticide properties and must be ingested by the insect or make the timber unacceptable. It is, however, extensively used in the USA against a wide variety of decay insects.

Water-based formulations (except for some pretreatments) have the disadvantage that they are not fixed in the timbers and may be leached out by further water penetration. They are generally not thought to be suitable for high-hazard situations (see Section 3.5).

Figure 4.17 Defrassed principal rafter braces at Salisbury Cathedral. This technique removes the damaged sapwood so that the underlying heartwood can be treated. The heartwood is not, however, at risk, and will not readily accept the preservatives.

4.4.3 Injection

The problem of beetle emergence in decay pockets can be overcome if the pockets are located and treated by pressure injection. Joinery injectors (developed for window joinery) fitted with one-way valves are frequently used for this purpose, and have been found to be effective. Injectors may be knocked below the surface, and the holes filled when treatment has been completed, or the injectors may be left for retreatment if required. Injectors must be installed at centres close enough to provide a reasonably uniform treatment.

Maxwell Lefroy investigated the use of timber injector valves during the Westminster Hall treatment (see Section 4.1) and was not impressed. He found that the chemical moved large distances along the open conducting vessels within the timber, but that movement across the grain was poor. This potential problem is readily under-standable from a consideration of hardwood structure, and it would be advisable to drill the holes to a greater depth than the injectors, and to stagger their centres in the timber.

Injection of preservatives into flight holes has been practised in the past. Notable in this field, and a good example of the practical approach, was C.E. Bebbington, joiner, cabinet maker, under-taker, parish clerk and sexton of Weaverham, Cheshire. Bebbington evolved, and commercially utilized, an exotic formulation which was injected into flight holes and sealed in with a filler. He apparently developed this treatment around the turn of the twentieth century and his formulation may even predate that of Maxwell Lefroy. The formula remained a secret throughout his life-time, but it is given in a document retained by his grandson. It can now be reported that it was a volatile poison containing camphor, formalin and oil of cassia mixed in wood naptha and diluted with

Figure 4.18 C.E. Bebbington applying a filler to timber damaged by death watch beetle (1920s).

methylated spirits prior to injection. Holes and cavities were then filled with an 'earth' composed of sheppy glue diluted 1:6 with water, which was mixed with sawdust and coloured with brown umber or yellow ochre to match the timber. A small quantity of formalin was added prior to use, in order to speed up the setting. The injection mixture must have been extremely smelly and must have produced a very unpleasant working environment, yet it was apparently successful and Bebbington continued to receive commissions throughout his working life (Figure 4.18).

4.4.4 Paste treatment

Deeper preservative penetration may be achieved by means of a paste which may contain fungicides, insecticides or both, a technique first described in a US patent in 1955. These pastes are emulsions of immiscible chemicals in an organic solvent base which are applied as a thick paste to the timber. The emulsion breaks down slowly at the timber surface, allowing slow and deep penetration. In some formulations the paste forms a skin that prevents evaporation of the carrier chemical, and thus allows greater penetration over time. This skin remains at the surface after treatment and may be brushed off or washed off with hot water. Residues of skin from earlier treatments are sometimes found and may lead to confusion. The author recently found that fragments of paste skin in a roof in London had been described by a remedial surveyor as the fungus *Poria placenta*.

The extent to which these paste preservatives will penetrate is debatable, but none should be used within several centimetres of decorative paintwork or plasterwork because of the risk of staining.

Holland and Orsler (1992) carried out a preliminary investigation in which they tested five formulations containing various combinations of lindane, tributyl tin oxide (TBTO) and pentachlorophenol on blocks of pine sapwood conditioned to 10% moisture content. The paste was applied at a loading of 0.43 kg m^{-2} on a tangential surface, and the depth to which each active ingredient had penetrated was assessed on a single replicate sample when all traces of the emulsion

had disappeared. This was after 1, 2 or 4 weeks, depending on the speed of absorption. Samples were also examined after 10 weeks, to discover whether penetration improved after the initial penetration phase. These results showed that the insecticide (lindane) penetrated well (greater than 8 mm) but that the fungicide (TBTO) content dropped below the required toxic value for the chosen fungus (*Coniophora puteana*) after only about 1 mm depth. Increasing the initial loading by a factor of 10 (to 4.3 kg m^{-2}) did not markedly improve penetration.

Pastes may be applied to the top surface of timbers with a caulking gun or a trowel. They are sometimes applied in thin strips to the underside and sides, and may also be held against the wood by polythene sheeting. Paste may also be caulked into holes bored into the timber at closely spaced (100–150 mm) centres.

4.4.5 Smoke treatment

Smokes are based on pyrotechnic formulations which are ignited on a tray and release particles of insecticide into the air which settle as a surface layer on the timber. The mode of action is unlike that of conventional organic solvent liquid treatments as the smoke particles affect only adult beetles, and then only after emergence. The residues of crystalline insecticide do not penetrate into the wood and have only a short effective life. Treatments are applied annually at the beginning of the emergence period for at least the maximum theoretical duration of the larval period, i.e. 10 years.

Harris (1977) analysed data from a 13-year field trial of lindane/dieldrin smoke in the fifteenth-century roof of the Chapel of King's College, Cambridge. He showed that the number of beetles collected fell from over 1300 in 1962 to 80 in 1975. Harris believed that perhaps 20 annual treatments would be required to eliminate the beetles. These results appear to be encouraging, but the use of dieldrin, which is more persistent than lindane, is no longer permitted, and the drying effect produced by reroofing at the commencement of the trial must also be taken into account.

Other smoke treatments have been rather less

successful. The nave roof at Salisbury Cathedral, for example, was smoke treated for many years, but investigation along the wall plates produced 541 beetles in 1991 and a further 257 in 1993. The former Clerk of Works assured us that the number of beetles emerging has dropped considerably since the treatment commenced, although once again timbers are probably drier because the heating system within the cathedral was also made more efficient at the same time as the treatments were commenced. The smoke generators used would have contained a mixture of lindane and dieldrin until recent years. Generator size was calculated for roof space volume in accordance with the manufacturer's recommendations.

Both tests indicate that annual smoke treatments will reduce beetle populations, and the fact that the insecticide was at least partially effective was confirmed by analysis of beetle extracts. In neither case, however, was extermination achieved. Recent commentaries on treatments by the Building Research Establishment (1986a and 1987) consider smoke treatments to be effective for the control, rather than the elimination, of beetle populations. Although there is some doubt about the stability of the insecticide, Building Research Establishment Information Paper 19/86 (1986a) suggests that smoke treatments should remain effective during the normal emergence period from mid-April to mid-June, if applied shortly before the beetles started to emerge.

There is thus plenty of evidence that annual smoke treatments will deplete a beetle population, but no evidence that they will eradicate the insects. One reason may be the emergence into cavities as discussed above, but another is undoubtedly the fugitive nature of lindane, the only active ingredient recently available in smokes registered for timber treatments. Harris (1969) showed that lindane levels on test timbers remained adequate to control the beetles throughout the emergence period. His samples were, however, placed in a store room and he states that persistence may not be as satisfactory under field conditions. A field trial conducted by Ridout Associates in 1993 at Wells Cathedral by analysing lindane deposition on randomly sited papers, demonstrated that

lindane levels on timber surfaces at the end of the beetle emergence period were 14 times too low to destroy the insects, and six times too low to have any visible effect on their behaviour, when compared with published toxicity levels (Coleman, 1978). Formulations containing pyrethroids may be obtained for killing 'crawling insects', and these might be beneficial against death watch beetle in small roofs. Coleman (1977, 1999) presented data that demonstrated that these smokes could be effective, but that high, open roofs in churches would require a special formulation to maximize plume height and minimize insecticide loss caused by the heat of the ignition mixture.

A further reason why the smoke treatments tested failed to eradicate infestations concerns smoke deposition and beetle emergence patterns. Harris (1977) showed that lindane deposition on the top surfaces of timber was about ten times that on a side or the underside. The author's investigations of medieval cathedral roof timbers have shown that the density of beetle emergence holes is frequently greater on the sides and underside of timber components.

Natural predation may limit beetle activity in a reasonably healthy roof (see Section 14.5.1). Unfortunately, spiders, which may be the major predator, are susceptible to insecticides, and are far more exposed to the treatment than are the beetles. The Wells Cathedral experiment produced a plethora of dead spiders.

4.4.6 Insect traps

Recent research carried out by Ridout Associates and Birkbeck College has shown that death watch beetle fly freely and are attracted to light (Belmain et al., 1999). Preliminary trials using commercially available ultraviolet insect traps have been very encouraging. Large numbers of death watch beetle were trapped, the majority of which were mated females. Further trials are needed to establish the optimum size of protective grills to ensure that there is no danger either to bats or to non-targeted insect species. Light traps may prove valuable in reducing death watch beetle populations without the use of chemicals in some situations.

CHAPTER FIVE

Furniture beetle or woodworm (*Anobium punctatum*)

5.1 Brief history of the beetle and its treatment

The common furniture beetle or woodworm (Figure 5.1) is indigenous to, or has been introduced into, most of the temperate world. Its similarity to the death watch beetle (*X. rufovillosum*) has always been recognized and in older texts it is frequently regarded as a small death watch beetle. Not until 1925 did Gahan discover that the insect does not tap, and that the name 'death watch' was misapplied.

Figure 5.1 The adult furniture beetle emerges from a 1–2 mm diameter circular flight hole.

The furniture beetle has the same natural habitat – the decayed portions of trees – as the death watch beetle, but unlike the death watch beetle it does not tend to confine its attentions to hardwoods. It is mostly restricted in building timbers to the sapwood of both hardwoods and softwoods, and will only attack heartwood which has been modified by fungal attack or is of a species that has little natural durability. Thus Richardson (1993) recorded it as attacking the heartwood of birch and beech.

Stephens (1839) noted that the beetle was common in old buildings, but the insect does not seem to have been considered a serious problem, and was apparently mostly treated by the application of paraffin oils, turpentine or, frequently, linseed oil (Girdwood, 1927). More curious formulations have also been recorded: Britton (1875) quotes an old recipe from Pliny, consisting of garlic boiled in vinegar, and an Indian formulation comprising coconut oil made into a putty with shell lime and diluted to a varnish with mustard oil.

Furniture beetle treatment in the twentieth century commenced once again with Maxwell Lefroy's work at Imperial College, London. Professor Lefroy, as discussed earlier, was probably the first to devise a complex preservative specifically for the control of wood-boring insects. His work on the eradication of death watch beetle at Westminster Hall attracted considerable publicity, and in 1923 he decided to exploit the commercial possibilities of his formulation. A patent for the formula for use as a spray treatment was applied for under the name Entokil, but objections were made on linguistic grounds, and eventually the product was marketed in 1924 as Rentokil. Lefroy commenced operations with freelance assistants from Imperial College and was joined by Elizabeth Eades, who assisted with the invoices and book-keeping. Miss Eades was soon running the commercial side of the company, and continued the business after Professor Lefroy succumbed in 1925 to the effects of hydrogen cyanide gas, with which he was experimenting for the control of blowflies.

Miss Eades was soon to employ a chemist and entomologist called Norman Hickin (whose unpublished manuscript, *My Life with Woodworm*, is the source for the information on the history of the Rentokil company given here). Dr Hickin was a man of considerable energy and talent. He perceived during the immediate post-Second World War years that furniture beetle infestation had become a major problem, and he masterminded a vast and successful nationwide campaign to alert home owners and to tackle the situation. This included intensive advertising and lecturing, mobile exhibitions, and an advice centre in Bedford Square, London. He also believed that the government of the day should perceive furniture beetle as a potential national disaster.

The reasons for an upsurge in beetle damage are not difficult to understand. Little good quality timber had been obtainable since the 1914–18 War to supply a substantial boom in housing and, during the 1939–45 War, building maintenance and repair had a very low priority. Shortage of fuel resulted in colder, damper buildings, and many were shut up for most of the war years. All these changes favoured the insects.

Furniture beetle was originally seen as primarily a pest of furniture (hence its name) and most early treatments were designed to control infestations in that class of item. Ealand (1916) summed up the generally accepted philosophy when he stated that heavily infested furniture should be destroyed.

The early post-war remedial industry did a great deal to counter this belief by demonstrating that even heavily infested items could be treated with insecticides. The housewife and her furniture became the targeted market for the early 'woodworm killer' promotions. Doubtless, as discussed above, the furniture beetle was present in large quantities and treatment was justified according to the philosophy of the day. This high industry profiling, however, produced an awareness of furniture beetle which was undoubtedly novel. Most people had not noticed furniture beetle, but now that they had been told what to look for, and told furthermore that this was a pest of national importance, they found beetle holes almost everywhere they looked. Not only did the home owners not want their furniture destroyed, but they could not abide the thought that they shared their home with insect infestation.

By the early 1950s the commercial importance of woodworm-killing fluids began to shift from furniture to structural timbers. Timber treatment was no longer a job for the householder or local builder, but a task for the specialist remedial firm whose surveyors would identify the problem and undertake the treatment. The concept that furniture beetle was a rapidly expanding nationwide problem became inculcated into the minds of home owners, surveyors and architects alike, and because no one perceived a health risk from insecticides their use could be maximized.

Nowadays we might look carefully for current insect activity before specifying preservative treatment, but in previous decades this has been considered both foolish and dangerous. Hickin (1966) quoted a legal case which apparently became known as 'Boland's Piano' – a story worth retelling because of the insight it provides into precautionary treatments, although this author must acknowledge that he has been unable to trace any official reference to the case.

Apparently a second-hand piano was purchased from a dealer who guaranteed that it was free from furniture beetle. Six months after purchase, flight holes appeared and after a lengthy correspondence the problem was taken to the courts. The dealer lost the case, and the judge is reported to have said: 'How stupid to give a guarantee that the piano had no furniture beetle just because it did not show any external evidence'.

What this case illustrates is the problem of primary colonization. A female furniture beetle might land on timber and lay a batch of eggs in a suitable site. If all was well for the larvae, then the beetles and accompanying flight holes would appear a year or two later, but in the intervening period there would be no indications that infestation was present. It is therefore theoretically impossible to be certain that there is no furniture beetle in any suitable and susceptible piece of timber, from easily visible external evidence. The conclusion is inescapable, if you have available a product that is perceived to be both efficacious and safe: all timber should be treated. The belief of many architects and other interested parties that old timber requires at least precautionary treatment must thus be seen as a legacy from the early post-war years.

At about this time a further marketing boost was given to the industry by the provision of 'guaranteed treatments', and this subject is discussed in Section 14.3. The guarantee stated that if further decay occurred then the timbers would be retreated at no further expense to the client. The guarantee applied only to the timber previously treated because of the problem of primary colonization as outlined above.

But what became of the nationwide furniture beetle epidemic, and why did so many untreated old house timbers and items of furniture stubbornly refuse to become peppered with furniture beetle holes as the decades passed? Many would claim this as a triumph for the preservative industry, and their claim might have some validity given the quantities of insecticides pumped into buildings since the last world war. Yet the mild voice of doubt and disquiet was raised even at the second annual convention of the British Wood Preserving Association (BWPA) in 1952. J. Price, who described himself as a 'dealer in wood, a lover of wood and a crusader for wood', stated:

> preservative publicity has not in my opinion been too subtle. The preservative industry will flourish best in a timber-conscious community, not one which has been scared into believing that wood in any situation, anywhere, is in imminent danger of disintegration from beetles or fungi.
>
> (Price, 1952, p. 37)

And Dr Fisher of the Building Research Establishment, whose work on death watch beetle has already been discussed, asked:

> Is there not a tendency to go a little too far without full and accurate knowledge of the biology of the insects, of the conditions determining whether the timber is liable to attack, and indeed whether or not a preservative treatment is really essential?
>
> (Price, 1952, p. 44)

Whether Fisher's words were justified at the time is a matter of opinion, but they were certainly prophetic. The remedial industry, once established, expanded rapidly, and although a core of companies based their work on the Code of Practice produced by the BWPA, very many others were operating using largely untrained labour. For these, any hole was a beetle hole, and any beetle hole was an excuse to treat the entire building.

Now, if we wish to redress the balance, we must pursue the concepts stated by Price and Fisher some 40 years ago.

5.2 Biology of the furniture beetle

The biology of the furniture beetle (*Anobium punctatum*) has been investigated in rather greater detail than has that of the death watch beetle.

According to Bletchley (1952) the female beetle lays, during the middle of the day, an average of about 28 eggs, and other researchers have reported similar numbers. This number of eggs is rather low for a wood-boring beetle (a factor of some importance, as discussed later) but their fertility has been found to be high. Rosel (1952) obtained an average of 20.8 eggs during his experiments, with a fertility of 95% (cultures maintained at 27 °C, 75–80% RH). The favoured sites for oviposition appear to be within the pupal chamber from which the female beetle emerged, or in the end grain of a suitable wood. Any roughened surface, particularly cracks and cavities, may however be chosen if necessary. It has been observed (Hickin, 1975) that females frequently mate and lay eggs while still within their exit holes, and this would clearly reduce the efficacy of surface treatments. The conditions required for eggs to hatch have been studied by several authors. Becker (1943)

suggested 65–70% RH as the lower level of viability in the northern hemisphere. Spiller (1948a) found that hatching is independent of humidities above 65% RH (at 22.5 °C) but is impaired between 50% and 60% RH. No eggs hatched at 45% RH and below. Bletchley (1957) found little influence of humidity above about 56% RH (22 °C) but noted that drier conditions were less suitable, and that few eggs hatched below 40% RH. These results are broadly in agreement, and are shown in Table 5.1 with probable associated moisture contents (Siau, 1995).

The incubation period is temperature dependent and has been measured as 2.0–2.5 weeks at 22 °C (86% RH) and 4.5–5.5 weeks outdoors.

The minimum relative humidity and moisture content required for growth and development of *Anobium* have been investigated to a limited extent (Becker, 1942). Williams (1983) provided considerably more information on a closely related North American anobiid *Xyletinus peltatus*, a rather larger insect. Both sets of data are included in Table 5.2. The Becker figures are the minimum for growth, whereas the Williams data represent conditions under which no young larvae survived.

Both series of experiments were conducted under temperature regimes favourable to development.

These data suggest that a timber moisture content of about 12% is probably the lowest that newly hatched anobiid larvae, including furniture beetle and probably death watch beetle, can tolerate. Williams believed that anobiid infestations will die out if timber moisture contents remain below about 12% throughout the year. The optimum for growth does not seem to have been established. Bletchley (1957) grew 'exceptionally large' larvae at 22 °C, 86% RH, which would be equivalent to a moisture content of about 18–19%.

Table 5.1 The relationship between egg hatching and relative humidity in *Anobium punctatum*

Observations	Relative humidity (%)	Moisture content in timber (%)
Hatching may be impaired	>56–65	>10–12
Few/no eggs hatched	<40–45	<8–9

Table 5.2 Reported environment which halted larval growth in anobiid beetles

Species	Temperature (°C)	Relative humidity (%)	Timber moisture content (%)	Reference
A. punctatum	20	65–70	12.0–13.5[a]	Becker (1942)
X peltatus	25	59.1±2.6	11.6±0.7	Williams (1983)

[a] estimated

Becker (1942) stated that larvae grow best at or above fibre saturation (28–30%).

The young larva burrows into the timber through the base of the egg and in so doing fills the egg capsule with faecal pellets. As it brushes against the surface of the egg it picks up yeasts, essential to nutrition, which have been deposited on the egg by the female. These yeasts will become established within its gut. Yeasts are killed at 26 °C, which is a factor liable to restrict the development of *Anobium* infestations in some roofs.

Rates of feeding, and therefore rates of growth, are increased by temperature. Williams (1977) found that tunnels produced by *X. peltatus* were 70–80% shorter in colonies maintained at 10 °C than those maintained at 24 °C and larval weight gain was 50–75% less.

Larval growth and the duration of the larval stages depend upon temperature and humidity, but nutrition is also highly important. The scarcity of nitrogen in dead timber is thought to be a major reason why larvae have to burrow so extensively. Baker (1969) investigated how furniture beetle digested sound Scots pine sapwood, and noted that 26–29% of the swallowed wood was digested, and that this comprised 7–8% of the lignin, 40% of the cellulose/hemicellulose and most of the soluble protein. He also found that the amount of nitrogen acquired by larvae during their growth was up to two-and-a-half times that provided by the wood, and this supported an idea explored by Toth (1952), who considered that symbiotic organisms living within the digestive system of the larvae must be able to fix atmospheric nitrogen.

Furniture beetle larvae are very similar in appearance to death watch beetle larvae (Figure 5.2). The larval stage usually takes 3 or more years to complete but may be considerably shortened if an abundant source of usable nitrogen is available. One such source was blood-casein glues used historically in the cheaper grades of plywood. Cymorek (1965) obtained beetles after 8 months on an artificial medium which contained blood glue. Modern adhesives are of no nutritional value to the insects.

The presence of fungus has been shown to increase larval growth, though not to shorten the duration of the larval stage. Bletchley (1966) studied the relationship and concluded that the presence of white rot increased the rate of growth, but decreased the rate of survival. Brown rots allow some increase in growth at lower timber weight, but significantly reduced the survival rate. He concluded that the diminution of the survival rate might be due to changes in nutrition or cannibalism due to the breakdown of walls between tunnels.

Less favourable conditions which prolong the larval stage tend also to produce smaller adults (Meyer, 1970). Spiller (1948b) investigated the numbers of eggs laid by large and small females (size not defined) and noted that small females produced fewer eggs (Table 5.3).

The observations of several researchers thus show that conditions which are less favourable to the larvae prolong the larval stage, thereby retarding population increase. The adults produced are also smaller, and may be selected against by the opposite sex (Goulson *et al.*, 1993). These also lay fewer eggs and therefore decrease population viability. This combination of factors may explain why a furniture beetle or death watch beetle infestation tends to die out at low moisture levels, as predicted by Williams (1983) and observed by several authors, including Maxwell Lefroy (1924).

Figure 5.2 The furniture beetle larva closely resembles that of the death watch beetle.

Table 5.3 Numbers of eggs laid by different sized *Anobium punctatum* (Data from Spiller, 1948b)

Size	No. of adults	Average no. of eggs
Large	126	11.3
Small	93	3.6

When fully grown, the larva burrows towards the surface and excavates a pupal chamber known as a puparium. Usually only a thin veneer of timber remains between the pupa and the surface of the timber. The pupal stage lasts about 8 weeks, and the adults emerge between late May and August, with a peak in late June and July. Beetles tend to stay within their exit holes during cool weather and the females frequently mate without emerging, by positioning themselves so that their abdomens protrude from the emergence holes. They are active fliers and may therefore enter buildings through open windows.

5.3 Monitoring current activity and population

Furniture beetle, although probably present, was not much of a danger to structural timbers in past centuries. Where sapwood is present in oak building timbers it is usually only a small proportion of the whole, and even when softwoods were used the amount of sapwood was frequently insignificant (except perhaps in floorboards) and the dimension of the timber was generous. Sometimes roofs were constructed using poles and in these situations far more sapwood will be present. In general, however, the presence of a few decayed sapwood edges, or even decayed thin section joists, in an otherwise sound roof, implies historical damage which may be safely ignored, provided that it has no structural implications, rather than ongoing infestation which must be treated.

The method of converting historical timbers by squaring the sides and sawing through the heartwood frequently produces a distribution pattern for furniture beetle that is even more distinctive than the distribution pattern for death watch beetle. Thus a quarter-sawn post may exhibit axe marks accompanied by extensive furniture beetle holes in the sapwood timber on two sides, while the other two sides are free from damage. Furniture beetle damage in this situation will be shallow, probably old, and of no consequence (see Section 11.8).

Hickin (1975) and others state that building timbers have to be aged before they are attacked. Hickin suggests about 20 years for softwoods and 60 years for oak. Bletchley (1957) disputes this for furniture beetle, noting that the beetles are quite capable of attacking fresh timber. He considers that the observed time lag is caused by the low number of eggs produced, and the length of the life cycle. An infestation initiated by one or two beetles might not become noticeable for many years.

Active furniture beetle can be recognized by the presence of sharp-edged holes with interiors the colour of freshly cut timber (Figure 5.3), and lemon-shaped bore dust. This is usually accompanied by dead beetles on floors and window sills. Old damage does not require treatment. In time, oxidation causes the interior of the holes to darken and the sharp edges of the flight holes are lost. If there is doubt concerning the activity of furniture beetle this can be resolved by fastening tissue paper tightly to the timber surface for a flight season, as described in Section 4.3. Active beetles will punch

Figure 5.3 Active furniture beetle infestation is indicated by bore dust the colour of freshly cut timber trickling from the holes.

holes through the paper. An alternative method, particularly useful with furniture, is to use a polish that clogs up all the old holes. New holes are then readily visible.

There has been an increasing interest in non-insecticidal control methods in recent years, as public concern over preservative treatments has increased. One field of enquiry that has proved useful with other (non-timber decay) pest insects has been pheromone traps. Pheromones include chemicals dispersed by the sexually mature beetles in order to attract the opposite sex. A drop of the appropriate chemical is placed in the centre of a simple sticky or pitfall trap, and will usually attract many beetles. A wide variety of chemicals are used by different insects, and the isolation and identification of these chemicals is a complex task. White and Birch (1987) showed that the sex pheromone used by furniture beetle was similar to that used by the closely related biscuit beetle, and the pheromone has been investigated (Burkholder and Phillips, 1988). Synthesis of the active ingredient proved difficult, but in 1995 lures for furniture beetles were produced, and a sticky trap based on these lures was marketed. Trials have shown that these traps will attract furniture beetles (Pinniger and Child, 1996), and they thus make a useful and inexpensive method of detecting current infestation. If used in conjunction with effective repair and maintenance, they may assist in the eradication of beetle populations.

5.4 Methods of treatment and control

Section 5.2 discussed how a poor environment for the furniture beetle increases the duration of the larval stage, reduces the size of the resulting beetle, and reduces the number of eggs laid. Thus a furniture beetle colony living at the lower levels of moisture tolerance or in nutritionally depleted timber is likely to decline in numbers. This is the reason why beetle populations tend to die out if the timber moisture level remains below about 12%, even though individual larvae will be able to tolerate drier conditions. A dry roof will tend to maintain moisture levels of about 12–15% depending on the time of year so that a well-maintained roof is only marginally suitable for colonization. A beetle infestation may therefore decline if all sources of dampness are halted and the timbers remain dry. The treatment of historical damage caused by an infestation that is no longer active cannot be justified, but if active infestation is rife then some form of insecticidal treatment may be required.

5.4.1 Spray and injection treatments

Spray treatments have generally been employed where preservatives are considered necessary, and these should probably be more successful against furniture beetle than they are against death watch beetle because most furniture beetle damage is in the sapwood. The surface retention of insecticides is maximized during spraying by keeping the lance close to the timber (30 cm or less) and using a relatively low pressure. Fine sprays and high pressures produce fogs of chemical in the atmosphere. Fogs may also be produced intentionally, as discussed in Section 5.4.2. They are more difficult to control than sprays, and the depth of fluid penetration within the timber will probably be shallower. Paste treatments are not normally specified.

The injection of insecticides into flight holes has been popular for many years, and Hickin (1949) discussed and illustrated a rather elegant device (constructed from copper and rather similar to an old-fashioned blowlamp in appearance) called the Rentokil Fetcham injector (Figure 5.4). This has now been supplanted by the plastic injector bottle, a less attractive but more economical alternative.

The injection of flight holes is sometimes dismissed on the grounds that the beetle has clearly emerged and the treatment is therefore useless. However, the pupal chambers within the emergence holes are the preferred site for egg laying, and the preservative will penetrate along the grain into adjacent galleries. Emergence holes may also be the only way to impregnate timber if the surface

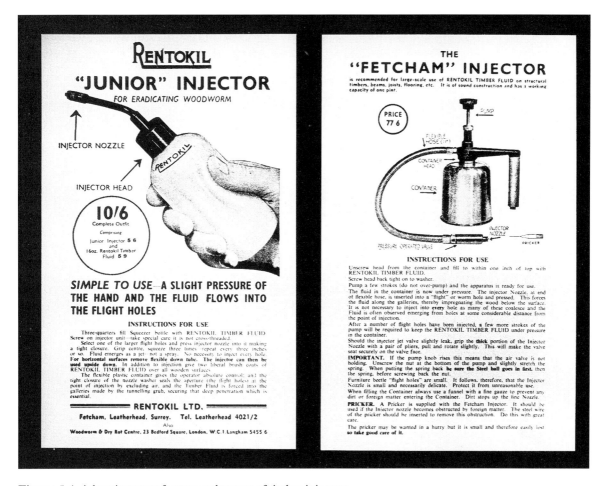

Figure 5.4 Advertisements for two early types of timber injectors.

finishes must not be disturbed. It is advisable in the latter case to test the preservative on a small and inconspicuous area of the item first, to ensure that there are no undesirable surface effects.

The National Trust Manual of Housekeeping (Sandwith and Stainton, 1984) recommends injection into holes at about 5 cm intervals. Eye protection should be used in case the fluid spurts from adjacent holes and excess fluid should be wiped off. Unfinished surfaces should be brush treated with the same preservative. The manual recommends repeating the treatment the following year and the authors stress the need for regular inspection.

5.4.2 Fogging

Fogging treatments have been devised in order to reduce the quantities of preservative used. Fogs are particularly indicated where large or inaccessible spaces are to be treated.

Catt (1991) states that the treatment is designed to kill the eggs, rather than the larvae or emerging adults as in orthodox spray treatments. One problem here may be the beetles' tendency to lay eggs in cracks, crevices and old emergence holes. In practice the pesticide might not contact a high proportion of the eggs. Another problem, common to both fogging and smoke treatments, is that the pesticide is not targeted directly onto the affected timber.

5.4.3 Freezing/heating

The deep freezing of furniture and other artefacts in order to destroy infestations is worth consideration, if a minimum temperature of –20 °C can be achieved. It should be noted, however, that this temperature may not be low enough to kill all the eggs, and Hansen (1992) recorded two beetles emerging from 'sawdust biscuits' which had contained eggs subjected to –30 °C (79.8±30.4 eggs laid on each biscuit).

The items are kept at room temperature prior to treatment so that the furniture beetles are active. They are then placed in polythene bags containing a little silica gel to absorb excess moisture and positioned in the freezer so that air can circulate around them. A temperature of –20 °C or lower should be maintained for 48 h and it would be usual to monitor with temperature probes to ensure that the correct temperature has been reached.

The temperature after removal should be allowed to rise slowly over about an eight-hour period while the item remains in the polythene bag. Some authorities suggest that the freeze–thaw cycle should be immediately repeated. This is because eggs and larvae have a natural tolerance of low temperatures, which enables them to survive in dead trees during harsh winters.

Heating timber will eventually kill wood-boring insects, but the method has the disadvantage that timber may shrink or crack. This disadvantage has been overcome by a new process which slowly raises the wood temperature to 55 °C and then lowers it again over an 18-hour cycle while maintaining a constant humidity. The system seems to work well for furniture and other items which may be placed in a suitably designed chamber. The method is currently being adapted for use on building timbers but there are few test data available at present on which to judge the process in the building context.

5.4.4 Fumigation

Museums have commonly fumigated infested objects with a range of insecticides, many of which have proved to be highly toxic or to adversely affect some objects treated.

In recent years attention has focused on high concentrations of carbon dioxide, which act on the insects' central nervous system, and high concentrations of nitrogen, which excludes oxygen from the air. The efficacy of both gases is reduced at temperatures below 30 °C , and prolonged exposure may be necessary to kill the beetle eggs and larvae. The use of nitrogen produces particular difficulties because furniture beetle may be adapted to withstand low oxygen concentrations within their tunnels (Paton and Creffield, 1987). Pinniger and Child (1996) provide data to show that 13% of furniture beetle larvae survived a 0.3% oxygen concentration after three weeks' exposure, whereas 4% survived a five-week exposure (normal air oxygen content is 20%). In spite of these difficulties treatments are commercially available for portable objects.

CHAPTER SIX

Minor decay insects

6.1 House longhorn beetle

This beetle (*Hylotrupes bajulus*) (Figures 6.1 and 6.2) is one of a large number of beetles that comprise the family Cerambycidae and is a large insect, the females reaching about 25 mm in length whereas the males are rather smaller. They derive their common name, 'longhorn', from the greatly elongated antennae found in most species. Most of the longhorn beetles require a high timber moisture content, and these attack green and un-seasoned timber. Only a few affect seasoned wood, and are able to continue their development after the timber has been utilized in building construc-tion, furniture or manufactured goods. Larvae of these species may be very persistent, and adults have been known to emerge from timber up to 40 years after the log was converted. Very few are able to re-infest converted timber.

The house longhorn can re-infest building timbers. The beetle attacks the sapwood of recently felled softwood, although some instances of damage to hardwoods have been recorded. Becker (1976) believed that the egg-laying females were attracted by particular extractives (diterpenes) present in fresh pine wood. He also suggested that the beetles were unable to attack older timber because of changes in the amino acids it contained.

The house longhorn beetle is widely distributed throughout northern Europe, where its status changed from uncommon insect to serious pest during the first half of the twentieth century. This change coincided with the loss in quality of new building timbers. In Britain it is now restricted to an area which includes north Surrey, parts of London, north Kent, south Essex and Hampshire. The problem still seems to be centred around the towns of Walton, Weybridge and Camberley (Lea, 1994). Infestation does occasionally occur elsewhere; Hickin (1957) records the beetles in floorboards in a house in Lisburn, County Antrim. These isolated infestations seem to have been present when the timber was imported, or to derive from other, more recently imported items. There is evidence that the beetle was more widespread in the past, and it has been suggested that its distribution became more restricted during the nineteenth century because of smoke pollution. Certainly historical damage (which does not require treatment) is frequently found, particularly in London. Larvae are some-times imported unintentionally, in packing cases and orange boxes, notably from Spain, and the current localized distribution may reflect these accidental re-introductions. Progressive infestation (as opposed to accidental introduction) may also be limited by the temperature required to provoke flight. Beetles appear to fly rarely at temperatures below about 25 °C, and the optimum is recorded as 30 °C (Cymorek, 1968). Beetle flight has been observed on a hot summer afternoon in Camberley, Surrey (Duffy, 1954), an area that has a good proportion of high summer temperatures.

Around 140–200 eggs are laid within narrow shrinkage cracks on the surface of the timber. The eggs hatch in about 5–10 days, depending on temperature and humidity, and the larvae burrow

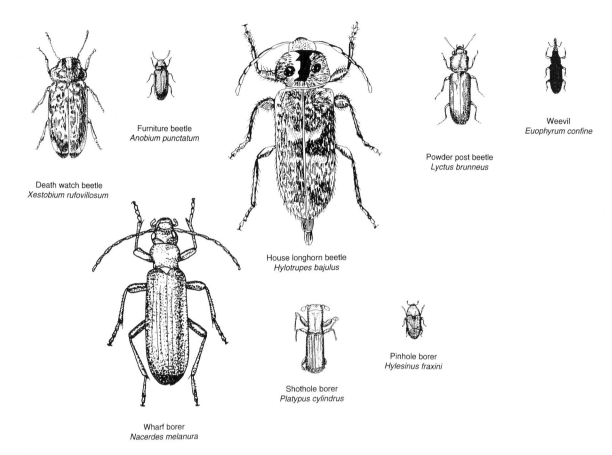

Figure 6.1 Relative sizes of wood-boring insects. The adult house longhorn beetle is about 15 mm in length.

into the timber. The average length of the larval stage is 3–6 years, but this may be considerably extended if conditions are unfavourable. Growth, as with the other beetles discussed, is stimulated by a low level of brown rot decay. During the growth period the larva may reach a length of 25 mm and achieve a weight of 0.5 g (Figure 6.3). The larva is therefore robust and capable of inflicting considerable damage on the timber. Optimum temperatures for growth appear to be 28–30 °C at moisture contents of 26–50%. The insect thus likes damp timber, but it has the ability to grow at much lower moisture contents. Schuch (1937) showed that survival was possible at a timber moisture content of 8–10% in pine sapwood and that this seemed to be a lower limit

for development, whereas Körting (1975) found that infestations could be maintained at a moisture content of 12% for a considerable period of time. Pupation takes place around May and the beetle emerges between July and September.

House longhorn attack may be recognized by characteristic oval emergence holes (6–10 mm long axis; Figure 6.2). These holes are packed with bore dust which contains small cylindrical pellets, and plugs of coarser fibres (Figure 6.5). The presence of bore dust in the holes is said to be diagnostic, and allows differentiation between house longhorn, and the wide variety of so-called forest longhorn beetles, which may emerge as accidental introductions in buildings. Forest longhorn beetles have no ability to re-infest building timbers.

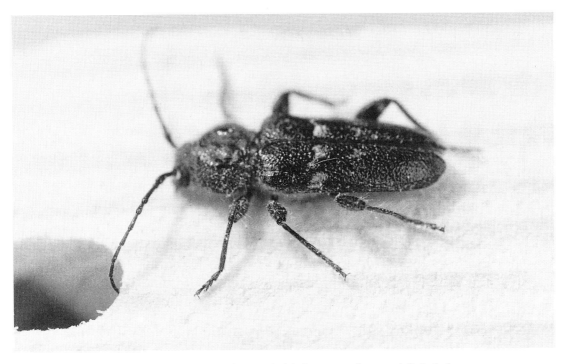

Figure 6.2 The house longhorn beetle (*Hylotrupes bajulus*) emerges from oval flight holes.

One other longhorn beetle is worth recording here, and that is the two-toothed longhorn *Ambeodontus tristis* (F). This is a New Zealand insect that causes damage to a wide range of timbers. It has only been recorded once in the UK, when it was found to be infesting ground floor joists in office premises in Syston, Leicestershire (Kennedy and Jeffries, 1975). It appears that the beetles were introduced into the building in New Zealand pine (*Dacrydium intermedium*) and thus they could presumably occur again.

6.1.1 Methods of treatment

Spirit-based, micro-emulsion or paste formulated insecticides are usually effective against house longhorn beetle. Forest longhorn beetle does not require treatment. Infestation is mostly confined to buildings constructed during the 1920s and 1930s. Use of pretreated construction timber is mandatory under the Building Regulations in the area where the insect is prevalent, and more recent

buildings have not been affected since these regulations were introduced in 1952.

The furniture beetle, death watch beetle and house longhorn beetle are the only three resident species able to colonize and maintain an infestation in seasoned building timbers. All may be controlled to a greater or lesser degree by preservative treatment if effective and flourishing infestation is in fact present.

Other timber-feeding insects are found in buildings, but these are either only capable of attacking the cell content of fresh timber and therefore have limited ability to re-infest, or they are dependent on fungal decay and high moisture contents.

6.2 Powder post beetles (Lyctidae, Bostrychidae)

These insects (Figure 6.1) are known as powder post beetles because they burrow into the sapwood

Figure 6.3 The house longhorn beetle larva feeds in the sapwood of modern softwoods, and may reach a length of 25 mm.

of susceptible hardwoods until nothing is left but dust held in place by a thin veneer of timber. The insects do not package the dust into frass pellets, so that frequently the expanded volume of dust ruptures the surface veneer (Figure 6.6). The exploded surface so formed is distinctive, and a good hand lens will confirm the absence of lemon-shaped pellets, as produced by furniture beetle.

Figure 6.4 The timber infested by the house longhorn beetle becomes filled with galleries packed with bore dust. Exit holes may be infrequent, and an uneven surface on the timber may be the only indication that beetle damage is present.

Furniture beetle frass pellets also give the bore dust a gritty feel when rubbed between the fingers, whereas powder post beetle frass feels silky. Both insects produce 1–2 mm diameter emergence holes.

Lyctus species have a world-wide distribution. The only indigenous British species appears to be *Lyctus linearis* Goeze, but a further four species of *Lyctus* and one species of *Trogoxylon* have been introduced (Hickin, 1975).

At least two of the species were introduced from America in the years following the 1914–18 War. This occurred because large quantities of timber had accumulated, and become infested, in American wood yards due to the disruption of shipping during the War. A survey undertaken by the Forest Products Research Laboratory in docks and timber merchants' yards during 1929 and 1930 showed that infested timber was regularly

Figure 6.5 Frass pellets of the house longhorn beetle are visible amongst the bore dust as short cylinders.

Figure 6.6 Powder post beetles (*Lyctus sp*) do not package dust into frass pellets, and so the surface of the timber explodes.

imported into the UK from Europe, America and Japan. The spread of *Lyctus* was thus attributed to the increase in overseas trade, and threatened at one time to seriously affect the hardwood trade with America. The problem was eventually diminished by site hygiene, kiln sterilization and the use of preservatives (Forest Products Research Laboratory, 1962).

Lyctus are elongate, slim beetles (2.6–6.0 mm in length) which lack the cowl-shaped projection of the thorax that protects the heads of furniture beetle and death watch beetle (Figure 6.1). The insect feeds on the starch in the sapwood of hardwoods, and does not have the ability to attack the wood cell wall. Hickin (1960) stated that eggs are not laid if the starch content of the timber is less than 3%. If the timber is air dried then much of the starch will be used up in respiration by the ray cells, which remain alive for some time after felling. Kiln drying was advocated by the Forest Products

Research Laboratory (1962) during the post-war years. Although kiln drying will indeed destroy any larvae present in the wood, it also kills the ray cells so that the starch is fixed within the sapwood. The timber may thus be susceptible to further attack for many years, and any risk of cross-infection from other timber must be avoided. Hickin (1945) perceived this problem and recommended that all converted timber and furniture should be treated with an insecticide.

During the decade 1940–1950 *Lyctus* was considered to be the most important wood-damaging beetle in the UK. This appears to have been because reserves of hardwood were poorly stored for extended periods during the war years, and became infested. The restrictions of the war and post-war years then promoted the production of utility furniture, which was constructed from every scrap of hardwood available in the wood yard and from air-seasoned logs. Beetle damage became extensive. The preventative spraying of susceptible timber with the new contact insecticides DDT, and later lindane, controlled *Lyctus* in the home and in the wood yard and by the 1960s the impact of the beetles had been reduced. The problem emerged again in the 1970s, particularly in hardwood flooring (which frequently incorporated sapwood on the underside so that a hardwood face could be presented as the wearing surface) and in furniture components stored on pallets. Pallets were traditionally made from elm and were frequently found to introduce infestation. The wide variety of tropical hardwoods imported during the last few decades has increased the number of potential hosts for *Lyctus*.

Eggs are laid by means of an ovipositor which is almost as long as the body of the insect. These eggs are placed by the female to a depth of about 5.0–7.5 mm in the earlywood conducting vessels of a large variety of hardwoods (Parkin, 1934). The female often makes space for the eggs by biting grooves in the surface of the timber. Only timber species with large vessels can be utilized because, although egg diameter can be varied, the ovipositor must fit into the vessel. This ovipositing behaviour precludes the infestation of softwoods and many hardwood species.

The 30–50 eggs hatch within about 8–20 days, depending on temperature, and the young larvae at first feed on the remaining egg contents before moving down the vessels. The range of moisture content required is said to be between 6% and 32%, depending on species. Parkin (1943) indicated that the lowest humidity *Lyctus linearis* could grow at was 40%, whereas Gay (1953) found a lowest timber moisture content of 7% for *Lyctus brunneus* larvae. Under favourable conditions the adult stage is reached within 8–12 months. Adults fly readily and are attracted to light, but infestations usually commence in the stockyard.

6.2.1 Methods of treatment

Infestations will die out within a few years as the starch within the cells becomes depleted. Microemulsion-based or solvent-based insecticides and pastes may be useful – if they will reach the infestation.

6.3 Weevils (Curculionidae)

The weevils (Figure 6.1) are one of the largest families in the animal kingdom, with about 60 000 described species. Many are serious pests of crops, stored food products and forestry, but in Britain only four species occur in building timbers. *Euophryum confine* and *Euophryum rufum*, both introduced from New Zealand and first recorded in the UK in 1937 and 1934 respectively, appear to be more successful than *Pentarthrum huttoni*. This weevil was apparently first described in 1854 from specimens caught in Exeter. Linscott (1967) suggested that it had been introduced from Chile. *Caulotrupodes aeneopice*, the fourth species, is rather uncommon.

Weevils attack hardwoods, softwoods and plywoods, but only in damp conditions where the timber has been modified by fungal decay (Figure 6.7). Completely sound timber is never attacked and so weevils are classified as a secondary pest. The spread of weevils into slightly decayed timber has been reported, and they have therefore been considered as vectors for the spread of fungus.

70

Figure 6.7 The wood-boring weevil (*Euophryum confine*) attacks timber which is already decayed by fungi. Note the distinctive elongated head, typical of weevils.

situations is interesting, because attempts to make the beetles fly have failed (Hum *et al.*, 1980). The characteristic damage of all species is recognized by small (1 mm diameter) emergence holes and ragged tunnelling along the direction of the grain. Tunnels frequently break the surface of the wood. These tunnels, created by both the larvae and the adult beetle, are loosely filled with granular bore dust which is finer than that of *Anobium*. Recent research has indicated that the larvae feed on cellulose and hemicellulose, leaving the lignin to be excreted in the frass (Pitman *et al.*, 1994).

6.3.1 Methods of treatment

The larvae are easily killed by drying the infected wood. Adults have a tendency to migrate to other areas when conditions become unfavourable, but this should not present a problem as colonization of sound, dry wood is not possible.

Insecticidal treatment is not required to control weevil infestations, provided that the associated fungal decay is arrested.

Moisture and fungal decay requirements vary between species. Baker (1970) stated that *E. confine* can live in structural timbers containing only about 20% wood moisture and less than 5% weight loss from fungal decay. *C. aeneopice* requires far damper and more intensely decayed conditions.

Studies of the life cycle of *P. huttoni* at 25 °C and 95–100% RH have demonstrated that the eggs, which are laid in cracks in the timber or holes made by the female, hatch after 16 days (Hammad, 1955). The pupal stage occurs between 6 and 8 months later and lasts about 16 days. The adults are easily distinguished from other wood-boring beetles, being almost cylindrical and having the head prolonged in front of the eyes, forming a well-defined snout. They are 3–5 mm long and brownish-black in colour. Adults live for about 16 months after emergence and can be found all year round. Dead weevils are frequently found in large quantities on window sills or around lights, and these assemblages suggest the presence of concealed wet rot decay. Their presence in these

6.4 Wharf borer (*Nacerdes melanura*)

Nacerdes melanura is believed to have originated in the Great Lakes area of North America, and has been introduced to all other parts of the temperate world by the passage of shipping. The common name, wharf borer, is attributed to its frequent occurrence in timber just above the high water line. It has been found widely distributed in the British Isles, but is particularly associated with the Birmingham canal network, the River Avon, and the estuaries of the South and South-east. Timber on bomb sites in London was frequently attacked, and infestations are still found in London in piling, structural timbers and buried debris in damp basements. Recent work on this insect (Pitman *et al.*, 1993) was prompted by infestation of stored timbers from the warship *Mary Rose* in Portsmouth. This infestation originated with beetles that were already present in the cellars in which the timbers were stored.

71

The wharf borer most readily attacks softwoods although, if conditions are favourable, oak and other hardwoods may also be infested. Like the weevils, it is not a primary pest of timber as it is associated with the early stages of fungal decay, and it will not attack completely sound wood. Although not entirely restricted to saline conditions, the wharf borer seems to prefer timbers impregnated with salt water, and it has been reported at the base of telegraph poles and fences which have been wetted with dog urine. Infestations have also been found in the structural timbers of St Pancras Parish Church, London (Hickin, 1952) and at the bases of lavatory pans in London (Hickin, 1963a). The infestation in the church, which apparently also included dead beetles and was some distance above ground, had previously been recorded as house longhorn beetle infestation. The author recently found the beetles infesting skirting boards in a first-floor bathroom at Deptford, London.

Adult beetles are usually seen in summer, sometimes invading buildings in large numbers. They are 7–15 mm in length and yellowish-brown with black tips to the soft wing cases. Females are rather larger than males. After mating, the females lay their eggs on timber with a high moisture content. Hickin (1975) states that the moisture content should not be much in excess of fibre saturation. However, Pitman et al. (1993) found that the moisture content of damaged timbers ranged from 130% to 670% of the dry weight. The greyish-white larvae, up to 30 mm in length, can be found all year round in irregular tunnels filled with plugs of wood fibres. Emergence holes are round or oval, and may be up to 6 mm diameter. This damage may be mistaken for that of the house longhorn beetle, but the presence of wood fibres in the tunnels, absence of cylindrical frass pellets, and a high timber moisture content, should distinguish the two.

6.4.1 Methods of treatment

Insecticidal treatment is not required providing the source of water is excluded and the associated fungal decay is arrested. Decayed timber should be replaced and sound timber dried, so that re-infestation will not be possible.

6.5 Pinhole and shothole borers (Scolytidae, Platypodidae)

More than 1000 species of beetles in these families attack stumps, logs and occasionally overmature trees in most forests of the world. They differ from the other wood-boring beetles considered in that it is mostly the adults that produce the tunnels. Baker (1956), who studied the British species, stated that the female is attracted by the burrowings of the male. After mating the female continues to bore a network of straight tunnels, 1–2 mm in diameter, while the male ejects the bore dust. Eventually, when their work is completed, clumps of eggs are laid within the burrows during the autumn and early winter months.

The larvae feed on fungi introduced by the female and form a lining on the tunnel wall (Beaver, 1989). This feeding behaviour has earned them the alternative name Ambrosia beetles, after the food of the gods in Greek mythology. The larvae take between 1 and 2 years to complete their development, and in some species all stages, including adults, may be present in a tunnel complex.

The names pinhole borer and shothole borer have been given by the timber trade, and reflect the size of the holes produced by different species. The holes resemble those of the furniture beetle, but may be distinguished by the absence of bore dust, and by the dark discoloration of the walls caused by the fungi. Damage may be restricted to the sapwood, or penetrate quite deeply into the heartwood.

Their reliance on fungus means that these beetles are particularly susceptible to dry conditions which will destroy the mould growth. They cannot therefore infest seasoned timber. Pinhole and shothole borers are not themselves a problem in buildings, but the damage they have caused in individual timbers may sometimes result in unnecessary treatment with insecticides.

6.6 Risk of termites in Britain

In 1994 a remedial technician in North Devon was somewhat startled when he removed a skirting board in order to install a damp proof course and exposed a well established colony of *Reticulotermes lucifugus*, a termite. This colony contained thousands of individuals and had clearly been present for many years.

Termites are frequently imported into Britain, but most are tropical species and have no chance of becoming established. There are, however, a few European and North American species which are more tolerant of cooler conditions, and the distribution of these might expand to include Britain if the climate became a little more favourable, or if they were accidentally imported into a suitable environment, for example a heated greenhouse or conservatory.

By altering the surface of the Earth and adding heat-trapping gases to the atmosphere, the expanding human enterprise is, without question, changing the climate (Samuels and Prasad, 1994). Biodiversity is the resource that is most threatened by the rapid climatic change likely to result from global warming (Wyman, 1991). Changes in climatic conditions will lead to distribution differences in both flora and fauna. Plants and animals whose habitats are restricted by low temperatures, for example, will expand into new territories as global warming takes effect. Thus in the UK we may expect to see the spread of Mediterranean/subtropical flora and fauna as temperatures rise. One particular group of insects, the Isoptera (white ants or termites) may pose a significant threat to the stability of the built environment in Britain; thus some background information may be appropriate here.

Termites feed on cellulitic materials including wood, plants, paper, cotton etc., but will also chew up vast quantities of plastic for no apparent reason. Underground electricity and communications cables have been penetrated even when an appreciable thickness of lead has been used as a covering. These materials are not used nutritionally, or even taken into the alimentary canal; they are just 'chewed off and spat out' (Hickin, 1971).

About one-third of the timber produced worldwide is lost due to various biodegrading agents. In tropical and subtropical conditions, termites are one of the major causes of this breakdown, and are responsible for heavy economic losses (Edwards and Mill, 1986). The approximate cost of the treatment of termites worldwide in 1986 was around US$200 million.

About 2000 species of termites are known, mostly from tropical areas, but only around 70–80 cause significant damage. They live in communities which may be complex (several million individuals) to simple (a few dozen). They are broken down into six groups, but species known as pests fall into three main categories, subterranean, dampwood and drywood.

Subterranean termites
Subterranean termites build their nests in the soil or on the sides of trees or transmission poles and rely on the soil for moisture. They desiccate easily, and so construct shelter tubes in their searches for food above ground to create a more humid environment, thus protecting them from the drying effects of the air.

Dampwood termites
These live in old tree stumps, rotting logs and pieces of buried timber (either structural or waste). Once established, however, they can move into sound wood in the structure of the building.

Drywood termites
Drywood termites live entirely within dry wood, and unlike the other groups are less dependent on an external source of moisture. They can thus survive above ground in most timbers and do not need access to soil.

It is members of the subterranean termites (Rhinotermitidae) which have become established in Europe, some species naturally and some following accidental introduction. These are more primitive termites with a relatively simple social organization. A recent paper (Serment and Pruvost, 1991) reporting on the growth, geographical spread and treatment of termites in France, reported that two species and two subspecies, all of them subterranean, are spreading through France (*Reticulitermes santonensis, R. lucifugus lucifugus, R. lucifugus grassei* and *R. lucifugus baryulensis*). The presence of termites has been officially recorded in France since the end of the eighteenth century. They were recorded in 1953 in the south and south-west of France, and by 1981 had spread considerably throughout all the Mediterranean south-west coasts. In the west and south-west, *R. lucifugus* communities thrive and re-infest regularly, but in the more northern areas they are very local, suggesting that their introduction is accidental. Termites have, however, been recorded in Paris since 1945. It is in such urban areas that the termite has found favourable conditions for survival in the more northern latitudes. Such conditions include:

- plentiful supplies of cellulose (wood, paper, boxes, tissues);
- high humidity (due to poor construction, building failure or proximity to water courses);
- warmth.

Thus although the termite's natural environment is the warm humid south-west, central heating in buildings in urban areas of the north has enabled them to establish populations.

The nest of *Reticulitermes* spp consists of a group of chambers, large or small according to circumstances, connected by runways. A mass of irregular honeycomb-like carton (excreta containing a large proportion of undigested or partly digested cellulose from the wood that has been eaten) is constructed, which increases living space and may play a part in regulating temperature. A special queen cell is formed, and covered runways leading to food sources are often widespread. As the colony increases in size, eggs and larvae are gradually carried further away from the main part of the nest, and hence away from the influence of the primary queen. Small groups of termites thus become isolated and therefore supplementary reproductives are produced to form the nucleus of a new colony. This is a common method of division in lower termites, especially *Reticulitermes* in Europe.

The spread of termites is generally governed by the formation of alates (winged reproductives).

Flight occurs at certain seasons, local critical climatic conditions appearing to be important. In the tropics, alates are formed just prior to the annual rainy season. It is possible that temperature and relative humidity differences in the soil or wood around the colony trigger this production. Alates do not appear to be formed in the accidentally introduced colonies of *R. lucifugus* in northern France and Britain, although the recent British infestation in North Devon appears to have spread from a greenhouse to timbers in outbuildings throughout the ¾ acre site. The infestation had affected not only wall plates and the base of studwork, but extended almost to the roof approximately 3 m above. However, had this infestation involved the more hardy termite species *R. santonensis* greater problems might well have arisen. *R. santonensis* can tolerate colder climates, can survive outside and are able to form alates. They are currently moving steadily northwards in France by establishing colonies on the wooden pilings of railway tracks (Dr Helaine Black, National Resources Institute, personal communication).

Further reports have suggested that subterranean termites are spreading northwards in the USA, aided by the trend towards milder winters (Synder, 1961) and that the dampwood termite, *Zootermopsis angusticollis*, can be found extensively up the Pacific coast of Canada (Hickin, 1971).

It therefore appears that should global warming have a significant effect on the climate of Britain, several species of termites would almost certainly become established in our built environment. Britain's buildings would then be subject to the destruction which is currently wrought in other parts of the world by this highly organized insect. Timbers such as teak heartwood may be resistant to termite attack, though even this can quickly be rendered vulnerable by wood-decaying fungi or bacteria. In living plant tissue, termites are also often secondary pests. The initial defect is often of minor importance, but after termite attack the plant may be completely destroyed or reduced in value as a crop. It is also worth noting that softwoods exported from North America and Northern Europe to areas with indigenous termite populations are ultimately destroyed by them (Hickin, 1975).

Even without the risk of global warming, however, recent changes in customs checks within the EU are likely to increase the chances of accidental termite infestations within Britain. From 1 January 1993, customs checks at the internal frontiers between member states of the EU were abolished. Harmonized plant health controls within the single market started on 1 June 1993. From this point onwards checks were focused on the country of origin of the plants. The directive requires that most controlled products moved within the EU have a plant passport attached, to show who has consigned the product and was therefore responsible for making sure that any special requirements (e.g. kiln drying) have been met. However, there is no control on, for example, pot plants brought in from France, or indeed the transporting of portable outbuildings. There is therefore a significant risk that insects, including termites, may be unwittingly introduced. This may well have been the case in the recent North Devon infestation.

6.6.1 Methods of treatment

A very well developed remedial industry can be found in countries where termite damage is a familiar occurrence. There is generally a great diversity in termite treatments; chemicals are used in the soil, in timber, in bait blocks (as antifeedants, repellants, attractants or arrestants). Insect growth regulators are also under development, together with other control mechanisms such as fluoro-lipids, chitin synthesis inhibitors and protozo-acides. Biological controls, including nematodes, fungi, fungicides and predators, are employed. Physical non-polluting methods include an electrical system which uses high-voltage electricity to 'zap' termites in their tunnels within the timber (Edwards and Mill, 1986).

In summary, it appears that the most immediate danger from R. *lucifugus* in Britain is likely to result from accidental introductions following the recently relaxed customs checks. These termites could easily establish colonies in buildings, though their spread would be slow. The more hardy termite R. *santonensis* is moving northwards unaided, and would fairly readily adapt to climatic conditions in England. The accidental introduction of this species would therefore be more serious.

CHAPTER SEVEN

Dry rot

7.1 History of dry rot and early treatments

In 1759 shipbuilders along the Thames were asked to give an opinion on the comparative durability of English and French ships. They concluded that the English ship of war should long outlast the French (Bowden, 1815, p. viii). By the beginning of the nineteenth century, however, the situation was reversed. Matters came to a head in 1810 when the *Queen Charlotte* was launched at Deptford (Ramsbottom, 1937). Close examination revealed that all her upper works – 'the ends of most of the beams, carlings, and ledges, the joinings of the planks etc.' – were infected with 'the dry rot'. The situation was investigated by A. Bowden of the Navy Office, who published his conclusions in 1815 as *A Treatise on the Dry Rot*.

Two main forms of timber decay were recognized in Bowden's day, and these were common or wet rot and a relatively new phenomenon they called 'dry rot'. The same terms are still used but the meaning is rather different, and it is important that this difference is understood.

In the eighteenth and early nineteenth centuries common or wet rot was seen as a form of decay which progressed inwards from the surface of the timber and was caused by the actions of wind, heat and water. The damage was thought to be chemical or mechanical. The resulting modified timber was thought to offer a particularly suitable substrate for fungus.

The earliest records of the term 'dry rot' date from the second half of the eighteenth century. A particularly useful description of the damage was published in the early nineteenth century:

The wood at first swells, after some time it changes colour, then emits gases which have a mouldy or musty smell. In the more advanced stages of it, the mass arises, and cracks in transverse directions. Lastly it becomes pulverulent, and forms vegetable earth, and generally in some of these stages of decay, the different species of fungus are found to vegetate on the mass.

(Wade, 1815, p. 3)

Dry rot was also observed to attack the timber from the interior outwards and to frequently leave only an apparently sound outer skin, unlike wet rot, which, as previously noted, progresses from the surface inwards. The term 'dry' was applied because of the crumbly mass that remained, and because it was not generally accepted that the decay was caused by water although it was exacerbated by warm, close and moist situations. Bowden stated that 'dry rot exists where there is no external moisture to produce it' (Bowden, 1815, p. 56). The cause was thought to be the fermentation of saps and vital juices within the timber, which was frequently provoked by heat. Bowden and others thought that these vital juices, which produced leaves and branches in the living tree, became destructive when the timber was converted because they then produced fungi (Bowden, 1815, p. 33). Internal pressures could, however, be alleviated if, as sometimes happened, the juices produced an external fungal growth (Bowden, 1815, p. 28). Wade was scornful of this theory and considered that fungus sometimes occurred on the damaged timber as a parasite. It was not accepted that either 'wet' or 'dry' rot was caused by fungi, although the result was frequently suitable as a basis for fungal growth.

A clear practical example of the way in which the name 'dry rot' evolved, and of the explanations engendered because of ignorance of the real cause, was given by a Mr J. George in his book *The Cause of Dry Rot Discovered*, published in London in 1829. At the back of his house in Chancery Lane were two 'subterranean vaults', which he wished to use for wine cellars. He chose the drier of the two and constructed a pine door in an oak frame. What happened next is best told in his own words:

> In October 1826 while locking my new, and, as I supposed, still sound door on coming out of the vault I fancied I perceived that the door in one part of it had a little given way, or was a little warped or shrunk inwards. I instantly applied my thumb nail to the part, and was exceedingly surprised to find that it penetrated the wood as easily as if it had been the cut part of a cheese. What can this be thought I? How can it have happened? The door has met with no rough usage, and it was new four or five years ago. I tried with my nail again on another part, it was equally soft. Surely it must be what we hear so much of as making such havoc in the Navy, it must be dry rot! How dry it looks! It cannot be the wet that has done it.
>
> (George, 1829, pp. 10–13).

The following week he investigated further and concluded:

> It cannot, as I have said before, be the wet because the wet has never touched the decayed part. The paint on the door has kept the wet even from touching any part of this timber itself.

If it were the wet must it not have decayed the outside first, just as it rusts iron, while the interior remains sound.

Eventually he believed that he had found the explanation:

> I have it! I have found it out! It is the heat which is so constantly working its way in such a quantity through the timber of the door, in the one direction or the other, and which now that some frost has come, is working its way out, and leaving behind it all that wet which it has deposited against the inner side of the door within the vault, and which is now running down so plentifully, and making a little pool of water in the ground, that has caused the decay.

George dismissed any connection between the dry rot and water because the decay was progressing from the inside of the timber outwards. We note, however, that the cellar was moist enough to cause excessive condensation in winter, and that therefore the timber was damp. George and most of his contemporaries evidently did not understand that water absorbed by, and held within, the timber could cause decay.

The concept that heat changes produced dry rot had been propounded earlier by Bowden and by Lingard, and a quote from Lingard (1819) will serve to show how a lack of understanding resulted in the wrong cause being attributed to the decay, even though all the required facts were observed:

> For instance what can be more to the prejudice of timber, or more hostile to the idea of its preservation or continuance of health and soundness, than using it in the manner in which it is perpetually employed for boarding kitchens and other rooms on the ground floor, where three sides of the joist, and the lower face of the flooring are bedded in earth so moist as to amount almost to positive wet, while the upper side of the joists and the upper face of the flooring is perfectly dry, and exposed only to the effects of heat from a large fire perpetually burning?
>
> (Lingard, 1819, p. 29)

The author attributed the decay to the movement of heat and not to the damp.

A comparison of our descriptions of brown rots given in Section 3.4.4 with the earlier descriptions of dry rot strongly indicates that Bowden and Wade's 'dry rot' was in fact brown rot, and 'common' or 'wet' rot was white rot (Figures 7.1 and 7.2). The application of two different names is understandable, because the two forms of decay do not look alike, and each progresses in a different fashion from the other. It is also important to note that the term 'dry rot' was used for all brown rots, and would therefore have encompassed a wide variety of fungi which we would now consider to be wet rots (e.g. cellar rot). The demise of the Navy's ships is also easily explained when it is remembered that brown rots particularly favour softwoods in humid environments.

The second half of the eighteenth century, and the first decade of the nineteenth, were periods of protracted warfare which were very costly in ships. At the same time the seamen were demanding better living and working conditions. These factors caused the following, according to Bowden:

- Large section hardwood for ship building was in short supply and sappy timber, together with large quantities of imported softwood, was used. Softwood was cheaper, and produced a lighter, more manoeuvrable, ship.
- The demand for new ships was heavy and there was not time to season the timber.
- A process for the rapid shaping of timber by steaming was devised, so that even if timber was seasoned, it was frequently rewetted.
- Methods of heating were devised to improve living conditions in cramped and poorly ventilated areas. This produced a dank atmosphere, ideal for fungal growth.

The changing pattern of building throughout the eighteenth century also encompassed a far greater structural use of softwoods; thus dry rot (brown rot) in houses became an increasingly serious problem, although it never reached the epidemic proportions experienced in the muggy, damp ships of the Navy.

Figure 7.1 Brown rots tend to leave a sound outer skin of timber. They are more common in softwoods than in hardwoods.

The scandal of dry rot (brown rot) in the Navy produced the first 'remedial industry'. The *Encyclopaedia Britannica* (4th edition, 1824) provides the following:

All the newspapers and journals of the day were filled with this alarming fact [dry rot in the *Queen Charlotte*] and, in consequence thereof a multitude of dry-rot doctors proffered their assistance, one having a nostrum for eradicating the disease where it had made its appearance, and another for preventing its farther approach. Some of these specifics were expensive and inconvenient, many of them impracticable of application, and most of them futile and objectionable in one way or another.

A good example would be the experiments of Mr Lukin, who constructed a kiln at Woolwich

Figure 7.2 White rots are more common in hardwoods than in softwoods. They generally require more water than brown rots.

Dockyard, the purpose of which was to drive water from timber and replace it with the distillate from sawdust. The kiln was charged with several hundred loads of timber and heated. The resulting explosion killed eight men, wounded twelve others and demolished the building.

Particularly notable was a publication produced in 1815 entitled *Practical Observations on the Dry Rot in Timber* by Mr Ralph Dodd, a civil engineer. This work was actually an advertisement for his 'Dry Rot Preventative'. Unsurprisingly, given his desire to promote his product, Dodd was at pains to emphasize the difficulty of eradicating dry rot:

If wood is highly impregnated with the dry rot it is impossible to stop it, nothing but the cutting away of the parts or amputating them will do. We may as well strive to smother fire with gunpowder, or stop spreading flames by a wall of pitch, as to stop it when this destructive Dry Rot takes place.

(Dodd, 1815, p. 18)

This statement, and similar opinions, were probably fair when applied to timbers in dank ships, and in some festering domestic situations (for example where ground floor timbers were covered with oiled floor cloth, a common practice). Unfortunately, their legacy remains with us today, when conditions are frequently very different.

The fact that fungi caused the decay rather than just living on it was not firmly established until work by the German botanist Robert Hartig was published in 1874. Considerable research into decay fungi ensued, not all of which was relevant to practical building situations. The conclusions reached, however, stay with us and have been woven into the mythology of dry rot.

The original term 'dry rot', as discussed above, included a range of brown rots. Gradually throughout the nineteenth century the term became restricted to fungi which produced substantial mycelium, and even during the first half of the twentieth century there was a tendency to include the mine fungus *Antrodia vaillantii* as a dry rot. Eventually, however, the name referred to only one fungus, *Serpula lacrymans*, and this became known as the 'true dry rot'. All other decay fungi (brown and white rots) were lumped together as wet rots.

Dry rot, like furniture beetle, became more prevalent during and after the First World War because of poor building maintenance and the use of inferior quality timber (Dewar, 1933). The Second World War produced even greater problems, as discussed in Section 5.1, because buildings were sealed up for long periods of time, maintenance had low priority, and bomb damage resulted in saturated masonry. Deliberate actions which had an unfortunate effect on the building environment and particularly encouraged dry rot included the blocking of vents as a precaution against gas attack, and the piling of sandbags against walls to reduce bomb damage. By the end of the war decay was rife (Cartwright and Findlay, 1952).

E.H. Brooke Boulton could be considered the chief adversary of post-war dry rot (Figure 7.3). Brooke Boulton had been a lecturer on forestry at Cambridge before becoming technical director of the Timber Research and Development Association, a post which he held for 14 years. During the mid-1940s he left the TRDA and established a company called Pestcure Ltd in order to tackle the dramatic increase in dry rot and other forms of timber decay which had resulted from the war.

Brooke Boulton carried across the British Isles his message that timber replacement for dry rot treatment had cost the nation £1 million in 1937, but that in 1949 that cost had risen to £20 million. He argued that the harbouring of dry rot should be made an offence unless its presence was notified and treatment was applied.

The origin of *Serpula lacrymans* in the British Isles remains obscure. The fungus does not occur outside of buildings over most of its range across the temperate regions of the world, and the few records and herbarium specimens from fallen trees in Europe, USA and Australia all seem to refer to a closely related species, *Serpula himantioides*, as far as these can be verified. However, Bagchee (1954) found the fungus growing on tree stumps at an altitude of 3000–5000 m in the forests of the Western Himalayas and further investigations have shown that, though uncommon, it is found growing wild within a wide zone in Northern India. Singh *et al.* (1994) reveal to us that large amounts of timber were imported from the Himalayas to England during the period 1850–1920 but, as they indicate, this trade commenced at too late a date to explain the presence of the fungus in the UK from the late eighteenth century. One might argue that the early dry rot was caused by other brown rots, but there is little doubt from contemporary illustrations and descriptions that *Serpula lacrymans* was present. It seems quite logical to suppose that dry rot, which had presumably spread from India across Russia to the Atlantic (it is common in buildings across Northern Europe), reached these shores in infected timbers from Europe. We know that the fungus attacked softwood on ships, and we also know that fungus had frequently to be scraped off cargoes of softwood when they were landed. Many cargoes of timber from the New World and from Europe had been largely destroyed in the ships' holds before they reached port.

Dry rot is a destructive fungus whose history and name has left a legacy of confusion. Many still consider any cuboidally cracked decay to be dry rot, and the implication in the name, that dry rot needs less water than wet rots, has frequently had disastrous consequences, at least for buildings. But conditions within buildings now are often far different from those in the past. Does the fungus always need vigorous and destructive treatment, or are there more sensitive methods of control that may be tried? In order to answer this question we must examine the biology of the fungus.

7.2 Biology of dry rot

The fresh dry rot fruit is rust brown with a white margin (Colour Plate 3) and a cratered or folded

Figure 7.3 A selection of press cuttings discussing the decay problem caused by the Second World War.

spore-producing surface (see Section 8.4; Figure 7.4). These craters are only found in a few closely related species (the others are rarely found in buildings), and are an important diagnostic characteristic. The dry rot fruit turns black as it ages and dries but the outlines of the craters or folds remain visible. Fruits are normally flat but corky; bracket-shaped forms may sometimes grow (Colour Plate 4), particularly on the external surface of walls in sheltered corners.

Fruiting may occur naturally when the fungus has grown sufficiently, but is frequently a response to exposure works. Thus the fungus may be induced to fruit by removing wall plaster or lifting floorboards.

Millions of rust-brown spores are liberated when the fruit is mature and it has been calculated that a fruit body of 100 cm³ would produce about 50 million spores in 10 minutes (Falck, 1912).

These may form a conspicuous dust layer, and sometimes this is the first indication of a concealed dry rot infestation. The fungus is reproductively inefficient, and only about one-quarter to one-third of the spores are viable. The rest appear to have a disorganized internal structure, often with no nucleus. Germination of fertile spores requires a timber moisture content close to the timber fibre saturation point (28–30%) and a relative humidity above 95–98%, depending on temperature (Viitanen and Ritschkoff, 1991a). Spores are resistant to desiccation and may be capable of germination when they are several years old, although viability decreases with time. Airborne spores are present in most buildings, but the spore loading increases considerably following a dry rot outbreak. This is a major reason why some buildings seem particularly prone to dry rot infestation. Architects and surveyors are frequently

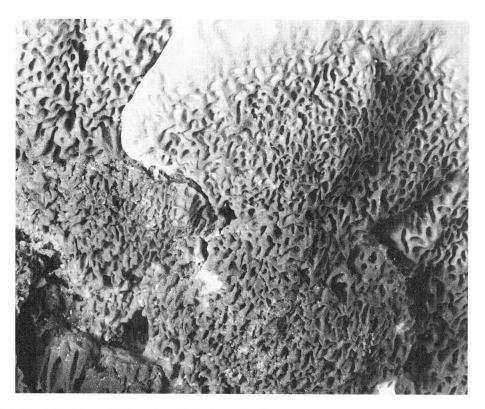

Figure 7.4 The folded (merulioid) surface of the fungus is diagnostic. It is only found in a small group of closely related fungi, of which only dry rot is commonly found in buildings.

concerned about the risk from carrying dry rot spores home from an infected building on their shoes and clothes. Spores are undoubtedly transported in this fashion, but the chances of a viable spore lodging in a suitable habitat, and growing, are very slight.

Frankland and Hay (1951) reported a more significant problem: the possibility of an allergic reaction to dry rot spores. Fruits should therefore be carefully removed and destroyed. A protective mask should be worn by anyone involved in this operation.

If conditions are suitable then a spore may germinate, and a microscopic fungal thread known as a hypha will appear. Hyphae then spread and grow together to form an aggregate structure called a mycelium.

The growth rate of dry rot under experimental conditions has been studied by several authors (Bravery, 1991), and rates of 5–9 mm per day have been established over inert substrates at optimum temperatures under laboratory conditions. Coggins (1977) observed a growth rate of 2.25 mm per day at temperatures approaching 20 °C in a building.

A variety of different mycelia are formed depending on environmental conditions (Colour Plates 5–9). Cotton wool-like growth may occur in cavities where the humidity exceeds about 95%. Rosettes are sometimes formed on wall surfaces where boundary humidities are high because of damp masonry. Leathery surface growths may appear where there is some air movement but the humidity remains high.

Thick conducting strands, sometimes referred to as rhizomorphs, are produced. These may cross inert surfaces and penetrate deep within masonry. This ability reflects tolerance to moderately alkaline conditions. Fresh mortar is too alkaline, and repointing in some situations may be sufficient to contain dry rot within a wall. Other fungi will also grow through walls if the alkalinity of old mortar is sufficiently reduced, and the ability is not, as frequently stated, a unique characteristic of dry rot (Figures 7.5 and 7.6).

The fungus does not assimilate nutrients from bricks and old mortar, but it does appear to be dependent on the calcium content in the following

Figure 7.5 Most fungi that produce strands have some ability to grow through walls. This photograph shows strands of an unidentified poria fungus.

manner (Bech Anderson, 1991). Brown rots (including dry rot) commence their attack on the cell wall by producing an acid to break down the hemicelluloses which ensheath the cellulose fibre bundles. Dry rot uses oxalic acid, but this is rather a strong acid and needs to be controlled. Control is affected by calcium, which reacts with the oxalic acid to produce insoluble calcium oxalate. The latter is deposited as harmless crystals on the hyphae. Other fungi investigated seem to use alternative and perhaps more efficient methods to control acid-mediated degradation. It has been recognized for many years that dry rot is commonly associated with damp masonry or ceiling plaster, and this may reflect the requirement for calcium. Certainly a degree of alkaline tolerance in the fungus, and a rich source of calcium within the buildings, would seem to be good reasons why an apparently unsuccessful woodland fungus should be far more successful in buildings, albeit within a narrow range of environmental conditions.

Figure 7.6 Roots may sometimes be confused with dry rot strands in walls, particularly if the rest of the plant has been removed.

The fungus does seem to require a stable environment in order to thrive, but temperature and moisture content requirements do not differ greatly from those of many other decay fungi. A recent compilation of environmental data for a variety of fungi, and from several sources, provided the data for dry rot and cellar rot given in Table 7.1.

The minimum moisture content figures provided for dry rot (*Serpula lacrymans*) and cellar rot (*Coniophora puteana*) seem unusually low, and decay would be extremely slow at these levels. In practice dry rot sometimes attacks timber with a moisture content down to about 22%, but probably only from a far wetter source. Cellar rot does not normally cause much damage below about 25% moisture content. A study reported by Viitanen and Ritschkoff (1991a) provided an optimum timber moisture content of 30–70% for both fungi.

The widely accepted principle that timber is not decayed by fungi if kept at a moisture content below 20% was devised by Cartwright and Findlay in 1946. This rule contained a safety margin, as the authors believed that the minimum moisture level required by wood decay fungi in most practical situations was probably 22–24%.

The data presented in Table 7.1 provide no support for the commonly held belief that buildings dry through a stage unsuited to wet rot but suitable for dry rot attack. It frequently happens that wet rot has caused damage at roof level within a building and dry rot occurs further down the walls (this should always be checked for), but the distribution may reflect the vigour of dry rot growth once established in a calcium-rich environment as much as any difference in moisture tolerance.

It is often stated that dry rot can sustain itself on metabolic water from the breakdown of wood, and can thus continue after the source of water has been removed. This story is sometimes used as a further argument for expensive treatment. In fact it seems to have originated with work carried out in 1932 by Professor Miller in Leningrad (Miller, 1932).

Miller placed infected wood samples in unventilated glass jars and recorded that a large quantity of water was produced by the total breakdown of wood. The phenomenon he noted would be common to all brown rot decay fungi under restricted growing conditions, and not just dry rot. The total breakdown of wood does produce large volumes of water, but in practice, amongst other complications, subunits from the wood are utilized by the fungus as it grows, and so not all the products of the wood are totally broken down. The volume of water produced by Miller would not be produced in a building – and the water that is produced tends to be lost by evaporation and diffusion.

It is also said that dry rot can 'wet up' dry timber by conducting water from a source of moisture. There is no doubt that the mycelium strands of dry

Table 7.1 Moisture requirements of dry rot and cellar rot (data from Viitanen and Paajanen, 1988)

Fungus	Temperature °C			Timber moisture content (%)		
	Min.	Opt.	Max.	Min.	Opt.	Max.
Serpula lacrymans	−5 to +5	15–22	30–40	17–25	20–55	55–90
Coniophora puteana	0 to +5	20–25	40–46	15–25	30–70	60–80

rot do conduct liquid, but this is largely a nutrient solution that distributes essential products around the fungus. Any ability to wet up timber by this method is very limited.

Savory (1964) conceived the concept of statically dry and dynamically dry environments in order to take into account the limited ability of the fungus to influence conditions. In a statically dry situation there is no air movement to encourage evaporation and the fungus is able to transport or produce water faster than it is lost. These environments develop in small, sealed spaces and are rather uncommon. More usual is the dynamically dry situation, in which water is lost from the substrate by evaporation or diffusion, so that the fungus cannot elevate the moisture content of a dry food source.

A dry rot attack then is usually limited to the zone of damp walls and timber (Colour Plate 10), although this may be extensive if there has been a major or long-term fault (Colour Plate 11). The primary remedial measure must be to locate and remedy all sources of moisture. This alone would kill the fungus once the wall had dried out. Chemical treatments should be used where necessary to control an infestation while the structure dries out, but little reliance can be placed on chemical treatments alone if the structure remains wet or future water penetration occurs.

Those who still adhere to the belief that dry rot is an immortal and unstoppable fungus contend that treatment only fails if it has not been vigorous enough. This attitude is summed up by Richardson (1977) who suggested that the fungus might be taken seriously if it was called 'malignant cancer of wood'.

The logic behind the argument does make a certain amount of sense. The fungus is capable of growing through brickwork and over inert surfaces away from a colonized source of damp timber if surrounding equilibrium moisture contents allow. If it encounters further damp wood, for example bonding timbers behind plaster, more decay may be expected. It is frequently impossible to be sure that no concealed timber lies buried in the walls, and much of the timber embedded in external walls will have a moisture content at least marginally suitable for attack. But for every serious and extensive outbreak there will be dozens of small localized infections, many of which are dead, or will die out of their own accord when the source of water is halted without the occupant of the building being aware of their presence. Why, if the fungus can be likened to a cancer, is it frequently not more destructive?

There are probably several answers to this question. One basic factor is that strains of fungus seem to differ in their growth rates and decay potential. Another is probably the innate natural durability of many old timbers. Of more fundamental importance though, is dry rot's requirement for water, and its basic intolerance of drying conditions. Brown *et al.* (1968) found the threshhold of infection to be 90% relative humidity at 20 °C. Optimum humidity was 99%. These data are similar to those obtained by other authors (Coggins, 1991), who also found that optimum humidity was 99%. These humidities would equate with timber moisture contents at, or slightly below, fibre saturation point, i.e. about 26–30%.

The significance of these results to treatment must be assessed with care. The high humidities required by the fungus will be within the substrate and at the surface boundary layer, not necessarily away from the timber. Nevertheless, timber is only likely to be subjected to high humidities if the wall is generally damp, or if timber is located where there is periodic wetting. The latter might be caused by rain penetration, or interstitial or surface condensation. From a practical point of view the high humidities required for active growth mean that the effective ventilation of cavities and surfaces is liable to slow or halt the growth of fungus in timbers, particularly after the source of moisture has been removed.

Dry rot will become dormant and eventually die once the walls start to dry. In many cases the fungus will stop growing after a short period of time because it is very intolerant of drying conditions (Coggins, 1991). Dormancy, the period between quiescence and death, is of finite duration. Falck (1912) investigated activity in dry rot and concluded that it fell into three categories:

1. Acute stage, continuous activity.
2. Chronic stage (dormancy), growth ceases.
   (a) Inhibition: no growth, but no other effect. Growth resumes when conditions become suitable again.
   (b) Reduced: strands turn dark grey, they are still living but not very viable and they need time as well as considerable change in the environment to produce an acute outbreak.
3. Dead stage.

The length of time that the fungus can remain dormant in timber under dry conditions depends largely upon temperature. Bravery (1991) quotes 9 years at 7.5 °C, decreasing to one year at 22 °C. Findlay and Badcock (1954) concluded that strands within masonry would cease to be viable within a year once the wall was thoroughly air dry.

The above data suggest that in many cases a dry rot infection can be controlled by drying alone. Thick, damp masonry or brickwork may, however, take several years to dry and some form of timber or masonry treatment might be required to stabilize the decay during the interim period. In some situations masonry may never dry and timber removal or repeated *in situ* treatment will be necessary. It should be noted that these treatments will not remain effective for long under sustained damp conditions.

7.3 Traditional treatments

Traditional methods of treatment may be very destructive, and there is a growing perception that the level of damage is not always desirable or necessary (Bravery, 1991; Ridout, 1989a). The traditional approach should therefore be examined in some detail. The environmental control of dry rot is discussed in Section 14.5.4.

7.3.1 Exposing the full extent of the infection

This procedure is usually employed because concealed damp timbers might harbour infection and be a source of further problems. The presence of fungus behind plaster is not in itself a cause for concern. Many adjacent timbers are visible (e.g. window frames) and the locations of some built-in timbers are predictable (e.g. window lintels). The *Building Research Digest* No. 299 (1993) recommends the removal of a 300 mm zone around these in order to check their integrity and the spread of fungus if sound plaster is to be retained.

Bonding or levelling timbers present more of a problem, because these may occur at unpredictable intervals down the wall. Sometimes their positions can be deduced from exposure work already undertaken elsewhere in the building, and sometimes, as in many stone-built churches, they are unlikely to be present.

The risks from unexposed and therefore untreated wall surfaces and timbers, are that the fungus may travel further from its concealed food source, and may fruit or grow through the plaster to attack new joinery. Potential structural consequences will depend on the dimensions of the timber. These risks may be small and acceptable if the fungus derives from a defined water source which may be halted, the spread of the fungus is limited and the wall is not particularly wet. Saturated walls and extensive decay may, however, require extensive exposure work unless valuable finishes or other constraints justify a more cautious approach and the greater risks involved. An attempt to provide more detailed guidance is made in Section 14.6 and Appendix A.

7.3.2 Cutting back past the last signs of decay

Norman Hickin, in his book *The Dry Rot Problem* (1963b), recommended that all timber be cut back to a distance of 3 ft (1 m) past the last visible signs of decay. This was done because the hyphae attacking the wood cells are microscopic and therefore invisible except by laboratory examination. Hickin was following a policy which had been popular for many years (see for example Blake, 1925) and is frequently still proposed. Rigid adherence to the 'one metre rule' can be disastrously destructive, particularly to ceilings, and is rarely, if ever, necessary in historic buildings. There was never any generally accepted distance for cutting back, however, and *Forest Products Research Laboratory Leaflet* No. 6 (1947) recommended 12–18 in (300–450 mm). The British Wood Preserving Association (BWPDA) Code of Practice 1983 states 'cut out and removed from site all decayed timber together with a margin of at least 600 mm beyond the visible limits of fungal growth'. It did, however, add a note that recognized special cases where alternatives to removal might be appropriate. It also indicated that the suggested margin of 600 mm might be either inadequate or could be seen as excessive, depending on the extent of the fungus and the construction details. The BWPDA *Code of Practice for Remedial Timber Treatment* 1995 (which amended the 1983 Code) clarified this even further: 'At the discretion of the surveyor cut out and remove from site all decayed timber. Up to 600 mm of sound timber beyond the last visible limits of fungal growth may also be removed as a safety margin.' This advice is again supplemented with a note about the importance of recognizing alternative *in situ* treatments.

The most recent Building Research Establishment guidance (1993) suggests a margin of 300–450 mm, but states that this need not be interpreted as a hard and fast rule. In practice it is frequently only necessary to isolate timbers from the wall where possible, and to treat the remaining bearings with a paste preservative (see Section 7.3.4). All remedial works to structural timbers affected by dry rot must be in accordance with relevant Building Regulation requirements, and a structural engineer should be consulted.

7.3.3 Wall irrigation/toxic box treatments

The fact that the fungus readily grew through walls and the disappointing results of blowlamp treatment (see Section 7.3.6), suggested the need to saturate the wall with fungicide. This form of treatment was originally performed by removing a brick or stone and constructing a cement dam. The pocket thus created was filled with fungicide. The technique received a boost in 1951 from an article written by J. Bayley Butler in the *Architects Journal*. Bayley Butler had considerable credibility because he was Professor of Botany at Trinity College, Dublin. He also established a remedial firm called Biotox. Bayley Butler appears to have been the first person to realize the great advantage of the newly invented masonry bit for wall treatment, and wall irrigation became immensely popular during the decades that followed.

Walls were drilled at closely spaced intervals and a fungicide was gravity-fed into the wall or pumped in under pressure. Findlay (1953) suggested that 0.5 in (12 mm) diameter downward-sloping holes should penetrate to a depth of 6–9 in (150–225 mm) at 2–3 ft (600–900 mm) centres. Savory (1971) pointed out that:

Effective irrigation cannot be achieved on brickwork with open mortar joints or on masonry walls with loose infill cores. The irrigation process will provide an improvement on surface applications only when the treated volume of wall is thoroughly saturated with fungicidal fluid. This requires the introduction of large quantities of liquid which dries out only slowly and introduces the risk that efflorescence of salts will damage prematurely applied decorations.

It should also be remembered that the primary aim of any dry rot works must be to dry out the structure, and that this process is not assisted by the introduction of large volumes of water-based fungicide. One obvious solution was to reduce the quantity of fluid used:

The variant, recently practised, of using limited amounts of liquid reduces these secondary risks but gives rise to treatment failures to an extent which prompts the suspicion that this so-called irrigation is most successful when irrigation is unnecessary.

(Savory, 1980)

The Building Research Establishment recommended and still recommends (1993) the use of wall irrigation only in special circumstances. Their 1971 recommendations were transposed verbatim into the BWPA *Code of Practice for Remedial Treatment*. However, the industry largely took no notice, and wall irrigation is still routinely employed by many treatment companies wherever dry rot is found.

One problem with wall irrigation, a legacy from the use of some phenolic solutions through brickwork that was not replastered, is that brown, needle-shaped crystals of pentachlorophenol were deposited on the wall surface as it dried. These crumble and become integrated into the dust assemblage of the building, creating a potential health hazard. Cope *et al.* (1995) suggest that pentachlorophenol could also be precipitated from the water-soluble sodium pentachlorophenate, if the solution were acidified.

There are so far no indications that masonry biocides containing dodecylamine or boron can form hazardous surface deposits.

In recent years several firms have begun to offer the toxic box system. This restricts the use of wall irrigation to a band around the fungus, and the surface within the box is thoroughly spray treated. The problem with this approach is that it is difficult to be sure that the fungus is all contained within the box. This is frequently investigated by removing bricks from the wall to search for fungus strands, a hit-and-miss process which can be very destructive.

7.3.4 Spray and paste treatments

Once it has been accepted that fungus within a wall cannot be readily killed by chemical treatments, but will die if isolated from timber and/or water,

then a sensible treatment specification can be produced. Thorough surface spray treatment of the wall surface, sometimes also now called irrigation, is normally all that is required to stop the fungus from fruiting or from attacking new joinery, once the food and water sources have been removed and as the wall dries. If the wall is excessively damp, however, it is likely that no chemical treatment, whether administered by spraying or by injection, can stabilize the decay. Great care must then be taken during re-instatement works, to ensure that all new timbers introduced into the building are pretreated and isolated from the wall.

The spray treatment of apparently sound timber to control fungus has little if any value. Much of the decay will be inside the timber, and the chemical will not halt the fungus, although surface growth may be controlled. For most purposes a formulation which gives a greater depth of penetration, particularly in damp timber, will be required.

Paste formulations were discussed in detail in Section 4.4.4. Many of these contain fungicides and are of value for the treatment of timbers which are infected with, or at risk from, dry rot. A major difficulty, however, is that these pastes will not penetrate well in damp timber, and timbers which are at risk from fungi will usually have elevated moisture contents. The problem has been addressed by the production of formulations which contain borates in water-miscible, glycol-based solvents. These are said to give a good final depth of penetration when surface applied or injected into predrilled holes.

7.3.5 Fungicidal renders

During the early 1950s the Forest Products Laboratory and the Building Research Station decided to make a joint investigation into the possibility of developing a fungicidal render (Mack and Savory, 1952). The intention was to produce a barrier which would lock the fungus within the wall and provide a swift and effective seal against fungus which was too deep within the wall to reach with fungicides.

The most effective barrier proved to be a plaster

formed from sand and zinc oxide. The mixture was gauged with a zinc chloride solution which combined to form zinc oxychloride and produced a rapid set. To give a practical working time, the set was retarded by the addition of boric acid and ammonium chloride.

A zinc oxychloride formulation is still commercially available, and is useful provided that existing woodwork is removed prior to treatment.

7.3.6 Heat treatments

The surface application of heat from a blowlamp was popular for many years (and is still sometimes used), but experience showed that concealed and partially decayed timbers were inclined to smoulder, and there was a high risk of starting a fire. Experiments have shown that a surface temperature of about 1100 °C would have to be maintained for about 5 h in order to heat a 230 mm thick wall to a temperature lethal to the fungus. In practice, therefore, the blowlamp only has a surface effect, and the fungus (if active) will soon grow again. Attempts were sometimes made to improve on the heat of a blowlamp; the following, which follows the guidance of Cartwright and Findlay in *Forest Products Research Bulletin* No. 1, is from a report on dry rot treatment undertaken at the Sheepshanks Gallery in 1933:

> Whole of woodwork within an area of 6 ft beyond the portion affected was removed: plaster infilling removed; infected brickwork and joints burnt with the oxy-acetylene flame at a temperature of 2000 °C; surfaces then brushed and treated with a solution of magnesium silica fluoride; cornices and frieze re-instated with rift sawn and knotless Douglas fir after being immersed in solignum at a temperature of approximately 180 °F (82 °C).

In recent years hot air has been used in Denmark to kill dry rot in both timber and brickwork (Koch, 1991). The idea is to achieve a lethal temperature of 40 °C in the centre of timbers and brickwork, and to maintain it for 24 h. Results so far have been encouraging, but more time is needed to evaluate the technique.

7.3.7 Timber reinstatement

Saturated brickwork or masonry may take several years to dry even after the sources of moisture have been removed (see Section 12.7). Depending on the treatment philosophy pursued, original timbers within the zone of decay may have been discarded or treated, or reliance may have been placed on their inherent durability. Replacement structural timbers and new joinery will not be particularly durable in these circumstances (see Section 11.12), and pretreatment will be necessary. Structural timbers to be inserted into wet walls should be pressure impregnated with a water-based preservative containing copper/chromium/arsenic to BS4072 (see Section 9.2). Joinery may either be double vacuum impregnated with an organic solvent-based fungicide or dip treated (see Sections 9.3 and 9.5). In either case the timbers should be isolated from the walls with a suitable membrane (see Section 12.10).

7.4 Detection of dry rot with dogs

Dogs have been used in Sweden for several years to detect volatile chemicals (secondary metabolites) produced by fungi attacking transmission poles. In recent years this technique has been used in Denmark and the UK to locate active dry rot. Lloyd and Singh (1994) state that dogs have a working capacity which ranges from 2 to 4 h a day, and that they can search 20–50 rooms in an hour. The disadvantage they note is that the dogs only indicate active infection. Old damage, which may be extensive, will presumably not be detected. Other fungi which may have caused significant damage together with insect attack, may also not be located.

Bech Anderson (1991) states that dogs have difficulty in differentiating between the smells of dry rot and cellar rot because the fungi are closely related, but that they will not detect more distantly related fungi.

CHAPTER EIGHT

Wet rots and minor decay fungi

8.1 Identification of fungi in buildings

Many of the fungi that take part in the woodland timber decay succession are likely to occur in buildings if the type of timber, its durability and its moisture content are all favourable to fungi growth.

Manuals for the identification of fungi in buildings seem to follow each other in describing the same narrow range of species. Many of these species the author has never found, but he has located and identified a wide range that are never discussed or illustrated. This is not intended as a criticism of the available guides, many of which are excellent (Building Research Establishment, 1989; Bravery *et al.*, 1992), but is simply to show that the identification of decay fungi is frequently impossible without considerable specialist knowledge, even when the fruit body is present. For most practical purposes concerning the conservation of building timbers, precise identification is also unnecessary.

What is necessary, however, is that the architect, surveyor and property owner should recognize a fruit body as a fungus so that concealed decay may be detected, and so that they may have some idea of its potential to cause damage. Some fungi – slime moulds, for example – may produce large fruits but cause no damage at all (Colour Plate 12). This is far simpler than learning to identify individual species of fungus. Any unusual lumps and excrescences located on timber should be removed and carefully examined, preferably with a hand lens. The purpose of this examination is to ascertain the presence (or absence) and topography of any spore-producing surfaces, so that the fruit (if it is a fruit) may be placed in one of the categories described below. Although wet rot may be produced by any one of a number of fungi, the treatment is the same in all cases (see Section 8.7).

8.2 Category A: Moulds (Deuteromycetes)

Moulds (Figure 8.1(a)) appear as a coloured mass of spores and pigmented hyphae. They are the imperfect form of higher fungi, usually Ascomycetes (see Section 8.3). Imperfect fungi reproduce asexually rather than by the fusion of two nuclei and the exchange of genetic material. Many, perhaps most, of the moulds will have a sexual form described under a different name, but a great many of these associations have not yet been made.

8.2.1 Damage to timber

Moulds usually have little effect on timber, although they may spoil its surface appearance (see Section 3.4.1). Large quantities of airborne spores may cause a health hazard (see Section 7.2).

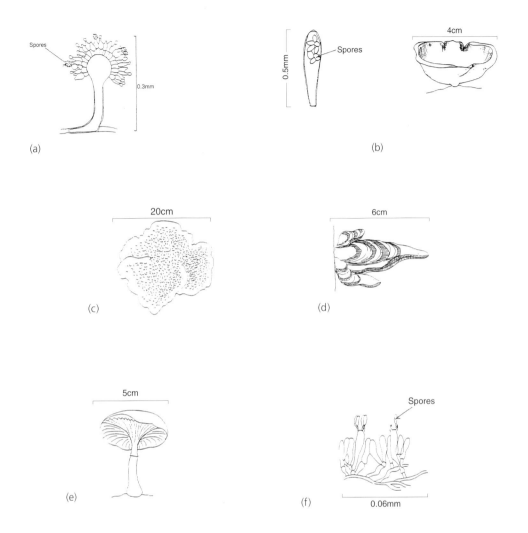

Figure 8.1 Examples of fungal fruits and their spore-producing surfaces: (a) moulds (Deuteromycetes); (b) Ascomycetes; (c) resupinate fungi; (d) pore fungi; (e) gilled fungi; (f) the spore-carrying structure for categories (c), (d) and (e).

8.3 Category B: Jelly fungi or plaster moulds (Ascomycetes)

Jelly fungi produce sexual spores that develop in a flask-shaped chamber called an ascus (Figure 8.1(b)). The spores are liberated when mature by the rupturing of the flask and thus the disruption of the fruit surface. This method of spore dispersal means that there is no distinctive sculpturing on the fertile surface prior to spore release. Jelly fungi therefore tend to appear as smooth and usually rather brittle fruits. Several types are very common in buildings following prolonged water penetration and two are worth describing here.

8.3.1 *Elf cup fungi (mostly Pezizaceae)*

These produce a cup which may in some species be up to 12 cm across. The colour is usually some shade of cream or brown but some genera produce orange or red fruits. All are more or less the same shape (Colour Plate 13).

The fungi live on organic detritus. The fruit becomes brittle and hard when dry, but should still be recognizable. Elf cup fungi are useful indicators of damp conditions where decay fungi may thrive. The extensive white mycelium they produce frequently causes concern but is harmless.

8.3.2 Pyronema *spp. (Pseudoascoboleae)*

These fungi do not have a common name. Their usual habitat is freshly burnt ground, but they inevitably appear rapidly in fire-damaged buildings. Considerable fine white mycelium appears on timber and masonry within a few weeks of the fire, and is frequently labelled as dry rot (see Section 12.5).

The fruit sometimes occurs as a convex red or orange lump 1 mm in diameter. These sometimes aggregate into a humpy, jelly-like patch.

8.3.3 *Damage to timber*

In most situations the Ascomycetes cause little damage to timber, although surface soft rots (see Section 3.4.2) may occur in some situations. Nevertheless, their presence does indicate conditions favourable to concealed decay, and they are frequently confused with dry rot. No treatment is required, beyond the drying-out of the affected timbers.

8.4 Category C: Resupinate fungi (Basidiomycetes: Corticiaceae, Coniophoriaceae, Stereaceae)

Resupinate fungi are usually flat and closely pressed to the timber or wall, with the spore-producing surface on the exposed face (Figure 8.1(c)). This surface may be variously sculptured, and common forms are described in Table 8.1. The fruits are persistent, but many curl up and darken when they have dried.

8.4.1 *Cellar rot (*Coniophora puteana*)*

This is said to be the commonest of the wet rots (Building Research Establishment, 1989), and is the name usually applied to any fungus not obviously dry rot. Cellar rot (Figure 8.2) is common throughout Europe and causes a brown rot in both softwoods and hardwood. It is thus a rather successful fungus.

The fruit is relatively common in buildings and when it is found it is invariably called dry rot. The surface is yellow to olive or olive brown, with a white margin (Colour Plate 14). The pigmented spore-producing area is covered with distinctive small bumps, never craters as in dry rot.

The mycelium may spread over masonry as distinctive black bootlace-like strands (Colour Plate 15). Occasionally white rosettes are formed under linoleum or other floor coverings. The fungus causes a brown rot, and the cubes tend to darken because the fungus converts phenolic extractives into the pigment melanin.

Table 8.1 Surface sculpturing of common resupinate fungi

Surface sculpture	Scientific name	Common name
Folded and cratered (merulioid)	*Serpula lacrymans*	dry rot (see Chapter 7)
Small bumps	*Coniophora puteana*	cellar rot (see Section 7.4.1)
Felty	*Asterostroma*	(see Section 7.4.2)

Figure 8.2 The fruit of the cellar rot (*Coniophora puteana*) is usually olive-brown with a white margin. The spore-producing surface is mostly unsculptured.

8.4.2 Asterostroma cervicolor

Asterostroma (Figure 8.3) is an uncommon woodland fungi which is found in the pine forests of North-west Europe (Hallenberg, 1985). Like dry rot and oak rot, it seems to have found buildings to be a congenial environment, and is frequently found in softwood joinery and structural timbers where water is plentiful.

The name *Asterostroma* means 'star body' and describes the curious form of the 'asterosetae' within the mycelium when viewed under a microscope. Most of the fungus seems to be composed of these thick-walled star-like structures. To the unaided eye the fungus produces large quantities of cinnamon-coloured mycelium. This seems inevitably to be identified as dry rot, with damaging and expensive consequences. It may, however, be readily distinguished from the latter fungus by the decay caused. *Asterostroma* produces a white rot, and dry rot produces a brown rot.

The fruit body is a loose-meshed felty brown structure and is not particularly distinctive (Colour Plate 16).

8.4.3 Damage to timber

Resupinate fungi probably cause the most commercially significant damage to *in situ* building timbers. The species noted above are particularly important, although *Asterostroma* is frequently not recognized. Dry rot and cellar rot are brown rots and can therefore tolerate relatively dry conditions although, in the case of dry rot, this is usually overstated (for treatment, see Section 8.7).

8.5 Category D: Pore fungi (Basidiomycetes: Polyporaceae, Hymenochaetaceae)

A large number of decay fungi produce spores in tubes, with an open pore at one end (Figure 8.1(d)). The fruit is usually an irregularly shaped

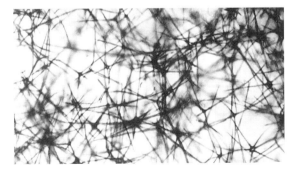

Figure 8.3 The hyphae of the wet rot (*Asterostroma cervicolor*) is formed from star-shaped structures (· 400).

white, yellow or brown excrescence, and the surface will be seen to be covered with pores when examined closely (preferably with a hand lens). Tubes will be revealed when the fruit is broken, although they may be restricted to a thin surface layer. A large number of species may occur in buildings, and sterile or misshapen fruits may lead to considerable difficulties in correct identification.

Since the early 1950s there has been a growing acceptance that fungi may be differentiated on their microscopic structure (the mitic system of classification; Pegler, 1996) and an expert may therefore be able to identify some of these misshapen poroid fruits.

In recent years we have collected pore fungi fruits wherever encountered and submitted these

Table 8.2 Pore fungi found on softwood building timbers

Fungus	Building	Timber
Poria stiptica (Pers. Fr.) Julich = *Tyromyces stipticus*	Salisbury Cathedral, Wiltshire	sarking boards
Diplomitoporus lindbladii (Berk.) Gilbn and Ryv = *Tyromyces cinerascens*	Somerset House, London	external cladding
	Tadworth Court, Tadworth, Surrey	tie beam bearing
	43 Eaton Place, London	roof timbers, wall studs
	Westcroft House, Carshalton, Surrey	wall stud
Postia floriformis (Quel.) Jul. = *Oligoporus floriformis* = *Tyromyces floriformis*	Victoria Pavilion, Morecambe, Lancashire	door frame
	Thorpe Coombe House, London	wall plate
Oligoporus rennyi (Berk: Broome) Donk = *Leptoporus destructor*	Park Place, Mitcham, Surrey	ceiling timbers
Schizopora paradoxa (Schrad. Fr) Donk	Salisbury Cathedral, Wiltshire	sarking boards
	21 Deptford Broadway, London	ceiling laths
	Birketts Building, Norwich, Norfolk	joist ends, wall plate
Schizopora flavipora (Cooke) Ryv.	Christchurch, Waterloo, Liverpool	valley gutter boards
Ceriporiopsis gilvescens (Bres.) Dom.	Aykley Head House, Durham	floorboards
Skeletocutis sp	The Stables, Sutton Montis, Somerset	floorboards
Antrodia vaillantii (DC: Fr.) Ryv. = *Fibroporia vaillantii*	Floral Hall, Stoke-on-Trent	dance floor
Antrodia xantha (Fr: Fr.) Ryv.	2 Powis Grove, Brighton, East Sussex	floorboards
Gleophyllum sepiarium (Wulf. ex. Fr.) Karst.	Widworthy Court, Honiton, Devon	ceiling joist (Colour Plates 17 and 18)

Table 8.3 Pore fungi found on oak building timbers

Fungus	Building	Timber
Phellinus ferruginosus (Fr.) Pat	21 Deptford Broadway, London	wall plate
	Salisbury Cathedral, Wiltshire	wall plate
Donkioporia expansa (Desm.) Kotl. and Powz. = *Phellinus megaloporus*	Old Court House, Coventry	wall plate
	The Dower House, Bristol	window lintel
	Stoneleigh Abbey, Warwickshire	wall plate
	Farleigh Hospital, Bristol, Avon	window lintel
Postia floriformis (Quel.) Jul. = *Oligoporus floriformis* = *Tyromyces floriformis*	Chatham Dock Yard, Chatham, Kent	ship's timbers under floor

to the Royal Botanic Gardens at Kew for critical identification based on microscopic characteristics. The list of species is offered here partly because the assemblage has not previously been recorded, but also because it demonstrates the range of fungi which may be found in buildings (Tables 8.2 and 8.3). Several of these had produced substantial surface growth and had been mistaken for dry rot. A few previous names (synonyms) have been included to indicate similarities between fungi, but no claim is made that this list of synonyms is exhaustive.

Some of these softwood fungi, particularly *D. lindbladii*, had caused considerable structural damage. All were, or had been, associated with considerable water penetration. Half of the samples belonged to a group of fungi previously aggregated within the genus *Tyromyces*. Most of the list are common species, associated with decaying softwood logs on the forest floor.

The only fungi from the softwood list that are usually mentioned as occurring in buildings are *Antrodia vaillantii* and *Antrodia xantha*. It is interesting to note that each of these fungi was only found once.

The two common species of oak rot recorded are closely related, and easily confused. The third, *Oligoporus floriformis*, has been reported from the

woodlands of North America and Europe, but only in worked timber in the UK.

All of these fungi may be adequately described as pore fungi. Two species are discussed further here as examples.

8.5.1 Mine fungus (Antrodia vaillantii)

This fungus is known as the mine fungus because it commonly occurs on pit props. The fruit is white/cream, flat and covered with small pores. Mycelium is usually prolific (Figure 8.4). Growth may be fern-like, and the strands may be thick and are brilliant white, unlike dry rot which is always greyer and more mushroom coloured. They are also flexible when dry, whereas dry rot strands become brittle. The fungus causes brown rot decay in softwoods. This species, in common with several other pore fungi, is fairly resistant to copper and is sometimes found attacking treated timber.

8.5.2 Oak rot (Donkioporia expansa)

In the early 1920s plaster was stripped from oak roof beams in the Louis XIII wing of the Palace of Versailles. The beams within the plaster were found to have been destroyed by a fungus which we

Figure 8.4 Typical fern-like white mycelium from the mine fungus (*Antrodia vaillantii*).

now know as *Donkioporia expansa* (formerly known as *Phellinus cryptarum* or *Phellinus megaloporus*). This fungus was investigated by Mangin and Patouillard (1922), who found that it was fairly common elsewhere on worked oak in cellars, mines, bridges and catacombs. They found no trace of its occurrence in standing trees or unconverted timber.

In 1933 Cartwright and Findlay of the Forest Products Research Laboratory reported the same fungus from buildings in Peterborough, Oxford, Abingdon and St Albans. Subsequent investigations have shown that the fungus is (and presumably always has been) rather common in the UK and Europe. It has also been reported from softwood. However, as with dry rot, it is mostly, perhaps totally, associated with worked timbers, predominantly in buildings.

The oak rot fruit body is covered with minute pores (3–4 to the millimetre) which are irregularly shaped, and are the external aperture of a deep tube layer in which, it is thought, spores are produced (Figure 8.5). Banks of tubes may become stratified by periodic cycles of growth. Fruits are produced freely in buildings and are usually the only visible indications of concealed decay. The fruit when fresh is buff brown (Figure 8.6), but as it ages the colour darkens and the surface collects

dust. The fruit then appears to be a nondescript knobbly excrescence on the surface of the timber. However, the true nature of the excrescence can be established by breaking a piece off: the tubes should be visible. The fruit is plate or bracket shaped and woody. It may be quite large. The specimen shown in Figure 8.6 was 27 cm long, 12 cm wide and 2 cm thick.

D. expansa causes a white rot decay in hardwoods, and has also been recorded from softwoods. Findlay (1953) considered that it caused more rapid decay in oak than any other fungus, but cultures under laboratory conditions grow vigorously while only producing a low timber weight loss (Esser and Tas, 1999). Nevertheless, substantial damage does occur in buildings – although probably over a long period of time and at high moisture levels.

Growth occurs between 5 °C and 40 °C with a temperature optimum of about 25–30 °C. Roofs of buildings are frequently very warm during the summer months, and this perhaps accounts for the marked stages of growth as showed by layered fruits. The minimum timber moisture content for growth is about 23–25% (Fuller and Moore, 1999).

Although the size of *D. expansa* spores (basidiospores) is recorded, they must be very rare, and

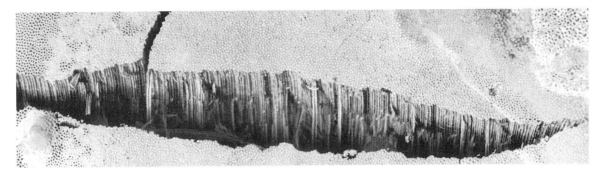

Figure 8.5 Spores of the pore fungi are produced within tubes in the surface layer.

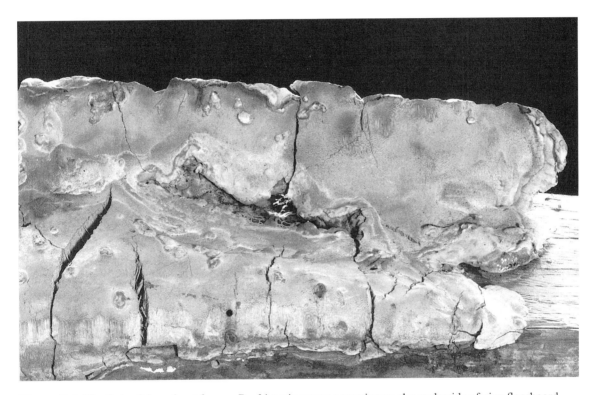

Figure 8.6 The fruit of the oak rot fungus *Donkioporia expansa* growing on the underside of pine floorboard.

most fruits are sterile. The fungus seems to be spread by asexual spores (chlamydospores) which some cultures of the fungus produce in enormous quantities.

Damage is usually concealed, either within timber bearings, or at the backs of plates, although sometimes polystyrene-like mycelium is formed (Figure 8.7). Damage may be detected, if its presence is suspected, by a dull hollow sound when the component is tapped, or by drilling.

8.5.3 Damage to timber

Pore fungi may cause white rots or brown rots, depending on the species of fungus present. The damage to structural timbers is frequently severe.

Figure 8.7 The oak rot fungus sometimes produces polystyrene-like mycelium.

Fruits are more robust than the majority of jelly or gilled fungi so that they may remain present and unshrivelled long after the fungus has died. High moisture levels must therefore be demonstrated before active infection is assumed (for treatment, see Section 8.7).

8.6 Category E: Gilled fungi (Basidiomycetes: Agaricales)

Many woodland fungi produce sexual spores on the gills of fruits which are commonly termed mushrooms or toadstools (Figure 8.1(e)). The gills are usually distinct when the fruit is mature. Most gilled wood decay fungi are only occasionally, if ever, found in buildings, but one genus, *Coprinus* (the ink cap fungi), has a few species that are frequently encountered. An ability to recognize these is essential.

8.6.1 *Ink cap fungus* (Coprinus *spp.*)

The ink cap fungi (Colour Plates 19–21) include a wide range of species, several of which may decay hardwoods in buildings (Orton and Watling, 1979). The common name derives from the liquefaction of the fruit margin as the spores mature. The toadstool-like fruit eventually becomes a dark strand with the shrivelled remnant of the cap still attached (Figure 8.8 and Colour Plate 21).

The group of ink cap fungi that occurs in buildings produce a dense brown mycelium. This was originally called an ozonium before the causal fungi were recognized, and the term is still sometimes used. Ozonium is, once again, frequently misidentified as dry rot, particularly as it is frequently found within walls.

Ink cap fungus may be plentiful on ceilings and in floor cavities following extensive water penetration (see Section 12.5).

8.6.2 *Damage to timber*

Coprinus causes a slow decay in hardwoods and is often associated with the destruction of ceiling laths. Other gilled fungi may cause severe decay in wet timber (for treatment, see Section 8.7).

8.7 The treatment of wet rots

The treatment of wet rots is traditionally less destructive than that of dry rot. Complications sometimes arise because of the erroneous but firmly entrenched view that wet rot somehow transmogrifies into dry rot as conditions dry. This is quite impossible, because the two types of rot are caused by entirely different fungi – although it has been suggested that dry rot spores germinate best on decayed timber because of an increase in acidity.

The primary remedial measure, as with dry rot, is the control of water penetration. Once this has been achieved the fungus will die. Decayed timber is usually removed, and structural repairs undertaken. Spray treatment with a fungicide is frequently employed, but this is of little value because it will not reach fungus within the timber. In most cases preservative treatment is probably not necessary. If the situation does warrant some form of *in situ* stabilization while the areas dry out,

Figure 8.8 Ink cap fungus attacking a window frame. Note the old fruit bodies that have stuck to the glass.

then paste treatments (see Section 7.3.4) with a fungicide would be appropriate.

Oak rot damage can be very severe when fully investigated, and considerable structural repairs may be required. Paste or injection treatments are all that are likely to be effective on large section timbers (once the source of water has been removed). Fungal decay in oak is frequently associated with death watch beetle attack (see Section 4.2) and the latter may continue to destroy the timber long after conditions are too dry for the fungus. Preservatives against oak rot should therefore include both a fungicide and an insecticide if there is active death watch beetle infestation present in the building.

CHAPTER NINE

Timber pretreatments

9.1 Brief history of pretreatments

Sometimes timber has to be repaired or replaced and it is useful to have some idea about the options for pretreatment. Preservative impregnation is likely to become more important in the future because efforts to grow timber more rapidly and convert it more economically are likely to reduce the durability of the end product. The current volume of timber that is treated with preservatives annually throughout the world exceeds 30 million m^3 and the total annual worldwide consumption of preservatives is estimated to be in excess of 350 000 tonnes of tar and 200 000 tonnes of water-based or organic solvent-based formulations. These preservatives are expected to increase the service life of the timber by between 5 and 15 times (UNEP, IE/PAC, 1994).

Pretreatment is not a new concept, and methods of treatment for the prevention of decay, rather than for its control, have been practised for centuries. The earliest modern processes for timber pretreatment evolved around the use of oils. This was a traditional concept in many parts of the world and may have derived originally from a variety of experiences. Thus staves of whale-oil casks were found to remain free from decay but to become brittle, whereas those of beef, pork and tallow barrels remained tough and sound. The first patented wood preservative process in the UK seems to have been a method devised by a Mr Emerson in 1736 (Britton, 1875). This involved the saturation of timber with boiled oil containing 'poisonous substances'.

The impetus for pretreatment experiments in the UK during the eighteenth century seems to have derived from the problems experienced by the Navy. They were evidently prepared to try anything once, and sometimes more than once. We have already noted Mr Lukin's disastrous misadventures with timber impregnation (see Section 7.1), but his was not the only failure. A London chemist by the name of Jackson, for example, obtained permission in 1769 to treat a large batch of timber with a mixture of salts and lime (Britton, 1875). These were then incorporated into several naval frigates, which rapidly fell apart. Other curious ideas included mopping the ship with a mixture of lime in glue and encasing the timbers in pounded lime followed by burial in soil. Saturating timbers with common salt was investigated because it had been observed that ships did not decay below the waterline. The timber so treated, however, became hygroscopic, thus producing a humid atmosphere in which metallic fastenings corroded rapidly (Bowden, 1815, p. 166).

Britton (1875) informs us that many ships were built during the eighteenth century with hollows cut in beam ends and stern posts to be kept filled with 'train oil', the intention being to prevent decay.

In 1817 Chapman published the results of his experiments with copper sulphate (blue vitriol) and mercuric chloride (corrosive sublimate) which seem to have been more promising (Britten, 1875) and in 1832 mercuric chloride was used in a pretreatment patented by a Mr Kyan. This was probably the first successful commercial pretreatment process. The architect Sir Robert Smirke tested timbers treated by Kyan, and his test procedure is worth restating in that it differs somewhat from the modern procedures as set out in the relevant British Standard:

I took a certain number of pieces of wood cut from the same log of yellow pine, from poplar, and from the common Scotch fir; these pieces I placed first in a cesspool into which the waters of the common sewers discharged themselves; they remained there six months; they were then removed from thence, and placed in a hotbed of compost, under a garden frame; they remained there a second six months; they were afterwards put into a flower border, placed half out of the ground, and I gave my gardener directions to water them whenever he watered the flowers; they remained there a similar period of six months. I put them afterwards into a cellar where there was some dampness, and the air completely excluded; they remained there a fourth period of six months, and were afterwards put into a very wet cellar. Those pieces of wood which underwent Kyan's process are in the same state as when I first had them, and all the others to which the process had not been applied are more or less rotten, and the poplar is wholly destroyed.

(Britten, 1875, p. 124)

Kyan was so convinced of the efficacy of his treatment that he approached the Admiralty, which allowed him to place a sample of treated oak in the fungus pit at Woolwich dockyard. The fungus pit was a damp, wood-lined capstan hole full of fungus, which was used for test purposes. The timber was removed in front of witnesses after three years and cut into three sections. Each was found to be sound (Faraday, 1836, pp. 23–4).

The original Kyan process entailed holding the timber submerged in a tank of corrosive sublimate solution for one week, followed by drying. The process was subsequently modified by using enclosed tanks and applying a pressure of 100 psi. Kyan's process was envisaged as a method of protecting timber with a low natural durability, in

which category he and Faraday placed Canadian and British home-grown wood.

The method was clearly effective, but suffered from the fatal flaws that it was expensive and that mercuric chloride is extremely poisonous and corrosive. The latter property was of particular importance, and Kyan's original tank had to be constructed from planks bolted together. Kyan's process was probably last used on a large scale in the 1860s (Richardson, 1993).

Other preservative pretreatments were developed during the early nineteenth century, including copper sulphate, patented by Margary in 1837 and subsequently used extensively in France in the Boucherie process (Richardson, 1993). But it was the advent of creosote, included in a process patented by Bethell in 1838, which had the greatest impact on pretreatments. Creosote was extracted from coal tar, and was impregnated into the timber within a pressure cylinder. Timber was placed in the vessel and air was drawn out from the cylinder (and thus from the pores of the timber) with a vacuum pump. Hot creosote was then pumped in and a pressure of 150–200 psi applied in order to force the required volume of creosote deep into the timber. Creosote is not of great importance in the conservation of building timbers because it has generally been avoided for interior use. This is because the treated timber becomes more inflammable, and because the smell lingers for several years. A rare example of its use in a building is Bristol cathedral, where the roof timbers were painted with Butler's Tar Distillate at the beginning of the twentieth century. Alan Rome, architect for the cathedral, learnt this from Sir George Oatley in 1948. The treatment was apparently applied by William Cowlin in the 1930s. Its main advantage was that it contained a wide range of substances toxic to fungi and insects. However, at least one fungus, *Lentinus lepideus* (a gilled fungus), is able to cause a heart rot in creosoted softwood transmission poles.

In 1838 Sir William Burnett (former Director-General of the Medical Department of the Navy) patented a process for the treatment of timber with zinc chloride impregnated into the wood in a pressure cylinder at 150 psi. In 1847 a large treatment cylinder was constructed at Woolwich dockyard and tests on this process were made in the fungus pit. Samples of Baltic pine, oak and elm were found to be free from decay after five years and the method was then used, to some extent at least, by the Navy. One problem that was encountered, and has always rather restricted the use of zinc chloride, is that it is soluble in water and easily leached from the wood. Nevertheless, it was also recommended for building timbers, although the extent to which it was used is unclear.

Little more of commercial importance was added to the repertoire of preservatives until 1907, when Wolman patented a formulation in Austria which contained fluorides. Various modifications followed and Wolman's Salts eventually consisted of sodium fluoride, dinitrophenol and sodium or potassium dichromate. This formulation became popular in the UK during the 1914–1918 War, when creosote was scarce. Unfortunately, though highly effective, it had poor permanence and was leached from the timber in damp conditions.

Various formulations were subsequently tried. Probably most widely used have been mixtures of copper, chromium and arsenic. The range of commercially available pretreatments was augmented in the 1960s by organic solvent-based preservatives, and, to a far more limited extent, by borates applied by the diffusion process.

The effective pretreatment of timber is not now regarded as a simple process, and the modern approach takes account of timber type, timber moisture content and intended usage. The preservatives in use and development have to fulfil the following criteria (UNEP IE/PAC, 1994):

1. Possess an adequate toxicity to wood-decaying organisms.
2. Penetrate into the timber.
3. Be chemically stable.
4. Be safe to handle.
5. Be economical to use.
6. Not reduce the strength of the wood.
7. Not cause significant dimensional changes within the wood.

9.2 Modern water-based preservatives for pressure impregnation

Copper sulphate, as noted in Section 9.1, had been first used as a patented preservative in 1837. It was very corrosive to iron and steel and easily leached from the timber, although a small proportion reacted with the cellulose and became fixed. The inclusion of chromium in the form of sodium dichromate improved the situation by the formation of chromium–lignin complexes (which chemically reduced the chromium, making it more reactive) followed by the slow production of copper chromate, which was stable. A formulation of this type was patented by Gunn in the 1920s. A further objection to copper as a wood preservative is that many fungi, particularly brown rots, can tolerate copper, and some are able to convert the toxin into insoluble copper oxalate. This problem was largely overcome by the incorporation of arsenic. A formulation containing copper, chromium and arsenic salts (CCA) was first produced in 1933 by an Indian Government research worker, Dr Sonti Kamesan, and was marketed under the name Ascu. Nevertheless, problems with tolerance still occur and some treated hardwoods, for example, may be attacked by soft rots if they remain wet.

The arsenic is also fixed into the timber by reactions with the chromium and copper, but fixation requires a careful balance of ingredients in order to avoid excess leachable free arsenic salts. In recent years free chromium salts have been perceived to be even more of an environmental hazard if the formulation is not correct. In practice the hazard to the user should be negligible provided the timber has been correctly treated and sufficient time has been allowed for the chemicals to fix and dry. CCA also prevents insect attack and has some water-repellent properties.

Bariska et al. (1988) have reported a structural weakening of CCA-treated poles by the separation of growth rings, and other changes in property have been recorded. In general, however, the effects are slight.

Several other water-based pretreatment preservatives have been tried in recent decades with varying success. An attempt was made in the late 1970s and early 80s to replace CCA in New Zealand with quaternary ammonium compounds, but staining microfungi detoxified the preservative and widespread failure occurred. This is an example of how a preservative can be effective under laboratory conditions yet still prove unsatisfactory because of some unexpected factor. Other preservatives have proved more successful, but none has rivalled CCA in worldwide sales; Connell (1991) has estimated that more than 100 000 tonnes of CCA are used each year.

Water-based preservatives (and creosote heated to reduce viscosity) are typically used in a high pressure impregnation system in order to enhance penetration. In this process the timber is loaded into the treatment vessel and subjected to a partial vacuum (usually −0.9 bar) for a specified period of time, which may vary from about 15 minutes to several hours, according to the type of timber and its cross-sectional dimensions. This, as in Bethell's 1838 process, draws air from the cells of the timber. The vessel is then flooded with preservatives and subjected to a pressure of 7–14 bar, which forces the chemical deep into the wood. Impregnation may be specified 'to refusal', at which point no further absorption occurs. When the process is completed the treatment solution is withdrawn and a final vacuum is applied to remove the surplus chemical. This is known as the 'full cell' or Bethell process (Richardson, 1993).

Empty cell processes exist for more viscous preservatives, typically creosote or pentachlorophenol in heavy oil. In these, the initial vacuum is omitted so that the cylinder is flooded with preservative at atmospheric pressure or under a low applied pressure. A high atmospheric pressure is then applied, which forces the chemical into the timber by compressing the air contained within the cells. These air bubbles expand when the pressure is released, thus forcing out the surplus preservative. Typically, a vacuum is applied at the end of the process in order to release any internal pressures which might cause preservative bleeding during service.

Two variations of the empty cell process are commonly used, and these are named after their inventors, Rueping and Lowry. Both are essentially similar, differing mainly in that the treatment vessel is flooded with preservative half-way through the pressure application period in the Rueping treatment, and a stronger vacuum is drawn at the end. Empty cell processes give a good depth of penetration but, as the name suggests, limit the quantity of chemical retained within the wood cells.

Oscillating pressure (OPM) and alternating pressure (APM) methods have now been developed, and these have the advantage that, unlike the other pressure methods, they may be used with unseasoned timber. These processes rely on repeated cycles of pressure and vacuum (OPM) or high pressure and atmospheric pressure (APM). The OPM treatment is sometimes preceded by steaming to improve permeability. The treatment of unseasoned timber reduces the space required for storage, and is particularly useful for those species that are difficult to treat when seasoned or that are particularly prone to stain fungi. The processes may also be useful for timbers that are too large in section to season cost-effectively.

9.3 Organic solvent-based preservatives for pressure impregnation

It became apparent in the 1960s that untreated joinery timbers were failing badly. This problem was, in part at least, due to the use of poor-quality timber with a high sapwood content. Pretreatments seemed to be indicated, but water-based pressure treatments resulted in dimensional changes, raised grain and demonstrated the need for post-treatment kiln drying.

Pressure treatments based on organic solvent preservatives were therefore developed and employed using a double vacuum treatment (often abbreviated to 'vac-vac' treatment). The active ingredient was dissolved in kerosene or white spirit, which gave greater depth of penetration in dry timber than water-based formulations, and did not cause dimensional change. They also allowed the incorporation of water repellants, colourants and contact insecticides which were insoluble in water. Other requirements might be cosolvents to increase the solubility of some active ingredients and antiblooming agents to prevent surface crystallization. Water repellants and antiblooming agents were commonly paraffin wax and a variety of resins (Hilditch, 1991).

The addition of a water repellant may cause difficulties with overpainting. Oil-based paints may take longer to dry and lose some of their gloss if preservative retention is high, whereas water-based paints may not adhere satisfactorily.

The double vacuum process requires the timber to be held in the treatment cylinder at an initial vacuum of −0.33 bar for about 3 minutes. Both vacuum and time may be increased if a pressure is to be applied subsequently in order to increase the rate of penetration. This pressure is commonly about one-tenth of that used in the full cell process. The vessel is then flooded with chemical and the vacuum released so that the preservative penetrates the timber. A second vacuum treatment of about −0.67 bar for 20 minutes draws out up to about 40% of the treatment fluid from the timber. This reduces costs, because solvent recovery is essential to the economics of the process, and avoids difficulties in factory paint priming. It also reduces solvent emission into the atmosphere.

Most light organic solvent preservatives perform well and do not have the disadvantages of some water-based systems. They can normally be overpainted when dry and are colourless unless otherwise formulated. They do not appear to affect the strength characteristics of the timber, are non-deliquescent, do not cause metal corrosion and are not leached by water movement. However, they are generally more expensive than water-based preservatives and therefore tend to be used where the properties they confer, particularly the reduction in timber distortion, offer a distinct advantage.

A recent variation in this technology has been the use of liquid petroleum gases, typically butane or isobutane formulated with isopropyl or polyethylene glycol as the carrier fluids. The low viscosity of the solvent produces a drier and more evenly treated product. The solvents are, however, expensive and hazardous to use without extreme care.

Pentachlorophenol (PCP) was probably the most widely used organic solvent preservative until accumulation in the environment resulted in restrictions on use.

In 1991 an EEC Marketing and Use Directive (91/173/EEC) was agreed, banning the use of PCP for most purposes in connection with buildings. It states that wood treated with PCP may not be used inside buildings, whether for decorative purposes or not, whatever the building is used for (residence, employment, leisure). This directive does, however, contain the following clause:

> By way of special exception Member States may on a case-by-case basis authorize on their territory specialized professionals to carry out *in situ* and for buildings of cultural, artistic or historic interest, or in emergencies a remedial treatment of timber and masonry infected by dry rot fungus (*Serpula lacrymans*) and cubic rot fungi [using pentachlorophenol].

The result is an ambiguity. It is not acceptable to treat timber with PCP in buildings (although timber pretreated with PCP is generally acceptable), but the preservative may be sprayed or injected *in situ* if dry rot or cubic rot fungi are present and the building is of sufficient merit. It seems that the risk from brown rot fungi (both wet rot and dry rot) outweighs the perceived toxic hazard from the preservative. The categories of buildings to be treated are broad and subjective, and the use of the word 'emergencies' in connection with dry rot treatment is unfortunate, suggesting as it does an urgency which is at odds with the ideal approach to dry rot treatment, which is a carefully researched and considered one. The Building Research Establishment has been contracted by the Department of the Environment, Transport and the Regions (DETR) to oversee the use of PCP, and must be notified of any intended usage in the United Kingdom on the appropriate form. PCP may therefore be used if its use is 'justified', but most remedial firms have so far shown a considerable reluctance to do so.

Tributyltin oxide (TBTO) came into use in the mid-1960s and was popular for the pretreatment of joinery because it was readily overpainted. It is a highly effective fungicide (Schweinfurth and Ventur, 1991), but its toxicity, particularly to marine organisms, eventually made it unacceptable, and its use in most remedial and in amateur products was prohibited by the Health and Safety Executive in 1990. It is still available, however, as an industrial pretreatment and in paste formulations.

A range of other organic pretreatment ingredients are now being used, notably acypetacs zinc and copper (which contain a mixture of linear and branched chain saturated aliphatic carboxylic acids derived from petroleum), and zinc versatate. The acypetacs group of acids have been used as synthetic replacements for naphthenic acids, which are derived from petroleum. Copper naphthenate, the original preservative based on naphthenic acids, was shown to be a wood preservative in Russia in 1880 and first marketed as such in Denmark in 1912 under the name Cuprinol (Broese van Groenou et al., 1951).

Frequently fungicides are formulated with the contact insecticides lindane or permethrin.

9.4 Diffusion pretreatments

Diffusion is a process in which compound concentrations tend to become equalized in a suitable medium. In timber pretreatments based on diffusion the compounds are usually an aqueous solution of boric acid–borax mixtures or of disodium octaborate tetrahydrate (Timbor). The preservatives become equally distributed in both the treatment solution surrounding the wood and the free water within the cells of the wood. Diffusion thus differs from absorption, although the latter may also occur if the wood cells are not saturated. Diffusion commences at fibre saturation point (see Section 2.1), and the speed of the process increases with the moisture content. This requirement for high moisture levels (about 50% water on an oven-dry basis) means that the pretreatment is more relevant to green timber. It is also important to note that the preservative is not fixed within the wood.

Diffusion processes occur in two stages. The first entails the application of the chemicals by one of a variety of methods, including dipping, spraying and soaking, in order to maximize preservative loading in the surface cells. The second stage entails wrapping and storing the timber under suitable conditions, and for a sufficient period of time, so that diffusion of the preservative to the required depth can occur. Storage time may be shortened by heating the treatment solution because the rate of diffusion nearly doubles for every 20 °C rise in temperature. Under normal treatment conditions about 4 weeks' storage is required for every 25 mm depth of diffusion.

The use of aqueous diffusion processes seems to have commenced in Australia and New Zealand during the late 1930s and 40s. By the mid-1950s New Zealand had become the major user of borates as wood preservatives, and by 1991 the annual volume of treated wood produced was about 1.4 million m^3 (Docks, 1991). Early efforts at marketing timber treated with borates in the UK were made during the 1960s, but supply difficulties, resulting from the necessity to treat while green before importation and therefore to order up to 6 months in advance, restricted success.

Inorganic borates have a wide spectrum of activity against fungi and insects, together with a low mammalian toxicity (Williams, 1997). Doubts have been expressed that the preservatives may be easily leached from the timber, but Dickinson and Murphy (1991) and Lloyd (1995) presented data which suggested that this should not be a significant problem unless the timber is wet and in contact with water or a suitable moist medium for a prolonged period of time.

9.5 Dip/immersion pretreatments

Dip and immersion processes in which the preservative is absorbed from a container into the timber provide a useful method of pretreatment. These processes have been defined by agreement between the BWPDA, the Building Research Association, the Timber Research and Development Association and the Nationwide Association of Preserving Specialists as follows:

- *Dipping*: Partial submersion of timber (likely to take place in a small vessel), such as fence post ends to be buried in the ground or cut ends of treated timber before assembly into structures.
- *Immersion (open)*: Complete submersion of timber in open tanks (likely to be large volume), such as immersion of window frames and fence panels in joinery workshops.
- *Immersion*: Complete submersion of timber in an enclosed tank, mainly industrial treatments plants, with some potential for professional use.

9.6 Preservative penetration

The depth of chemical penetration achieved by these processes depends on timber porosity, duration of contact with the fluid and type of solvent. Absorption will be greatest along the grain because this is the direction in which the cells (tracheids and vessels) are constructed to allow the flow of liquids (see Section 1.4). Water-based preservatives are not as easily absorbed across the grain as spirit-based preservatives. They may, however, slowly diffuse through the cells so that a good depth of penetration may be ultimately possible. The uniform absorption of preservatives is not always easily achieved and timbers vary considerably in their treatability.

Softwood tracheids (which make up the bulk of softwood) are sealed at both ends and the movement of liquids takes place through bordered pits containing a torus. These valves may close during drying, thus hindering treatment. The problem is more common in some species of timber (for example spruce) than in others, and is more pronounced in earlywood than in latewood. Pits may also be sealed with translocated extractives, a problem that has been reported with Douglas fir sapwood. Special drying and treatment schedules have been devised to combat these and other problems so that depth of preservative penetration is maximized. Sapwood pits will sometimes open again if the timber is soaked, and storage in water allows micro-organisms to break down the pit membranes so that the pits remain at least partially open.

The treatment of hardwood sapwoods is easy because the conducting vessels within the timber provide a more or less open system of transportation (see Figure 1.5). However, heartwoods may be impossible to treat because in many species (e.g. oak) the vessels become blocked with tyloses and other substances. Typical absorption values across the grain for a reasonably porous timber are presented in Table 9.1.

Data of this type are bound to vary considerably, but do provide useful guidance. Hilditch (1991) stated that European redwood sapwood penetration is about 15 mm by vac-vac treatment, but that preservative retention is about half of that achieved with a similar depth of penetration, by immersion.

Full penetration of sapwoods with CCA is easy to achieve, but heartwood is more difficult and may require additional processes, for example high temperature pretreatment seasoning. Preliminary trials have not been entirely successful, however, because of incomplete arsenic fixation in the heartwood. Future development may overcome this problem.

Table 9.1 Approximate depth of preservative penetration achieved in air-dry European redwood by dip or immersion treatments

Preservative type	Duration of immersion		
	3 min	60 min	24 h
Spirit-based	2 mm	6 mm	30 mm
Water-based	1 mm	2 mm	4 mm

9.7 Metal corrosion in pretreated timber

Some metals, in contact with some woods, will corrode and cause decay if water is present (see Section 3.7). This is an electrochemical process which will cause a bolt, for example, to shrink while the hole into which it is inserted expands. The process will be very slow if the moisture content of the timber stays below about 18%.

Organic solvent-based preservatives do not seem to cause corrosion, perhaps because the oil coats the fastening, but water-based preservatives containing copper can cause a problem because of soluble copper salts and the formation of sodium sulphate ions which aid conduction. The type and speed of corrosion, if corrosion does occur, depends on the type of CCA used. Salt formulations, based on copper sulphate, sodium dichromate and arsenic pentoxide, have been recorded to be more rapidly corrosive to galvanized steel nail plates, for example, than oxide formulations containing cupric oxide, chromic oxide and arsenic pentoxide (Cox and Laidlaw, 1984). This difference is apparently due to the formation of protective zinc corrosion products with the oxide formulation. Baker (1988) concluded that fastenings made from a metal which was cathodic to copper in the galvanic series would perform best in CCA-treated timber under high hazard conditions. He recommended type 304 and 316 stainless steel, silicon bronze, copper and monel nails. These fastenings are all very expensive and would probably not be a viable option except in special situations.

The risk of corrosion is negligible provided the timber is kept dry and the preservative was thoroughly fixed and dried when the components were fastened. There are occasionally cases of tiling battens, for example, still dripping with preservative, being fastened with galvanized nails. Such a practice may rapidly result in metal failure. At least one of the major UK manufacturers of CCA has now switched to production of the oxide formulation.

Cross *et al.* (1989) stated that the corrosion rates for mild steel, electroplated or galvanized steel, aluminium alloy and stainless steel were only a few micrometres per year in timber with a moisture content below about 19%, irrespective of treatment or lack of it. Corrosion could therefore be ignored.

The same authors stated that a surface corrosion rate of 0.2 mm per year occurred at about 26% moisture content in galvanized fastenings and zinc electroplate associated with CCA-treated timber, and that this increased to 0.5 mm per year for steel if the timber moisture content was increased to 30%. Stainless steel (type 304) and aluminium alloy (BS 6063) were pitted but otherwise unaffected, except that severe intergranular corrosion of the aluminium occurred in treated timber at very high moisture levels.

Boron preservatives, at least at the concentrations used in wood preservatives, do not cause metal corrosion. There may, however, be a substantial problem when boron and other salts are used at a high concentration in flame retardants, and further advice should be sought before these are used in potentially damp environments.

9.8 Selection and use of pretreated timber

The use of preservatives increases the cost of timber, may complicate its use on site, and may extend delivery times. They should therefore only be specified where some definite advantage is conferred. This is, however, frequently the case in the repair of historic buildings because walls retain residual moisture and sometimes fungus. Extra durability is therefore required while the structure dries, and longer-term resistance to insect attack may be an advantage if a high proportion of sapwood is unavoidably present.

The use of pretreated timber is subject to the usual health and safety controversies to be expected wherever biocides are employed. At one extreme are those who believe that any use of pretreated wood produces a potential, and unjustifiable, environmental hazard, while at the other is a commercial view that some restrictions in published guidance notes are unnecessarily alarmist. The technical literature is extensive, and shows the complexities of the subject without any generally accepted resolution of the issues involved.

In 1994 the United Nations produced a technical guide entitled *Environmental Aspects of Industrial Wood Preservation* (UNEP, IE/PAC, 1994). This has been taken as a suitably authoritative document on which to base most of the general information presented in this section and Section 9.9.

The guide recommends that the use of wood preservatives or impregnated wood within buildings should be minimized. The recommendations suggest that only constructional timbers should be impregnated, but this exclusion of joinery might sometimes have unsatisfactory consequences, given the quantity of sapwood present in modern timber. Wood preservatives should not be used for timbers which will be in contact with food or drinking water, or be in direct skin contact (man or animals).

Guidance on the specific selection of pretreatments for structural timbers is provided by British Standard 5268 (Part 5), 1977. Generally, fixed water-based preservatives (such as CCA) are recommended for common building softwoods in high hazard situations, which the Standard classifies as ground contact or other situations (e.g. timbers embedded in damp brickwork or masonry, sole plates, timbers below d.p.c. level) where timber is likely to remain wet. Elsewhere, either unfixed water-based, or double vacuum treatments are acceptable.

Ideally components should be fabricated prior to treatment, in order to avoid cutting through the protective shell of preservative. This may not always be possible, however, and any subsequently cut ends should be thoroughly brushed with a spirit-based preservative or the end treatment fluid recommended by the producing company.

9.9 Disposal of pretreated timber and waste

A high percentage of pretreated timber components will have a maximum service life of only a few decades, so that a substantial hazardous waste disposal problem is accruing. More waste may be generated by the fabrication process. Current options for disposal are not entirely satisfactory.

Timber pretreated with water-based preservatives has usually been machined after treatment in order to overcome any dimensional changes and to remove surface deposits of preservatives which might present a health hazard and impede overpainting. This process generates about 15% of treated waste, which has traditionally been incorporated into composite wood products. The practice has, however, been reviewed in recent years because of the potential hazard from dust if these composites are sanded.

Various proposals for disposal have been made, but burial on pre-designated sites seems to be a common current option in some countries (Vinden and Butcher, 1991). The problem of leaching over long periods of time as the timber eventually decomposes requires further investigation. Burial is also wasteful because considerable areas of land site may be utilized for a few per cent of hazardous material.

Burning would reduce the volume of waste, provided that the hazardous materials were broken down safely into elements deposited in the ash, and the furnace was equipped for efficient flue gas cleaning. Management of the resulting ash or slag would also be required, under the control of the appropriate environmental authorities. This is feasible but the difficulties involved in controlling furnace emissions are at present immense. It seems likely, however, that some form of chemical recovery and recycling will eventually be in use.

Legislation governing the disposal of treated timber varies from country to country; many countries have no regulation at all. In many countries local authorities control disposal as landfill, while incineration requires approved facilities. One of the commonest restrictions is to ban the burning of treated waste in domestic fires, because of the potentially harmful products released.

In Britain, pretreated timber from commercial enterprises is considered as 'special waste' and should be disposed of in landfill sites which have been appropriately licensed to accept it. There are no controls on householders disposing of domestic waste on their own property.

CHAPTER TEN

Regulations, legislation and charters

10.1 European Standards for wood preservation

At the time of writing, recommendations for the use of preservatives and treated timber in the UK are contained within a range of British Standards. Other countries have their own standards, which frequently differ significantly from each other. The Single European Act of 1 July 1987 required that member states should enact their own national legislation, harmonized by 279 European Directives, by 31 December 1992. The eventual legislation adopted by the European Commission would then be derived by a majority vote.

The Construction Products Directive (one of the 279) required products to satisfy six Essential Requirements if they were to be traded freely within the European market. The criteria to be satisfied related to:

- mechanical resistance and stability
- hygiene, health and the environment
- safety in case of fire
- safety in use
- protection against noise
- energy economy and heat retention.

The standards to be achieved in these categories were to be set out in Approved Technical Specifications, which would normally be European Standards.

The European Committee for Standardization was given a mandate by the European Commission to prepare specifications for wood preservatives (this term is imprecise and the EC includes them in the category Biocidal Products) and treated wood, and it undertook this task by organizing a series of working groups. Eventually, when specifications are completed, products that comply with the Essential Requirements will be entitled to carry a CE mark of conformity. The right to trade products, so marked, within the EU may not be hindered by technical and regulatory requirements (Bravery, 1992).

The new EU standards will differ significantly from the current British Standards in that they will classify wood preservatives in accordance with a scale of Hazard Classes (see Section 3.5). The loading of preservative and depth of penetration into a specific zone of the timber will also be prescribed. They will thus describe the performance required from the preservatives, rather than the procedures for their application.

10.2 Controls on the manufacture and use of pesticides

In 1974 the Health and Safety at Work Act required that suppliers of substances used at work should ensure, as far as reasonably practical, that the substances were safe when properly used. This duty was to be fulfilled by carrying out adequate toxicological testing and providing the resulting relevant information. The idea built upon the 1972 Robens report, *Safety and Health at Work*, which suggested that a statutory notification scheme should be established. Under this scheme, anyone marketing a new chemical for industrial use would have to supply the Government with basic toxicological data prior to marketing.

The 1974 Act was followed in 1977 by a discussion document issued by the Health and Safety Executive (HSE) and entitled *Proposed Scheme for the Notification of the Toxic Properties of Substances*. The scheme revived and amplified the ideas contained within the Robens report by recommending a basic package of toxicological data which would be required by the Government if the product was to be produced in quantities greater than one tonne per annum. This was seen to be a way in which manufacturers could fulfil the requirements of the 1974 Act. The HSE discussion document was, however, overtaken by the 6th Amendment of a 1967 EEC Directive which became known as the 6th Amendment Notification Scheme and had similar requirements.

The scheme related directly to individual chemicals, not to mixtures, and was not designed to approve formulations. That role was taken on by the Pesticides Safety Precaution Scheme (PSPS) which had been established in 1954 to cover the clearance of agricultural pesticides. The scheme was expanded to cover non-agricultural pesticides (including wood preservatives) in 1976. The PSPS required sufficient data to be passed to the appropriate department so that the safety of pesticides could be assessed by a team of independent advisers. Safety clearance would be granted if appropriate.

This scheme remained in operation until 6 October 1986, when the Control of Pesticides Regulations (COPR) came into operation and replaced the old voluntary scheme with statutory powers to approve pesticides. These regulations were a practical development from Part III of the Food and Environment Protection Act 1985, which introduced statutory controls on pesticides. It is illegal unless approval has been granted by ministers to:

1. Make up laboratory formulations of pesticides. Only approved pesticide formulations may be used.
2. Use pesticides in a non-approved way. The precautionary labels on proprietary formulations are mandatory and must be adhered to.
3. Store, supply or use non-approved pesticides such as arsenic, DDT or dieldrin.
4. Use unskilled or untrained staff to use pesticides unless the pesticides are cleared for household use. There is also a general requirement that reasonable precautions should be taken to ensure that preservatives are stored and used in a safe way.

Products that had Commercial or Provisional Commercial clearance under the PSPS were granted provisional approval under COPR. Products approved under the 1986 regulations and in subsequent years are listed in a monthly publication, *The Pesticides Register*, and in an annual reference book (*Pesticides*, first published in 1986). No legislation was repealed with the passing of the Food and Environmental protection Act 1985 and so duties under other Acts of Parliament (for example the Health and Safety at Work Act 1974, which amalgamated many pieces of health and safety legislation and was the enabling Act for other legislation) continue to apply. It is useful to remember that it is products that are approved by this scheme, not active ingredients, and that the product has been judged to be safe to use in the manner for which it has been approved.

The regulations specify three categories of use for wood preservatives and masonry biocides:

* amateur use
* professional use
* industrial use.

A professional is considered by the Health and Safety Executive to be 'a person who is trained in the use of the product and the equipment and applies pesticides as part of his/her job'.

10.3 Protection of bats

Concern has increased in recent decades because of the decline in bat numbers. There are several possible causes. Bats require a variety of sites, such as hollow trees, caves, mines and buildings, for maternity roosts in winter. Destruction of deciduous woodlands has reduced the numbers of hollow trees available, while caves and mines have been blocked up or become increasingly used for human leisure activities. Several wood preservatives were also found to be toxic to bats, and these were absorbed through the skin during roosting and grooming. The decline in safe and suitable roosting sites has also been accompanied by a decline in insect prey due, it is said, to changes in farming methods and the use of pesticides.

Efforts have been made to halt the decrease in bat numbers by giving them full protection under the Wildlife and Countryside Act 1981 (Nature Conservancy Council, 1991). This Act made it an offence to deliberately harm bats, or to intentionally destroy, obstruct or disturb any place which the bats used as a roosting site, unless the Nature Conservancy Council (now English Nature, Countryside Council for Wales and the Nature Conservancy Council Scotland) was informed and given reasonable time to provide advice. This advice would normally include recommendations for less harmful preservatives, scheduling of building works to months when the bats were absent from the building and, if ultimately necessary, the removal of the bats by licensed bat handlers. Any action which deliberately disturbs bats will require a licence (Stebbings and Jefferies, 1982).

The surveyor is in a particularly vulnerable situation with regard to bats, as it is against the law to disturb them. He or she should always check for their presence when inspecting roofs, cellars or similar spaces. The most obvious sign will normally be the presence of droppings, although occasionally dead bats or the sound of their chattering may indicate the presence of a colony and the need to contact the appropriate authority.

Bat droppings vary somewhat in shape and size, but are always distinctive (Figure 10.1). The bats' exclusive diet of insects means that the droppings break into a fine glistening dust of insect fragments when squashed, unlike mouse or rat droppings which are plastic or hard in consistency. Droppings may be scattered over the floor surface or deposited

Figure 10.1 Bat droppings can be differentiated from mouse or rat droppings by squashing. Bat droppings are composed of insect fragments, so they break into a glistening dust.

in heaps under roosts. The latter may be anywhere that there are cracks or crevices, for example where timbers join at roof ridges, under valley gutters or at gable walls (Hutson, 1987). Only two species, the Greater and Lesser Horseshoe bats, normally roost by hanging from exposed timbers, and these two bats are now both uncommon.

The two commonest species found in buildings are the Pipistrelle and the Brown Long-eared bat. The Pipistrelle ejects small elongate droppings as it flies, so that these are frequently found attached to wall surfaces. The Long-eared bat produces larger elongate droppings which are usually a mixture of shades of brown, frequently accompanied by numerous moth wings. There is no direct evidence to suggest that these animals eat wood-boring beetles, but it seems likely that they would do so if they encountered them.

Bat droppings are frequently said to be harmless, and to make good insulation. These assertions must, however, be treated with a little caution. There is certainly no reason to suppose that they would significantly harm the top surfaces of ceilings where they normally accumulate, but acids in the urine and accompanying faeces may damage wall paintings and other historic finishes in medieval churches for example. Faeces should be carefully removed with a vacuum cleaner without damage to the surrounding fabric (Paine, 1998).

10.4 Control of Substances Hazardous to Health (COSHH) Regulations 1994

The COSHH Regulations came into force on 1 October 1989 and have been subsequently updated and amended. They require an employer (self-employed persons are regarded as both employers and employees) to assess the risks which may arise from any work to be undertaken in which hazardous materials are used. A written record should be kept of the assessment unless the conclusions are obvious and easily demonstrated. The following notes are intended to provide a summary for anyone interested in the Regulations, and are selected to be relevant to timber treatments. They are not an authoritative guide to the law. The Regulations themselves should be consulted if further or more precise information is required.

Hazardous materials are those which may be included within the following categories:

1. Those which are known to be very toxic, harmful, corrosive or irritant, and were listed as such under the Classification Packaging and Labelling Regulations 1984 now superseded by the CHIP Regulations 1994.
2. Any substance which has been given a Maximum Exposure Limit or an Occupational Exposure Standard.
3. Substantial quantities of dust of any kind within the air.
4. Micro-organisms which may create a hazard to the health of any person.
5. Other substances which produce a comparable risk to the above.

Relevant exclusions are lead and asbestos which have their own separate regulations, and any substance which is only a hazard because it is explosive, flammable or at high or low temperature or high pressure.

The purpose of these Regulations is to ensure that the exposure of an employee to hazardous substances is avoided or adequately controlled and that, as far as is reasonably practicable, the use of these substances does not adversely affect any other person. Most of the duty placed on the employer also encompasses any other person who may be affected by the works, whether or not they are at work. When unacceptable exposure cannot be prevented within the working environment, then appropriate and effective personal protective equipment must be provided, and all reasonable measures must be taken to ensure that it and other relevant facilities provided are used, and used correctly. Every possible route of exposure must be considered and guarded against. The following are obvious and important examples:

- inhalation: provide masks or respirators
- skin contact: provide overalls, gloves and goggles
- ingestion: provide washing facilities.

Employees and any other persons who carry out works relevant to the employer's duties under these regulations must always be adequately informed, instructed and trained. There is clearly no benefit to the employee in informative labels if he or she has no ability to read or understand them; in such cases verbal instructions must be given. Further information on the regulations and their requirements will be found in the approved Code of Practice, *The Safe Use of Pesticides for Non-agricultural Purposes* (Health and Safety Commission, 1991). Other complications, for example defining responsibilities on multicontractor sites, are discussed in the publications of the Construction Industry Advisory Committee, while advice on assessments is provided in a range of Health and Safety Executive publications.

The Government policy on the remedial treatment of timber decay, based on the Regulations and other documents discussed above, is provided in a guide entitled *Remedial Timber Treatment in Buildings: A Guide to Good Practice and the Safe Use of Wood Preservatives* (Health and Safety Executive, 1991). This guide, which was produced by a working party chaired by the Health and Safety Executive, is intended for the use of professionals and other interested persons involved in the repair and conservation of buildings. It contains a considerable quantity of information on relevant topics, for example the labelling and safe storage of preservatives, which do not concern us here, but should be studied by all persons involved in the use of preservatives.

The COSHH requirement that the public should be protected from exposure is also amplified within the guide, and the measures to be taken are worth restating here in an abbreviated form. The guide itself should be consulted if more information is required. The precautions listed include the following:

1. Provide for the owner/occupier in writing before work commences, details of the type of treatment to be used, details of the preservative and of any potential risks, together with precautions to be taken by the contractor before and during treatment and the occupier after treatment. This information should also be provided for owner/occupiers of nearby properties if they are likely to be affected.

2. Access to the treated area during treatment and for a minimum period afterwards should be restricted to suitably protected personnel. Re-entry would not normally be recommended for a minimum of 48 hours or until the treated surfaces had dried. This period has recently been reduced for certain micro-emulsion preservatives. Evacuation of adjoining properties may also be required if there is a risk that the occupiers will be exposed to the preservative.

3. The very young, very old or those with respiratory problems will require special precautions to be taken before work starts, including advice from the responsible medical practitioner. The supervisor must also check to ensure that other

affected persons, including the occupiers of adjoining buildings, do not suffer from medical conditions which may be adversely affected by the treatment. If a potential health risk cannot be avoided then the treatment must not be used.

4. Notices must be clearly posted around the site prior to, during and after treatment which give warning of the chemicals used, and prohibit eating, drinking and smoking in the treatment area.

5. Remove fish and other pets from the treatment area and inform the appropriate authorities if there are signs of bats.

6. Cover all water tanks tightly to exclude contamination.

The basic underlying intentions of the policy are that preservative treatments should only be used where necessary, and that the minimum quantity of biocide should be used for effective pest control, compatible with human health and the environment. This places the onus on the surveyor or specifier to justify the remedial treatment to be undertaken, and the guide is intended to assist with this process.

The safe use of the preservatives is thus controlled by legislation, but the extent of any exposure works, timber removal and choice of preservative remain the decisions of the contractor although he or she may have to convince the client or the local planning authority officer of the need. Depending on the extent of the proposed work to the fabric of the building, it may be necessary to obtain consent from the various statutory authorities, including the local planning authority, the Diocesan Chancellor through the Faculty process, the Cathedrals Fabric Commission and the Department of Culture, Media and Sport. The extent of treatment works specified by different specialist surveyors or architects may vary considerably, and although they may remain within the framework of the Government guide or the BWPDA Code of Practice, they may result in an unacceptable loss of historic fabric. This is the point at which timber preservation meets building conservation; the two do not necessarily go hand in hand.

10.5 Construction (Design and Management) Regulations (CDM) 1994

On 31 March 1995 the Construction (Design and Management) Regulations (CDM) 1994 came into force. These implemented the EC Temporary or Mobile Construction Sites Directive 92/57/EEC and supplemented the Management of Health and Safety at Work and Provision and Use of Work Equipment Regulations 1992.

Within these regulations the role of a Planning Supervisor is defined and duties are allocated so that a comprehensive Health and Safety plan may be produced for the duration of a contract.

The aim is to eliminate all unnecessary health and safety risks and to control and manage those that are an integral part of the works. These regulations may apply to most building, civil engineering and engineering and construction works in accordance with the following criteria:

1. Large contracts which involve continuous work for more than 30 working days or more than 500 person days of work are 'notifiable' and HSE must be informed before work commences.
2. CDM applies to non-notifiable work if five or more people are working on site at any one time.
3. If four or fewer are working on site and the construction phase is less than 30 working days and involves less than 500 person days, then most of CDM does not apply.
4. CDM applies to all demolition/dismantling work of *any* size.
5. CDM will apply to design work of any size no matter how long the work lasts or how many workers are involved on site, unless the local authority is the enforcing authority for the work, in which case none of the regulations applies.
6. CDM does not apply to construction work where the local authority is the enforcing authority for health and safety purposes. This means that CDM does not apply where work is not notifiable and is:
   (a) Carried out in offices, shops and similar premises without interrupting the normal activities in the premises and without

separating the construction activities from other activities.
   (b) The maintenance or removal of insulation on pipes, boilers or other parts of heating or water systems.
   (c) Carried out for a domestic client, apart from the designer's duties and duty to notify where appropriate. However, where a domestic client enters into an arrangement with a business developer CDM will apply.

If CDM does apply then the following duties are imposed:

1. The client should be satisfied that only competent people are appointed as planning supervisor and principal contractor. This also applies when making arrangements for the appointment of designers and contractors. Clients should also ensure, as far as they reasonably can, that those they appoint have sufficient resources, as well as competence to comply with CDM so that the project is carried out safely. Duties on clients do not apply to domestic householders when they have construction work carried out.
2. The designer should ensure, as much as he or she can, that the proposed works are designed to avoid or, where this is not possible, to minimize risks to health and safety when they are being carried out and maintained. Where risks cannot be avoided, adequate information has to be provided. Design is not limited to drawings, but also includes the preparation of specifications.
3. The planning supervisor has overall responsibility for coordinating the health and safety aspects of the design at the planning and pre-tender stages of the Health and Safety plan and ensuring completion of the health and safety file.
4. The principal contractor should take account of health and safety issues (and in particular pre-tender health and safety plans provided by the planning supervisor) when preparing and presenting tenders or similar documents. The

principal contractor also has to develop the construction phase health and safety plan and coordinate the activities of all contractors to ensure that they comply with health and safety legislation. Principal contractors also have duties to check on the provision of information and training for employers and for consulting with employees and the self-employed on health and safety.

5. Contractors and the self-employed should co-operate with the principal contractor and provide relevant information on the health and safety risks created by their work and how they will be controlled. Contractors also have duties for the provision of other information to the principal contractor and to employees. The self-employed have duties similar to those of contractors.

Further information may be obtained from the Government guides listed in the bibliography, and from the BWPDA guidance notes (of March 1996), from which the lists of criteria and duties given above have been taken.

PART THREE

Effects of the Building Environment on Timbers

CHAPTER ELEVEN

Drying and wetting: A historical perspective on timber decay within buildings

11.1 Changes in moisture content after felling

Timber is not a homogeneous solid like a metal which contracts and expands equally in all directions. It has different internal arrangements along the grain and across it, so that it shrinks and swells unevenly as it loses or gains moisture. Green mature timber shrinks little along its length, more across the radial face and much more across the tangential face. Tangential shrinkage is usually 1.5–2 times as great as radial shrinkage. Unequal shrinkage causes stresses within the log that lead to splits along the weakest tissue, which is the rays. Sawn timber subjected to uneven drying will warp, the severity and type of distortion being dependent on the manner in which the log was cut.

Sawn building timbers therefore have to be dried to a level that does not suit the majority of decay organisms, but in a controlled fashion so that distortions are minimized. This process is known as seasoning, a term that probably derives from the practice of leaving oak logs and ships' frames for several seasons in order to rid them of saps liable to 'ferment' (Bowden, 1815, pp. 85–93). A report from a commission of inquiry set up in 1609 to investigate the condition of the Navy's ships concluded that timbers were putrefying because they were not properly seasoned before the ships were constructed. It advised that the timber be 'seasoned in water to sucke out the sappe and after dryed by the ayer and sonne and pyled uppe till thear be fit use of it'.

It became the custom to leave ships on the stocks for three or four years to season in the open air, but this clearly did not preserve the ships from decay. As Wade noted in 1815:

When a ship is built exposed to the weather, the lower part forms a grand reservoir for all the rain that falls, and as the timbers in that part are placed as close together as possible, the wet escapes very slowly. Those timbers are always soaked with moisture, and to some distance from the keel, exhibit a green appearance.

English shipbuilders subsequently adopted the practice, used by the Swedes, of building well-ventilated roofs over ships under construction (Wade, 1815). Stacked timber was also protected and, instead of being placed on logs resting on the ground, was rested on stone or iron supports. Small pieces of wood were placed between the timbers in the stack, to allow the free circulation of air. Seasoning was now understood to be a method of drying, rather than for the removal of fermenting saps. However, as oak when dried becomes very hard, the drying process was halted while the timber was still green enough to work.

Drying and a reduction in sap was thought to be enhanced by felling during the winter months when the tree was dormant. This worked to the disadvantage of the valuable tannin industry, which relied on oak bark, because bark would only strip easily in the spring. This was ascribed to the rising of the sap (Bowden, 1815, p. 26), but was more likely to have been due to the easier cleavage of the actively growing cambium layer (see Figure 1.9). The French took the practice further still and various directions, including a royal ordinance of 1669, limited felling to between 1 October and 15 April when the 'wind was at north' and 'in the wane of the moon' (*Encyclopaedia Britannica*, 4th edn, 1824). Desch and Dinwoodie (1981) have stated that there is no evidence to suggest that winter felling produces timber with a lower moisture content, and it seems unlikely that it could significantly, because sapwood relies on saturation to exclude air and thus decay fungi. Sap rise affects flow rate, but probably not the degree of saturation to any great extent, if at all.

Nowadays seasoning is usually undertaken in a more controlled fashion and its purpose is to make the timber as stable as possible with regard to both distortion and decay. Seasoned timber is also lighter (therefore less costly to transport), stronger, holds nails better and is easier to machine, paint and glue. It also usually accepts chemical preservatives readily because the wood cells are empty of liquid.

Ideally the less durable timbers should be converted as soon after felling as practicable because they are susceptible to a wide variety of decay organisms. This topic is complex, however, and advice may be conflicting. It has been suggested, for example, that the ray tissue, which remains alive for some time after felling until killed by drying, uses up nutrients which might otherwise be available to decay organisms and stain fungi. This perceived advantage is countered by recent research (Schmidt and Amburgey, 1994) which shows that log colour deterioration during storage, caused in some timber species by enzymes produced by the cells, could be avoided if the cells were rapidly killed. Felling during the cold season (if there is one) may also be advantageous because the metabolism of decay organisms, and hence their rate of colonization, will be slower.

If the bark is completely removed from the log before or after felling, then uneven drying and the release of stresses may cause severe permanent shakes to develop from the outside inwards. This reduces the amount of usable timber that can be cut from the log. However, if the bark is left on the log to retard drying, a different set of problems occurs; these include end splitting and staining as well as attack by wood-boring beetles and fungi.

Different timbers vary considerably in their anatomical structure and in their physical properties, and there is a wide variation also within any one species. It follows, therefore, that although the drying of all wood, regardless of its species and size, is governed by the same physical laws, there are great differences in the drying conditions that can safely be imposed. Water seasoning is worth a mention here even though it is not a method of drying, because it is an old-established practice. If logs remain waterlogged then starch is removed and with it the risk of powder post beetle damage when the timber dries. Fungi are also inhibited but bacterial attack may increase the porosity of the sapwood. This is not necessarily a disadvantage because it may aid the penetration of preservatives (see Section 9.6).

11.2 Air drying

Air drying (Figure 11.1) is probably the oldest technique available. The timbers must be stacked in a way that allows adequate, even air flow and prevents distortion. Correct stacking is of considerable importance, as the diameter of the felled trees decreases and the risk of distortion, particularly cupping, in the resulting smaller section timber increases (Wengert and Denig, 1995). Planks and other timbers are normally stacked horizontally with thin spacing timbers of uniform size, known as stickers, between them.

Stickers are placed so as to form vertical lines throughout the stack, usually at about 300 mm centres, in order to avoid unequal stresses. Stickers have to be kept thoroughly dry in order to avoid staining in susceptible timbers (Wengert, 1990). The rate of drying may be controlled to some extent by the thickness of the stickers and their distance apart. Heavy weights may be placed evenly on top of the stack to minimize distortion. If stacks are too large for adequate ventilation then the air becomes saturated and drying ceases.

Figure 11.1 Logs and stacks of air-drying timber.

Maximum dimensions have been given as 4 m wide and 5 m high with a 1 m minimum wide passageway between stacks. A suitable cover is constructed over the top to protect the stack from rain. The edges of the covering should extend beyond the sides of the pile to prevent rainwater from dripping onto the timber (Desch and Dinwoodie, 1981; Rietz and Page, 1975). The cover may be a shed, with or without fan-assisted ventilation (Figure 11.2).

If carefully piled, the timber may dry to a moisture content of about 17–20%. The time taken depends on numerous factors, including type and thickness of timber, season of the year (see Section 12.7), weather, and dry conditions within the yard. The latter is important because if the area around the stack is cluttered and damp then drying will be impaired. Good foundations (i.e. a flat surface that is sufficiently firm to take the weight of the timber) are also required to prevent deflection

(Food and Agriculture Organisation, 1986). If conditions are satisfactory, 25 mm-thick redwood should air dry in about 3 months. Hardwoods such as beech and oak of similar dimension may take 7 or 8 months, and it is usual to add one year for each extra 25 mm of thickness (Desch and Dinwoodie, 1981). End shakes are the most common form of defect during drying; they occur because of fast evaporation from end grain. They may be avoided by using a sealant, or by using some form of end covering.

11.3 Kiln drying

Natural seasoning does not produce dry enough timbers for many purposes and requires a large amount of yard space for a long time. The timber industry in many parts of the world is having to become more efficient and competitive. As the

121

Figure 11.2 Air drying under cover in a drying shed.

cost of logs and the demand for dry timber rise, storage time and drying degrade have to be kept to a minimum if profits are to be maintained. Kiln drying (Figure 11.3) is therefore frequently more economical, but a range of defects may still occur.

There are two conventional types of ventilated kiln. In the first the conditions are uniform and the timber remains stationary within the kiln for a set period of time while being dried by a current of hot, moist air. The second type of kiln is long and conditions become progressively hotter and less humid along its length. The timber is slowly moved from one end to the other as drying proceeds. The second type of kiln is more difficult to control, and is normally only used for softwoods, which can safely withstand faster drying than hardwoods. These kilns may assist in avoiding a high proportion of kiln-induced defects which have been shown to be caused by variations in moisture content in both the timber and the kiln. Defects

are mostly produced by localized variations in conditions within the kiln.

Timber is stacked in the kiln in the same manner as for air drying, but great care has to be taken because the risk of defects occurring is far higher under the more severe kiln-drying regime. It is essential to ensure that loads are composed of similar species and sizes. Different species of timber are dried according to schedules that have been developed by trial and error in order to hasten drying and reduce defects. However, the satisfactory kiln drying of timber depends ultimately upon the degree to which the individual pieces of wood are uniform in structure, upon careful monitoring and upon the skill of the kiln operator. It has not been unusual for up to 25% of pieces passing through a kiln to be subsequently downgraded due to kiln-induced defects (Hart, 1990). The cost implications of this may be substantial (data from Southern Pine Lumber Mills).

Figure 11.3 Drying kilns at Henry Venables timber yard.

Moisture movement from the core of the timber to the surface is a relatively slow process. If drying proceeds too rapidly because the air is too dry, then the outside of the timber may dry and set while the inside remains damp. The result is known as 'case hardening' (Figure 11.4), and differential drying when the plank is resawn will cause severe cupping (Stumbo, 1990). If case hardening continues too far then shrinkage of the tissue at the centre will be restrained by the hardened shell. The result is a mass of small shakes and defects at the centre which are invisible from the surface of the timbers. This defect is known as honeycombing (Figure 11.5).

If the timber is very green and evaporation of moisture occurs too rapidly, moisture is forced from the timbers faster than air can be drawn in to replace it. In this case the diminishing volume of water causes the cell walls to cave in, especially in the spring wood, and the whole timber shrinks and warps. This is known appropriately as collapse (Figure 11.6). Most of these defects can be corrected by changing the drying schedule, provided that they are detected early by careful monitoring, and that they do not derive from abnormalities in the wood (Lamb, 1990). Collapse may be avoided by predrying. Most modern kilns today dry a charge of softwood every 24 h although some operate on a 12 h drying cycle (McConnell, 1990). Hardwoods must be dried at a much slower rate if defects are to be minimized, and 25 mm thick oak dried from green will take about 5–6 weeks. This period may be halved if the timber is air dried first.

One problem with conventional kilns is that the water collected from the timber may contain up to 3% of organic extractives, some of which may be hazardous (Singer *et al.*, 1995). Waste disposal must therefore be taken into consideration. These condensates may also cause significant corrosion damage to the kiln (Little and Moschler, 1994).

Figure 11.4 Case hardening, a kilning defect caused by the outer layers of the timber drying too rapidly while the interior is still wet. It is detected by cutting a prong from a sampling board and watching the prong for deformation.

Figure 11.5 Honeycomb shakes are separations of the fibres caused by drying stresses. These occur after case hardening when the interior of the timber dries.

Several other methods of drying have been tried with varying success (an excellent overview is provided by Milota and Wengert, 1995). Drying by dehumidification seems likely to become of increasing importance, particularly for drying pretreated timber, and drying with vacuum kilns is becoming an accepted practice in many parts of Europe. Commercial vacuum kilns can produce a vacuum which halves the boiling point of the water within the timber; the moisture can therefore be driven out at a lower temperature than in a conventional kiln.

Timber is frequently dried to a moisture content specified for a particular end use, and its moisture content when supplied should preferably be within about 2% of that specified. Dimensional change for every percentage variation in moisture content may be small, but may nevertheless affect gluing because a glue layer may only be 0.23 mm thick (Taylor, 1994). Care must be taken after drying to ensure that the moisture content remains stable, and that it is not altered by inappropriate transportation, on-site storage, or other building works.

The average moisture contents that modern softwood timbers attain in dry buildings are generally about 12–15% in domestic roofs, and

Figure 11.6 Collapse is a kilning defect that occurs in some timbers if a rapid loss of moisture causes cells to deflate.

perhaps 12–14% in floor timbers (above ground floor) and joinery. Heating systems may reduce moisture levels to about 6–9%, when cracking or joint separation may occur, whereas suspended ground floor timbers may have moisture contents in excess of about 18% – high enough to allow insect attack if sapwood is present. Recent amendments to BS4978 and BS5268 (Part 2) 1977 concerning dry stress-graded structural timbers, under 100 mm thick and for interior use, require that they be graded at a maximum average moisture content of 20%. If these timbers are subsequently pretreated with a water-based preservative then they must be redried to the same level. Timbers must then be marked as 'Dry' or 'KD' (and 'Wet' if undried, and therefore for outdoor use). Kiln drying will make a substantial difference to the cost of timber for repairs. Kiln-dried oak costs about three times as much as green (Venebles, 1993).

Large-dimension softwoods also present a problem, and sizes over about 100 mm · 300 mm · 6000 mm are likely to be green and prone to shrinkage.

11.4 Moisture, the key to decay

Timber in buildings that are well maintained will be unlikely to decay. Unfortunately, many property owners seem disinclined to give structural matters the same attention that they give to, for example, their car. The latter is likely to be given frequent services, but houses are often left with blocked gutters, slipped slates and vegetation growing out of walls (Figures 11.7–11.9), even though these and many other faults may cause water penetration – and water penetration causes decay.

The terms 'dry' and 'damp' are often applied when porous building materials are discussed, but in practice they may be quite difficult to define. Dry materials in a strict sense have no moisture, but some that are porous, particularly timber, attract moisture from the atmosphere to some extent, and so the term 'dry' may have only a limited practical application. The property of attracting moisture from the atmosphere is known as hygroscopicity. Porous building materials may also hold moisture tightly by physical forces within small pores and are therefore by definition more or less damp.

The problem of definition is overcome by the concept of 'air dry', which means that all materials present reach their own particular moisture equilibrium when placed in air of a fixed moisture content. This is because the vapour pressures exerted by the air within the pores of the material and within the enclosing building space will strive for equivalency. We must not, however, expect the 'equilibrium moisture contents' so obtained to be all the same if the materials vary.

The concepts of air dry and equilibrium moisture contents enable the moisture-absorbing characteristics of one material to be related to those of another, but it is still necessary to define acceptably 'air dry' in terms of a building environment which is satisfactory both for the occupants and for the timber, or satisfactory for some other purpose or materials. Timber should remain stable if the moisture content equilibrates between about 10% and 15%.

Figure 11.7 Most building faults that cause timber decay are easy to recognize. The roots of this buddleia bush allow water in at the back of the cornice.

Figure 11.8 Shrubs growing out of walls behind gulleys indicate damaged rainwater goods or faulty drainage.

In practice, air within a building rarely has a fixed moisture content so that the material will tend to pick up moisture (adsorption) or lose moisture (desorption) as conditions fluctuate. These moisture contents, if plotted, produce an oscillating sorption curve with intermediate values. If the environment were to be stable for a few weeks then an equilibrium moisture level would be reached which would vary a little depending on whether the wood was wetting up or drying down. The difference in equilibrium moisture contents achieved by these processes is called a hysteresis effect, and is mostly of no importance. Occasionally the difference between moisture contents attained by adsorption and desorption may be significant because timber drying down in a repaired roof will equilibrate at a higher moisture content than replacement timbers which are wetting up. A dynamic relationship is thus established, and the range of moisture contents that a timber may experience is frequently more informative than the moisture content at any particular point in time. We may demonstrate this by considering the graph of annual timber moisture content fluctuation shown in Figure 11.10. Moisture meter readings taken during the summer months would indicate that the roof was acceptably dry, whereas readings taken during the winter months might suggest that it was damp and required further investigation. The timber is, however, only responding to

Figure 11.9 Shrubs at every level in this London building indicate major long-term water penetration. There was dry rot on every floor.

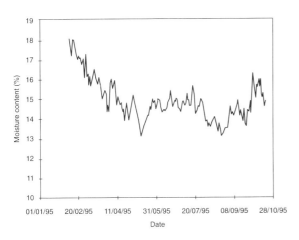

Figure 11.10 Annual timber moisture content fluctuations in modern softwood.

changes in seasonal ambient relative humidity, and moisture content readings do not indicate that more water is entering the roof.

11.5 Air temperature and relative humidity

Relative humidity is usually defined by the equation

$$RH = \frac{\text{Amount of water in a given quantity of air}}{\begin{array}{c}\text{Maximum amount of water the air}\\\text{can hold at that temperature}\end{array}} \times 100$$

Relative humidity is therefore expressed as a percentage where 100% represents saturation, and is the level at which condensation will occur.

The relative humidity of air containing a fixed volume of water can be varied by changing the temperature of the air. Warm air is capable of holding more water than cold, so that raising the temperature will lower the relative humidity. Conversely, lowering the temperature will raise the humidity until the dew point (saturation) is reached, and water condenses out. It is possible to control the relative humidity within a building by adjusting the temperature (Staniforth *et al.*, 1994), but problems may occur if rising damp or some other source of moisture is present. Raising the temperature will then draw more water through the structure so that the relative humidity remains stable, but the higher water loading in the atmosphere means that condensation is more easily achieved when the air cools.

The relationships between temperature and air moisture contents are described by a psychrometric chart. These are rather complex, but a simplified form will demonstrate the points under discussion (Figure 11.11).

A temperature of 18 °C and a humidity of 55% provides an excellent regime for timber, particularly antique furniture (A on Chart 1; Plenderleith and Werner, 1971). The lowest humidity level advisable would be about 45% (B), whereas if the humidity remained above about 65% for long

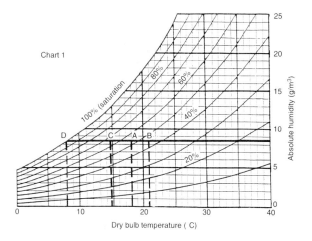

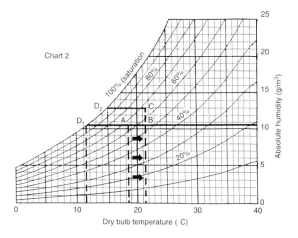

Figure 11.11 Controlling humidity by temperature changes.

periods mould growth and furniture beetle attack might occur (C). Water will condense on surfaces at about 8 °C (D). Therefore the aim would be to maintain the temperature within the building between 15 °C and 21 °C, as shown on the horizontal axis.

However, if the external wall (for example) of a room is damp then the humidity may be 65% at 18 °C (A on Chart 2). Theoretically it would be possible to reduce this humidity to 55% by raising the room temperature to about 22 °C (B) but in practice the elevated temperature might just draw more water from the wall so that the humidity

remains constant (C). Condensation in this example will then occur at 15 °C rather than 12 C (D_1) and little will have been achieved unless the excess moisture is also removed.

The inverse relationship between temperature and humidity is prominent in most environmental data as daily fluctuation. Figure 11.12 shows a typical example. Troughs of temperature during the day are accompanied by rises in humidity; the opposite occurs at night.

A similar effect, though frequently less marked, is found if the environment is monitored over the course of a year. Ambient humidity declines over the summer months as temperatures increase, and rises again during the winter.

11.6 Water absorption along the grain

Between 1975 and 1976 the Butser Archaeological Trust built a replica of an Iron Age roundhouse, 12.20 m in diameter. This construction was based around 27 oak posts, each about 300 mm in diameter, which were inserted into the ground in pipe holes, the rest of each post hole being filled with packing.

In 1990 the building was dismantled, and it was found that the bases of many of the posts had rotted away, and that the pipe holes had become filled in with debris. None of the posts showed any tendency to sink into the pipe holes, however, because all elements were fastened together and acted as a stable unit. The roof of the roundhouse rested on an inner circle of oak posts and an outer circle of stakes. These two sets of timbers were both partially buried in the soil, but the shelter provided by the building created two different habitats and the processes of decay differed accordingly. The comments that follow assume a soil which tends to retain water.

Outer stakes are exposed to the weather and also receive incremental water from the roof: a hypothetical instance is illustrated in Figure 11.13. The bases of the stakes are likely to be wet, with little oxygen, and therefore only subjected to slow chemical modification and probably attack by

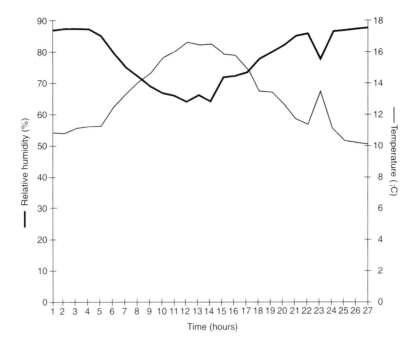

Figure 11.12 Hourly variations in temperature and relative humidity.

anaerobic bacteria. The stake ends may therefore be preserved. The integrity of the timber allows end grain absorption of water, and flow up the stake is driven by evaporation above ground level. The stake is therefore acting as a wick.

Further up the stake towards the soil surface the soil is better aerated and the surface of the timber will be eroded by soft rot fungi (see Section 3.4.2). It is at and around the soil–air interface that the greatest decay will occur, and this will extend up the stake as far as the dynamic water supply–surface evaporation relationship and exposure to the weather will allow. Eventually the stake will collapse.

Inner posts decay in a different manner. The ground surrounding the inner ring of posts is drier, because it is protected from the weather. In this situation the surface layers of soil will contain more air because the large soil pores are not all filled with water, and decay will therefore occur further down the post than in the outer stakes. Conduction of the smaller amount of water available becomes more difficult because water in the small pores, and

lining the large pores, is bonded to the soil particles and drier conditions will make evaporation from the post more efficient. Decay above ground level is therefore likely to be internal, and the post would snap off at the ground surface if unsupported. The newly formed end of the post would then be a tube of relatively sound wood with a rotten core.

A parallel with more recent building construction would be the decay of structural roof timber bearings embedded in damp brickwork and masonry. It is frequently found that, although several truss and joist ends embedded in the walls have decayed, the roof remains in place unless loadings are altered, because the various elements are fastened together and presumably continue to share the load. In this example the damp walls parallel the soil of our Iron Age dwelling because water is held around the timber. If the walls are made of brick or any other porous material and excess water penetration has caused free water to fill the large pores, then the water will travel easily along the end grain of the timber. Unlike the earthfast post, however, the roof timbers will not

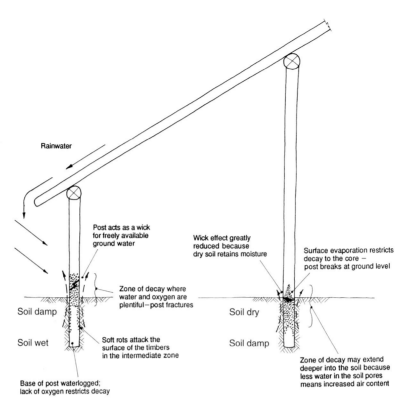

Figure 11.13 Hypothetical decay of posts in two different environments, as governed by differential water and oxygen availability.

usually be in anaerobic conditions and the fungi will consume the entire component end as far as the water entering the wall and evaporative loss will allow (Figure 11.14). This form of decay will continue for some time, even after the supply of water is halted, because until the large pores of the wall are empty of water there is a plentiful supply of free water within the wall.

However, if the wall is only damp then much of the water it contains will, as with the soil, be held by capillary forces in the small pores, and the amount of water that is available to the fungus is limited. The timber will still wet up and rot, but only the bearing within the wall will normally be lost. Decay caused by small leaks is therefore usually restricted, and will cease rapidly when water penetration is halted.

11.7 Water absorption across the grain

The earthfast post was always prone to rot, and this may have been one major reason why the technique of building timber frames with horizontal sill beams was developed (Figure 11.15). Many late medieval buildings had a sill beam, on which the posts rested, as their lowest element. This timber was placed horizontally and was therefore less liable to absorb water, because water movement across the grain is only a small fraction of that possible along the vessels (the major natural route) from the cut or hewn end (Figure 11.16). The beam would therefore tend to restrict water movement up the posts, and thus to act like a modern damp proof course.

(a)

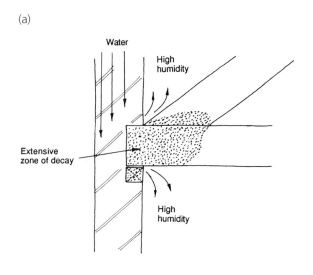

(b)

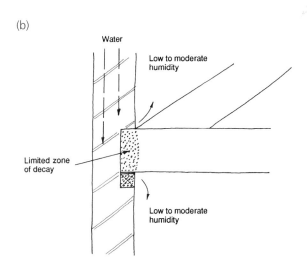

Figure 11.14 Hypothetical decay of truss ends in two different environments, as governed by water availability. (a) Large volumes of water enter the walls. Water in the large pores of the bricks is freely available to raise the humidity and saturate the timber. (b) Smaller volumes of water tend to be held by physical forces within the small pores of the bricks so that humidities are lower and decay is restricted to the embedded section of timber.

Many of the timber components, including the end grain of the sill beam, would be exposed to the weather, but exposed timbers do not necessarily decay because they become wet. If water gain is balanced by water loss then little damage will occur, although there might be some slow surface erosion. If water penetrates into the timber and becomes trapped, however, perhaps within loose joints or behind cracked impervious finishes, then rot will commence (Figure 11.17). This is demonstrated by many timber frames which lasted for centuries only to be destroyed in recent decades when they were covered with cementitious render. Fungus and death watch beetle can cause enormous damage in this situation because cracks inevitably appear in the render, water is driven in, and evaporation is impossible.

11.8 Some consequences of conversion

The methods by which building components were produced also have interesting effects on the decay observable in softwood and oak timbers in surviving medieval buildings. Components were formed by techniques which developed from squaring the log, usually with a side axe, and sawing or splitting with wedges. Squaring removed much of the vulnerable sapwood but, because the carpenter sawed each component from the smallest log that would provide the correct size, a layer of sapwood would remain, particularly at the corners (Figure 11.18). The thickness of this layer would depend on the width of the original log, because narrower logs have a greater depth of sapwood. Sawing or splitting would then penetrate the heartwood which, as discussed in the previous chapter, is less susceptible to attack.

If four timber components are derived from a squared oak or pine log then each will have two faces of sap wood and two faces of heartwood. Insect attack in the sapwood over the centuries will have caused two faces of the timber to be peppered with holes, whereas the other two remain more or less undamaged (Figure 11.19). Insect damage in a roof therefore requires substantially more

Figure 11.15 Horizontal sill beams rest on low stone walls and resist ground water because moisture absorption across the grain is limited (Pembridge, Hereford and Worcester).

investigation than making the observation that it is present. If holes are visible in some faces of old oak or softwood timbers and not in others then the damage is in the old sapwood layer, active infestation is unlikely, and the damage will not penetrate far into the timber unless it was of particularly poor quality. This does not mean that beetle activity is not present elsewhere within the roof, but it does mean that it will not normally be generally distributed in most of the readily accessible timbers. Whole roof treatment with insecticides, and particularly defrassing, will not be necessary.

Charles (1984) states that the cut surface was always set to the outside of a wall frame. This was done so that water entering the softer earlywood could not penetrate to the interior of the building because each earlywood half ring would be backed by latewood. He also states that erosion of the earlywood channelled rainwater runoff so that the wood dried quickly. The heartwood face in this position would also present the most durable surface to the weather. Richard Harris of the Weald and Downland Museum has amplified the topic with these comments:

I think the rule is best stated as follows: where a timber has been converted by sawing (either half, quarter or slabbing), the sawn surface was always used as the 'upper' or fair face of the frame, and in external frames this face was always placed outwards. But remember that whole trees (i.e. hewn baulks) were often used for main timbers, especially posts and tie beams, and in these cases a hewn outer face of the tree would necessarily have faced the weather.

(personal communication)

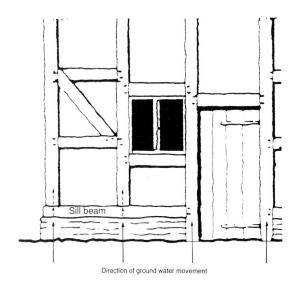

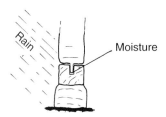

Figure 11.16 A horizontal sill beam acts as a damp proof course because of grain orientation. (a) Water absorption across the grain of the sill beam is only a small percentage of that possible along the grain of the door posts. The posts and studs jointed into the sill beam are therefore protected as long as the joints remain secure. (b) However, the mortice and tenon introduce a moisture pocket into the sill beam which can enter the end grain of the studs.

11.9 Timber replacement and re-use

Whether or not suitable materials for constructing timber-framed buildings were ever in short supply, as many authors have suggested, seems open to debate. Rackham (1990) states that a typical large fifteenth-century Suffolk farmhouse was found to

have been made from about 330 oaks. The diameters of all but three were less than 0.5 m and half were less than 0.25 m. This, he concludes, implies a rapid turnover of small oaks. It was only trees of greater girth, and of usable length in excess of 8 m, that were rare and expensive. Harris again offers some useful commentary:

> I think Rackham's emphasis on the number of small oaks used may be rather particular to Suffolk/East Anglia. My experience elsewhere suggests that most primary members were whole, half or quarter trees, but that most secondary members (particularly from the late fifteenth century and early sixteenth century onwards) were obtained as 'multiple conversion' of larger trees – wide but thin studs were slabbed, while squarish floor joists can be 4, 6 or more from a tree.
>
> (personal communication)

Nevertheless, there is ample visual evidence that building timbers were re-used. Many framed buildings contain a few timbers with joints cut in positions which now serve no purpose. Converted timber was evidently a valuable commodity, and sound components would be salvaged if buildings fell into disrepair. Now, in the twenty-first century, history has turned full circle and the question of timber re-use is with us again. This, as we shall see later, is because wild-grown eighteenth- or nineteenth-century softwood is more durable than its modern plantation-grown equivalent, without having been treated with preservatives. The same question may be asked about both medieval and modern re-use, namely 'what is the risk of infecting or infesting the building with decay fungi or wood-boring beetles?'. In both cases the answer must be that the risk is negligible, as long as the recipient building is made sound and weatherproof.

11.10 From oak frames to brick and softwood

Pine was not grown for building purposes in significant quantity in English soil until the first

Figure 11.17 If the sill beam becomes embedded in a later construction, water becomes trapped and the plate may decay.

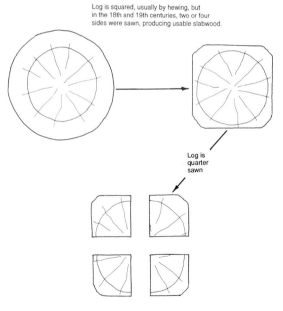

Log is squared, usually by hewing, but in the 18th and 19th centuries, two or four sides were sawn, producing usable slabwood.

Log is quarter sawn

Sawn faces were used as the 'fair face' of the timber frame and always placed outwards on an external wall.

Figure 11.18 Sapwood distribution in timber as a result of quartering.

Figure 11.19 This quartered post has beetle holes in the tangential side which was squared through the sap/transition wood. The radially cut side (left) is heartwood, and beetle holes are absent (see Figure 11.18).

attempts at establishing plantations during the late eighteenth century. All the eighteenth- and most of the nineteenth-century pine timber found in English buildings will therefore have been imported from overseas (some Scottish buildings were erected using native-grown timber, but the difficulty of identifying which timbers are native and which are imported makes it difficult to determine exact numbers).

A decline in the production of timber-framed buildings and increasing construction in brick and in stone reduced the quantity of timber used, and coincided with a change from using oak to using softwood for structural components. The change in timber type, at least in English brick buildings, tends to be fairly abrupt. Thus a house from the seventeenth or early eighteenth centuries will have oak roof and floor timbers, whereas after about 1740 these timbers will usually be pine. The situation in Scotland is less clear because softwood had been imported since the fourteenth century and by the seventeenth century this trade was extensive. Supplies of home-grown softwood were, however, limited in Scotland and non-existent in England.

Timber used in the construction of a brick or stone building is in a very different environment from that of a timber-framed building. In masonry construction, the bearings of timber components are inserted into a material which may retain water, especially if rainwater goods become blocked and locally saturate the walls. The conjunction of a change in construction type with a change in construction material brought brown rot fungi into prominence, with far-reaching consequences (see Chapter 7).

In Scotland arboriculture was practised to some extent during the seventeenth century. It was given a substantial impetus by an Act of Parliament in 1713 which gave bounties for the importation from Scotland into England of timber-derived naval materials, including rosin, Stockholm tar and masts. This encouraged the planting of large larch plantations. Larch was seen as a substitute for oak for many constructional purposes, including ship building. Sang (1820) stated that larch at 30–40 years old was in every respect superior in quality to fir at 100 years old. Durable it may have been, but there was widespread failure of the crop on many sites. This was partly due to inexperience and ignorance but also because of the trees' susceptibility to a range of destructive diseases.

The English home-grown timber industry seems to have started in 1766 with plantation experiments at Ocknell Clump in Hampshire (Nisbet, 1905, p. 199). In neither country, however, did the home-produced softwood make much impact on timber importations (Burnell, 1860).

Most of the softwood used during the eighteenth century came from Europe, and belonged to the common pine species *Pinus sylvestris*. This timber was variously named according to its colour and place of origin, thus it might be called Baltic fir or pine, Finnish red or yellow wood, redwood, red deal, Swedish red or yellow wood, or yellow deal.

Other exporting countries, including Russia and Poland, also gave their names to timber, but eventually it became more usual to call it redwood. Home-grown *Pinus sylvestris* was generally known as Scots pine.

Some attempt was made to import American softwood masts during the First Dutch War (1651–54) because the Baltic ports were blockaded, but the importation of New World softwoods for other purposes proved abortive because the cargoes frequently decayed during the voyage. In 1765 an Act of Parliament offered bounties on the importation of 'good sound and merchantable timbers from the North American Colonies' (Nisbet, 1905, p. 26) but the long duration of voyages effectively limited the quantity of timber landed. This problem was eventually overcome by improved ship design, and during the nineteenth century large quantities of timber were imported from Canada and the USA. By now, softwood was generally considered in the timber trade as the material for structural components, while hardwoods were used for furniture and sometimes for decorative finishes.

11.11 Some consequences of war

The home-grown softwood industry had declined dramatically by the beginning of the twentieth century, but that which remained was to play an important role in supplying Britain's timber requirements during the two World Wars, when foreign imports were largely unavailable. In 1914 no official organization existed in England in connection with timber supplies or forestry. The only information on stocks came from Ordnance Survey maps, which showed approximately 3 million acres of woodland. About 50% of hardwoods and 95% of softwoods were imported.

During the First World War large quantities of softwoods were used as trench and mine props (Stobart, 1927). The shortages thus created led to the establishment of the Forestry Commission in 1919 and the planting of large stands of conifers against future emergencies. The trees were, however, too small to be of use during the interwar years and most of the timber available from Europe was of poor quality. Nevertheless, large quantities of European timber were imported during the interwar period to meet the demand for low-cost housing. This timber was of such poor quality that sometimes fungus had to be brushed from stacks before it could be distributed from the timber yard (Dewar, 1933).

A census of woodlands undertaken by the Forestry Commission in 1939 provided more precise information about timber supplies than had been available in 1914. All stocks of cut timber were recalled, but the best of the home-grown mature timber had been cut during 1914–18 and only that planted in the immediate post-war years was large enough for pit wood and other essential requirements normally supplied by imported timber.

Before the 1939–45 War, timber was the country's largest dry cargo import. Home-grown resources provided only about 5% of consumption. When war commenced a Timber Control Board was set up (House, 1965), which centralized buying and developed a licence system governing distribution and use. By 1943 home-grown wood provided 75% of Britain's total timber consumption but demand steadily overtook supply and the use of low grade material remained inevitable. Much of the timber required could only be imported with considerable difficulty from abroad. Some exotics, for example balsa wood, which formed an essential part of the Mosquito aircraft framework and had to be imported from Ecuador, could not have been supplied from domestic sources.

The war and timber shortage also had a dramatic effect on building design. Before 1945 building was by traditional methods and it was rare for any timber structure to be designed on an engineering basis of calculated stresses. The Directorate of Constructional Design, part of the Ministry of Works, developed steel connectors and laminated skeleton trusses during the War. Anyone who wanted to use timber had to apply to the Directorate for a licence and was given the choice of using the light type of truss or not using timbers at all. Purlins and wall plates were mostly considered to be too heavy for their purpose and replacements for bomb damage repairs were usually reduced in thickness by 25–30% (House, 1965). Roof boards were banned completely except in Scotland, where traditionally they had been used for direct slating instead of battens. Common rafters were banned until the revival of permanent house construction at the end of the war so that only sheet materials such as asbestos could be used for roof covering. Ground floor joists and flooring were also abolished.

The war years were a period when building maintenance had a low priority. Some buildings were temporarily repaired or left derelict following bomb damage, and many others were left empty while their owners moved to safer districts. Unavoidable neglect coupled with several decades of construction and repair with inferior materials caused enormous decay problems which, in turn, promoted the growth of the timber preservation industry. This is discussed in later chapters.

11.12 Durability of old and modern softwood timbers compared

Wood in a dry environment is a highly durable material. For example, 4000–5000-year-old

Egyptian sycamore sarcophagi have been found to be in an excellent state of preservation when excavated (Nilsson and Daniel, 1990). Differences in the susceptibility of timber to decay in different climates, however, depend not only on the innate durability of the timber species but also on that of the individual trees.

It was generally accepted at the beginning of the twentieth century that English Scots pine was inferior to that grown in Scotland. This was attributed to soil quality (Stobart, 1927). In fact, most conifers are adapted to adverse conditions, and good climate and soil conditions will be liable to produce more rapid growth. Growth is also enhanced by increased space. When plantations are thinned to provide more growing room, the trees produce larger crowns to maximize light gathering and sugar production (photosynthesis). This in turn requires an increase in sap translocation from the roots. Softwood trees achieve this during the growing season by maximizing early-wood production, and wide rings are produced.

These effects were partially quantified by Henderson (1939) who noted that Sitka spruce grown in England tended to have about three or four rings per 25 mm, whereas in its natural and more rigorous habitats in North America and Canada this number increased to between 10 and 20. Baltic redwood grown in the wild tended to have 20–40 rings every 25 mm.

Increasing the width of growth rings may not directly influence the properties of the softwood timber. Thus attempts to relate density (and therefore some strength characteristics) generally to tree ring width do not produce significant results (Seco and Barra, 1996). As Aaron and Richards (1990) have commented, 'Coniferous timber displaying widely spaced growth rings has often been regarded as having inferior strength properties. This is a fallacy which has persisted despite the substantial volume of evidence to the contrary.'

Nevertheless, the percentage of the denser latewood present does affect density (Uusvaara, 1974; Wimmer, 1995) and it may be that meaningful comparisons within a species could only be made by comparing different trees of the same strain grown on the same site.

Indirectly, the consequences of wide annual growth rings are significant because the trees take a shorter time to reach a marketable diameter. This means that the juvenile core, with all its inherent weaknesses (see Section 1.5.1), will take up a larger proportion of the cross-section (Table 11.1). Elliot (1970) reviewed the literature and showed that growing pine at a high density slowed the growth rate and reduced the volume of juvenile wood.

The effect that an increase in juvenile core wood has on durability can be gauged from the distribution of extractives. The extractives that confer decay resistance in Western red cedar (*Thuja plicata*) have been investigated and found to be mostly thujaplicins and thujic acid. Nault (1988) studied extractives from six healthy old trees (260–710 years old) and 10 healthy second-growth trees (42–77 years old). He found that extractives increased from the pith to the outer heartwood and decreased in the sapwood. Older wood had more extractives than younger. He concluded that, 'Products made from the wood of younger trees, with reduced amounts of thujaplicins, will be less resistant to decay than those made from older trees.'

Rennerfelt (1945) showed that two phenolic compounds (pinosylvin and pinosylvin monomethyl ether) found in the heartwood of Scots pine were highly toxic to fungi, and Browning (1963)

Table 11.1 Potential juvenile wood content at the base of a Douglas fir at various growth rates (Data from Ramsay Smith and Briggs, 1986)

Age (years)	Diameter of juvenile core (mm)	Number of rings per 25 mm	Juvenile wood (%)
540	25	30	5
72	125	4	25
36	250	2	60

considered that these compounds are responsible for the durability of pine heartwood. If these extractives are distributed across the trunk of a pine tree in the same way as thujaplicins in red cedar, then this would explain why Carey *et al.* (undated) found that the adult heartwood of joinery grade Scots pine was significantly (0.1% probability) more durable than juvenile heartwood, and that both were significantly (0.1% probability) more durable than sapwood.

It is apparent from this discussion that the durability of softwood is largely dependent on the amount of mature outer heartwood present. Uusvaara (1974) sums up the evidence as follows: 'As the amount of heartwood seems to be associated simultaneously with age, growth rate and soil type, wood with a particularly low heartwood percentage will be obtained from young, fast growing pine plantations.' He concludes, 'The average percentage of adult heartwood in plantation-grown pine is only a half of the percentage in stems of natural origin.'

The amount of durable material in the stem of a tree is thus greatly dependent on the length of time it has been growing. A Scots pine tree felled in Britain after 60 years might, near its base, have 18 years of sapwood with no durability (see Section 1.5), 15 years of juvenile wood with low durability, and only 27 annual growth rings with increasing durability. Maximized durability will not be reached. The growth rings increase in width towards the core, so that the juvenile wood takes up a disproportionate volume, and the sapwood band becomes wider as the stem narrows because the volume of sapwood tends to stay constant along the stem. These characteristics mean that the mature heartwood that is present will only be in the lower section of the tree and that the rest will be all juvenile wood and sapwood. In practice, the outer mature heartwood, frequently accompanied by a high proportion of sapwood, is generally sold in Britain and Scandinavia as joinery grade timber, because its tighter growth rings and fewer knots produce a better finish and allow easier working.

Twentieth-century plantation-grown structural grade softwoods therefore have a durability greatly inferior to that of historically grown softwoods (Figure 11.20) because they are taken from trees that have not been grown for long enough to produce a significant volume of mature heartwood. This is not necessarily seen as a disadvantage because the modern timber readily absorbs chemicals, and pretreatments give an excellent depth of penetration. The modern material cannot, however, be considered as a like-for-like substitute for the original. Historical softwoods have very different properties, and are irreplaceable unless trees are grown for a greatly extended period. Their removal from buildings should be minimized on the grounds of both durability and historical authenticity.

The increased sapwood content in available timber was investigated by Linscott (1970), who examined 78 lengths of imported rough-sawn redwood obtained from a timber merchants in Sussex. She found that the majority of the timber contained more sapwood than heartwood. Sapwood averaged 66.3% of the surface area and 52.5% of the volume. In some pieces, however, these figures were as high as 88% and 90%, respectively. These results indicate that the timbers were converted from narrow logs.

The problem of obtaining a first-class traditional building timber should be restricted to softwood. As noted earlier, the 1914–18 War was a heavy drain on forest resources, and the subsequent concentration on the more speedily grown softwoods meant that oak was only available from private woodlands. These too diminished as stands of oak were sold to pay death duties, and few landowners could afford to resist the quicker returns to be made from softwoods. The Second World War led to still greater overcutting of forests already depleted by one war and by a complete lack of forest policy for private woodlands in the interwar years. Nevertheless, the demand for oak has not exceeded supply, and good quality British and European timber is available.

Timber is considered as a building material which can be replaced like for like. If softwood roof timbers are old, with perhaps a few worm holes, then many will consider it sensible and more economical to undertake wholesale replacement than to attempt localized repairs. In fact, the old

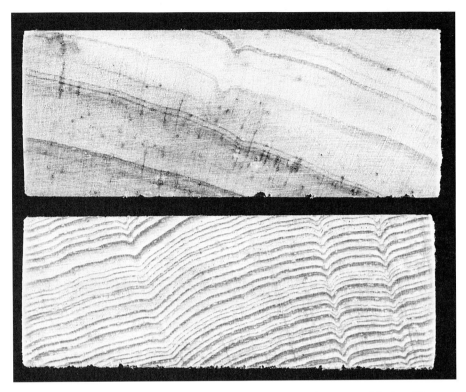

Figure 11.20 (a) Wide-ringed plantation-grown pitch pine cut from near the centre of the log. The natural durability is poor. (b) Close-ringed wild-grown pitch pine with a good natural durability.

timber removed may have a far greater natural durability than any modern replacement, and the slow-grown original, so lightly dismissed, is a vanishing commodity which will soon be irreplaceable. The durability of modern plantation timber may be bolstered by preservative impregnation, and pretreated timber has a vital role to play if the demand for timber is to be satisfied, but the new product is not the same as the original.

11.13 Use of second-hand timbers

Although softwood timber from earlier centuries is an almost irreplaceable material which should not be wasted, one still finds high quality imported softwood being removed from buildings that are being restored. If the argument for removal is irrefutable then there may still be an argument for

re-use. Objections raised normally fall into the following categories.

- *It may introduce decay into the building*: Assuming that the building will be restored to a weatherproof condition, the timber will not represent a hazard, provided that obviously decayed pieces are discarded.
- *The timber may contain nails and be difficult to work*: This may present a problem, and careful inspection will be necessary. The enhanced durability of the finished work should, however, make the extra effort worthwhile.
- *The re-use of timbers distorts the historical evidence presented by the building*: Philosophical arguments (see Chapter 14) must be tempered by the consideration of relative durability. All changes can be documented, and some form of inscription or plaque can be left if this is felt to

be necessary. The re-use of timber has a long historical precedent.

• *It may be difficult to establish the legitimacy of the source of second-hand timbers*: There is rarely any way of knowing where reclaimed timber from salvage yards comes from, or whether it was improperly obtained from other historic buildings. It might be argued that, even where such material is not illegally obtained, the existence of a demand for second-hand timber provides an incentive to obtain supplies by demolishing old buildings.

11.14 Timber and walls

In brick or stone construction many timbers – including beam, rafter and joist bearings, lintels and bonding timbers – were partially, sometimes totally, embedded into walls. All of these timbers would attain an equilibrium moisture content which would vary with that of the wall in which they were embedded.

The materials utilized in the construction of walls clearly differed considerably in their porosity, and the moisture content of individual elements would also depend on location. Thus a brick in the outer face of an exposed wall will be likely to have a higher moisture content than one in the interior face. The resulting moisture gradient will be reflected in that of any embedded timbers, and high timber moisture contents may therefore be expected if timber bearings are located within a zone of interstitial condensation, or where direct water penetration is possible. Timbers that achieve high moisture levels in this fashion will stay damp for as long as the wall moisture levels allow, and these will be very slow to change.

The decay potential for an embedded timber will therefore depend on its location, the properties of the surrounding construction, and the timber's own natural durability. The last factor is of

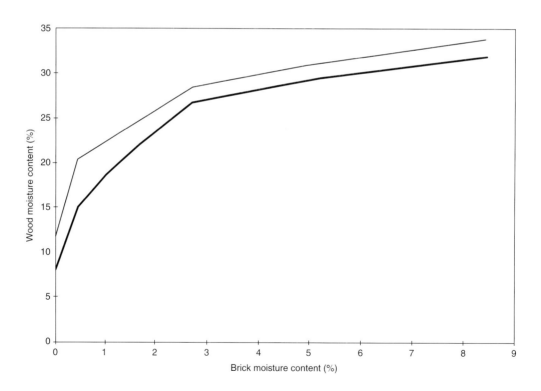

Figure 11.21 Wood and brick equilibrium moisture contents shown for two different bricks.

particular importance, and it will frequently be necessary to replace decayed embedded timbers with inorganic materials, or to isolate replacements from the wall, because plantation-grown softwoods used to replace historical timber elements will not have the durability to survive the damp environment.

The actual moisture contents induced in embedded timbers may frequently be surprisingly high. Figure 11.21 illustrates experimental data obtained by allowing pine dowel rods, sealed into soft red bricks, to equilibrate at a range of brick moisture contents. A moisture content of 3% in soft bricks is usually accepted as air dry, but appraisal of the graph shows that a timber moisture

content approaching fibre saturation may be produced. Thus, considered as an environment for the preservation of timber, the wall may be unacceptably damp for a timber of poor durability.

Dry brick or stonework will commonly have a variable moisture content around 1% or less. The steep first section of our timber wetting curve, which shows moisture absorption below fibre saturation, demonstrates that little extra water may be required in order to make the habitat suitable for the growth of fungus. It must be stressed, however, that wall materials are variable in their properties, and therefore in their wetting potential. Figure 11.21 is an example only and must not be taken as representative of all brick walls.

CHAPTER TWELVE

Fire Damage and Dereliction

12.1 Dry rot and fire damage

In 1982 a fire occurred in a large building in the north of England. The fire took many hours to fight and damp down. Five jets and six hosereel jets were used, and it was estimated by the Fire Brigade from their records that the whole process required 35 000 gallons (159 110 litres) of water. Financial considerations required that the building be back in use within the year, and the sum of insurance money eventually available was not as large as hoped. Compromises had therefore to be made with materials. Within 2 years of the fire dry rot was found, and over the next few years £87 244.00 was spent on treatment and consequent building works. The total plaintiff's damages claimed in the legal wrangle that ensued amounted to £223 173.17. What went wrong and how could dry rot have been avoided? These questions and others are addressed in the present chapter.

Very little has been published on the subject of dry rot and fire damage. No claim is made that what follows is a definitive text; it offers the conclusions drawn by the author from personal experience of a wide range of examples.

Fire damage is only an extreme example of building fabric saturation, but it does form a useful framework on which to base the discussions. Other examples include flood damage and dereliction, where the same principles apply.

12.2 Weatherproofing

The first priority following fire damage is to ensure that no further water enters the building. This should be accomplished with a temporary roof (Figures 12.1–12.3). The potential for further wetting is considerable because much of the British Isles has a high annual rainfall. The site described in Section 12.1 took 6 months to weatherproof because it was thought that the intended short duration of the restoration contract would make a temporary roof an unnecessary drain on limited resources. During these 6 winter months 37.8 cm of rain was recorded by the local meteorological station. The simple multiplication of plan area by rainfall suggests that 42 543 gallons (193 405 litres) of water fell on the fire-damaged site during that period. This is 7 543 gallons (34 295 litres) more than the water used to extinguish and damp down the fire.

The speed of temporary roof erection will be likely to depend on the quality of the building, the resources available and a wide variety of other complications. The roof over the King's Apartments at Hampton Court Palace took 18 days to erect, and the first scaffolding over Uppark House was also in place within a few weeks. The Milestone Hotel in London, however, took several years to protect and clear of debris because of protracted discussions about its future.

The type of roof used is also of considerable importance. Each has advantages and disadvantages which must be balanced. Table 12.1 indicates a

Figure 12.1 Open scaffolding allows plenty of ventilation, but may be unstable in high winds.

range of solutions and some of the problems that have been encountered.

In practice, decisions are likely to be based on factors that might include cost, time of year and location of building. Thus light, open scaffolding in an exposed area might be considered to be dangerous, and no weatherproofing might be an appropriate option if the new roof can be completed during the warm summer months in areas with a low rainfall.

12.3 Removal of debris and timber cleaning

The removal of all debris must be completed before any drying will occur (Figures 12.4 and 12.5). In practice this process may be delayed by insurance decisions, structural stabilization and, in the case of important historic buildings, by careful archaeological recording and excavation. This is important because in many cases where accurate replication of the original finishes is contemplated, the photographic record is found to be incomplete.

The structural engineer will undoubtedly be cautious about the removal of charred timbers because these may be providing support for the walls. The amount of damage that will have occurred to timber obviously depends on their size and position within the fire, but material loss can be quite small. The charring of the surface will tend to insulate the centre of the timber and afford it considerable protection. This was demonstrated by many of the roof trusses at Hampton Court Palace, which were sand-blasted to remove charring, and retained. It was interesting to observe that damage was most severe at joints – a phenomenon that may have structural implications (Figure 12.6). It is worth re-stating that sand-blasting, be it for treatment of fire damage or any other

Figure 12.2 An enclosed scaffolded roof is safer, but no significant drying will occur until it is removed.

purpose, produces an unpleasant ridged finish on softwoods because the softer earlywood is preferentially removed (Figure 12.7).

Floor-coverings must also be included within the category of debris unless they are important enough to dry and conserve. In either case they must be removed. Failure to do this will result in decay within the subfloor and distortion of the floorboards. Subfloor debris must also be removed, and this is discussed in the next section.

12.4 Stripping interiors

Those who walk around a historic building after a fire are frequently relieved to find that some at least of the finishes and joinery have survived. This is particularly the case in ground floors and basements when fires have commenced at upper levels. Unfortunately this pleasure may be short-lived because the water used to extinguish the fire can be

as destructive as the flames. Any type of wall-covering, be it plaster, paper or joinery, will retard drying to some extent, and joinery will distort and decay. All should ideally be removed if the walls behind are damp. Some, for example many modern plasters that contain gypsum, will not stay on the walls anyway. Consent may well be required for stripping of wall plaster in legally protected buildings.

It is sometimes possible to save interiors if they are important enough but this does require careful assessment and monitoring. The following are important considerations.

12.4.1 Position within the building

Finishes on upper floors are frequently easier to retain than those on the ground floor and in the basement. This is normally because fire-damaged material and water falls down through the building,

Table 12.1 Types of temporary roof

Solution	Advantages	Disadvantages
No weatherproofing (reinstatement of roof a priority)	cost of temporary roof avoided; ventilation maximized	continued wetting of structure until completion
Tarpaulins/polythene	inexpensive	only really suitable for limited damage; frequent removal and reinstatement probably necessary
Scaffolded roof, largely open at the sides	affords reasonable protection; maximizes ventilation and therefore drying	rain may blow in at the sides; risk of failure during gales
Scaffolded roof, enclosed sides	good protection from the weather; likely to be safe in gales	minimal air movement; little or no natural drying until removed

Figure 12.3 Most scaffolded roofs leak a little and require periodical adjustment. Condensation on scaffolding poles may be a problem.

Figure 12.4 As soon as archaeologists have completed their work, the debris should be removed as it inhibits drying.

Figure 12.5 The removal of debris should also be undertaken in areas that are wet, but untouched by the fire. Here an accumulation of wet debris around a beam end has allowed dry rot to develop. Note the dry rot fruit body developing against the right-hand side of the right-hand tie beam.

and the upper floors may stay relatively dry. Water on the wall surfaces evaporates because of the heat from the fire below, and subsequent air movement is greater around the upper walls of the building. The situation still requires monitoring, however, because considerable volumes of water can enter the heads of thick walls once the roof has been destroyed. This is particularly the case with rubble-filled walls.

A good example of the retention of finishes is Prior Park in Bath. The walls in that building were constructed from stone, and careful assessment showed that the water had passed through the building, leaving the upper walls relatively dry. A great deal of plaster and joinery work could therefore be retained. In other cases it may be appropriate to remove areas of plain plaster in order to increase the drying around more important finishes.

Rooms and wall surfaces that were not touched by the fire but were extensively damped down in order to contain it represent a considerable hazard, because undamaged decorations may prevent walls from drying out and therefore create ideal conditions for decay. Finishes may be retained, but drying should be maximized (see Section 12.9) and vigilance is essential.

Finishes at ground floor level and in basements will be very difficult to conserve *in situ*, but few tasks are impossible if sufficient thought is given to them. One problem with basements is that the walls may seem dry after the fire but they will not stay dry. Water will continue to migrate down within the walls for several months so that these walls will slowly become wetter. Good examples of this phenomenon occurred in the Colonnade at Hampton Court Palace and the ground floor rooms at Windsor Castle. The effect was particularly marked at Windsor because most of the principal floor constructions were solid.

Figure 12.6 Grit blasting the charred surface from an oak truss shows that charring is shallow, but that damage is more severe at the joints.

12.4.2 Floors, panelling, joinery and linings

These cause problems because individual timbers swell, and lateral restraint produces distortion. The cupping that results is largely recoverable if sufficient boards and panels can be removed to release the tension, but may become permanent if plastic deformation of the wood cells occurs as they dry.

It is generally advisable to remove boards in the vicinity of beam and joist ends, and at intervals across the room in order to assist drying. Difficulties may occur, and more boards should be lifted, if there is subfloor sound insulation (pugging or deafening). This may be almost any material laid on boards as an intermediate layer between floorboards and ceiling. Pugging usually retains water so that the floor remains wet, and the pugging boards create a concealed ceiling void that may

only be accessible with fibre optics. Pugging should be removed if at all possible, but it is sometimes practical to remove a few runs of floorboards together with pugging boards at either end of a room. Inspection and through-ventilation of both subfloor voids is thereby facilitated. This approach is particularly useful when high quality floorboards are connected together by tongues or pegs. This type of floor seems to be particularly difficult to lift intact, and is, in our experience, rarely relaid. In some cases it may be preferable to sacrifice the ceiling below the floor in order to speed drying.

Panelling has the advantage that it is usually removable entirely or in part. Sometimes, as at Hampton Court Palace, the individual panels may be removed, leaving the frame *in situ*.

Joinery is usually constructed from softwood and therefore theoretically more prone to decay. This risk can be reduced if layers of gloss paint are

Figure 12.7 Grit blasting softwood removes the softer earlywood and leaves ridges of latewood.

stripped in order to allow vapour movement and drying. Stripping may not be possible, or may be incompatible with the need to preserve layers of historic decoration, in which cases it may be possible to increase vapour loss from the surrounding walls by removing plaster.

Dry linings, stud partitions and fixings may decay if they are constructed from modern softwood. It would be best to expose these as far as possible. Decay is unlikely to occur in historic linings and embedded timbers unless decay fungus is already growing in the vicinity, and their removal as a precaution would seldom be contemplated. Nevertheless, frequent inspection, with fibre optics if necessary, is advisable.

12.4.3 Storage

There is little point in salvaging floorboards, joinery and other items unless they can be put back in the right place. The material should be recorded on drawings prior to removal, labelled according to an adequate numbering system that is cross-referenced to the drawings, and appropriately stored. Labels should carry a code relating each item to its exact location, and should be firmly attached.

Storage facilities are also important (Figure 12.8). Items should be sorted by size and type and stacked as in a drying pile with regularly arranged and carefully positioned spacer sticks. It may be necessary to pad the sticks if high quality decorative joinery is involved. Stacks should be above the ground, perhaps on pallets, and there should be adequate room to walk around them.

The environment within the store should be dry and well ventilated, or controlled to 45–60% RH at 18–20 °C. Regular inspections are necessary to ensure that these conditions are being maintained. If a suitable store cannot be found it may, in many

Figure 12.8 Careful stacking in a well-ventilated room or outbuilding is the best way to store salvaged panelling that will be reinstated.

cases, be better to leave the items *in situ* and risk deterioration.

12.4.4 History of dry rot

Water used to extinguish fires may or may not cause dry rot – this depends largely on the way in which the subsequent works are organized – but it certainly will spread fungus which is already extant and viable. The heat from the fire will not be anywhere near hot enough to kill fungus within the walls. This problem must be anticipated and guarded against. All available information on past outbreaks should be obtained, and particular attention paid to those areas where dry rot has occurred. It may be necessary to dismantle joinery as a precaution. It must never be assumed that previous chemical treatments have destroyed the fungus, and dry rot, once growing vigorously through wet walls, will be very difficult to contain.

The spread of dry rot from extant sources explains much of the problem with the example in Section 12.1. This house had a history of small dry rot outbreaks which had been a relatively frequent nuisance. The architect concerned with the restoration works after the fire had been associated with the building for many years and had therefore dealt with most of the fungus as it was located. Unfortunately he did not realize that the majority of dry rot outbreaks are ultimately destroyed by drying rather than chemical treatments, and that there is frequently a residue of fungus, perhaps deep within the structure, which remains unaffected by the fungicide. In cool damp parts of the building this fungus may remain viable for several years. A comparable example of fungus spread by wall washing is discussed in Case study 3 (Appendix B).

12.5 Progression of fungal assemblages

A range of moulds will appear within a few days of the fire. The type of mould will depend on the substrate, but the first intimation of the growth to be anticipated is frequently given by the salmon pink globular fruits of *Pyronema* sp. (Figure 12.9; see Section 8.3.2), which may appear within a week or two of the fire. The sudden proliferation of *Pyronema* will produce massive, perhaps alarming, amounts of white surface growth which is frequently mistaken for dry rot. However, it is too early for the decay fungi to grow. After a while the *Pyronema* is joined by, and eventually overtaken by, a wide variety of moulds. Those that appeared at Windsor Castle during the first year included the following genera: *Aspergillus*, *Cladosporium*, *Penicillium*, *Fusarium*, *Trichoderma* and *Sporotrichium*. These do no harm to the fabric, but spores of some species, notably *Sporotrichium* sp., *Aspergillus niger* and *Aspergillus fumigatus* in the Windsor assemblage, can produce a significant health hazard if present in sufficient quantity (Figure 12.10). This did not happen at Windsor,

Figure 12.9 Mould growth and the jelly fungus (*Pyronema* sp.) are usually the first to appear after the fire. *Pyronema* may produce large quantities of white growth and be mistaken for dry rot.

but *Chrysosporium* sp. was so prolific at Hampton Court Palace that the workmen were advised to wear masks before removing debris. This is always a wise precaution if mould growth is plentiful.

The most obvious fungi to appear during the first 6 months are the jelly fungi *Peziza* and related genera (Figure 12.11; see Section 8.3.1). These plaster moulds usually grow vigorously on subfloor debris (Figure 12.12). Their white hyphae may be particularly conspicuous.

The first to appear of the fungi with a significant ability to degrade cellulose is often *Chaetomium globosum*, which is frequently found on wallpaper. This fungus produces a mass of white hyphae with black speck-like fruits in it. Among the fungi that can cause damage to timber, the first to appear are *Coprinus* spp., the ink cap fungi (Figure 12.13; see Section 8.6.1). *Coprinus* usually appears after 8 or 9 months, although this will depend on the time of year. *Coprinus* can damage hardwood ceiling laths and is frequently a problem in subfloor voids.

Serious decay fungi, which would include cellar rot (*Coniophora*; Figure 12.14), *Asterostroma* and

Figure 12.10 Spores from some moulds may produce a health hazard if the fungus grows prolifically.

dry rot, do not in the author's experience normally become prominent until about 2 years after the fire. Spore germination should not occur if debris has been cleared and there are no enclosed and stagnant cavities. However, as discussed above, dry rot will spread rapidly from an extant source, and considerable care must be taken if the building has a history of dry rot (see Appendix A.4).

Most moulds and minor fungi can be controlled by surface application of a fungicide if necessary. Dry rot may need extensive chemical treatment and the isolation of all adjacent timbers.

12.6 Dereliction

Dereliction produces effects that are similar in many respects to fire damage, and the same

Figure 12.11 Elf cup fungi (*Peziza* spp.) appear within a few weeks of the fire. These are plaster moulds, and do not cause damage.

Figure 12.12 Ceiling cavities below pugging boards are particularly difficult to dry, and should be exposed along walls to allow frequent inspection and ventilation. Note the elf cup fungi growing on the pugging material.

principles apply for restoration. The decay fungi assemblage present will, however, be very different. The fabric will probably be saturated, and will have been in that condition for a long time. This is the way in which woodland debris decays and many of the fungi from the forest floor will occur within the building.

Much of the remaining timber, particularly lintels and other components built into walls, may be too decayed to retain. Much of the fungus will probably be a wide assemblage of white rots with a high moisture requirement. Brown rots with a lower moisture tolerance, perhaps including dry rot, may also be present in more sheltered parts of the building. It is possible that increased timber acidity caused by wet rot damage may enhance dry rot spore germination, but in general there is little evidence to suggest that buildings dry through a zone significantly favourable to dry rot, and none to suggest that wet rots somehow transmogrify into dry rot as the structure dries. Dry rot may become established at any time during the restoration works, while walls are wet, if reinstatement is incautiously undertaken.

12.7 Modes and rates of drying

The question most frequently asked when a fire-damaged or semiderelict building is restored is 'how long will it take to dry?'. Unfortunately there is no clear answer, and certainly not one which the owner will wish to hear. The satisfactory drying of brickwork and masonry may take years to complete. Any measures taken to accelerate the

Figure 12.13 Ink cap fungi (*Coprinus* spp.) destroy ceiling laths if ceilings are not encouraged to dry. These are usually the first decay fungi to appear after a fire.

process will probably be expensive, and it is therefore important to ensure that they are effective (see Section 12.9).

Modes of drying in porous building materials have been extensively studied in laboratories, and complex formulae have been derived. These relate drying to the physical parameters of the material, but unfortunately they give little information on the speed of the process in a practical situation. Rule-of-thumb measurements such as 1 in (25.4 mm) per month for drying can be dangerously misleading, particularly where walls are thick. There are, however, a few general points that can be made, and these may be of some use.

12.7.1 First-stage drying

If a brick is saturated with water under vacuum, and its weight loss as it dries is recorded, then the relationship shown in Figure 12.15 is observed. The first part of the plotted line is straight, and shows that there is a steady loss of water over time. This part of the plot represents first-stage drying, and illustrates the loss of moisture from the large pores within the brick. The steady slope shows that evaporation is unhindered by any forces within the brick, and is in fact similar to evaporation from a free water surface (Hall *et al.*, 1984).

The significance of this phenomenon, which is also found with timber, is that most of the free water is easily removed, and under reasonable drying conditions will be lost within the first year.

12.7.2 Second-stage drying

Reference to Figure 12.15 shows that eventually evaporation starts to slow down and the slope of the line becomes much shallower. The brick has

Figure 12.14 Major decay fungi do not usually appear for a year or two after a fire, unless they have spread from an existing source. Here cellar rot (*Coniophora puteana*) is fruiting through a cask.

now entered second-stage drying, and water vapour is dispersing from the small pores. The rate of vapour loss slows because it is now restrained by forces within the pores. The same relationship occurs with timber, and in that case the water is bonded within the cell walls.

Second-stage drying, particularly in walls, is a long slow process, and is not easily accelerated by environmental modifications. The moisture content at which it commences is variable, and depends on the pore structure of the material. In medium-density brick it will commonly be at about 4%, whereas in timber it will probably be at about 28%.

The relationships between the drying of a brick and the drying of a wall are likely to be complex and variable. Figure 12.16 shows a drying curve obtained from dowel rods inserted into a wall. The drying process illustrated by this curve is reasonably clear, but this, unfortunately, tends to be the exception. Second-stage drying in particular may

become excessively prolonged as excess water migrates from the centre of the wall, and little if any drying is recorded for a long period of time.

12.8 Drying by increased ventilation

Air flow will dry brickwork and masonry, provided that there is an appropriate vapour pressure gradient from the wall to the surrounding air. The air must be able to accept moisture from the wall. In many practical building situations there are unfortunately conflicts of interests that inhibit this process. Scaffolding, for example (see Table 12.1), is frequently enclosed at the sides for safety during high winds, and this effectively halts vapour loss from the structure. Windows may have to be boarded up for security, which will also impede drying. The air if heated may accept moisture from the walls but there will be no air exchange to remove it from the building. The end result is likely to be excess condensation when the temperature drops, but no drying. The rebuilding process itself will not help because large volumes of water are used by the various trades and these will maintain high humidities.

None of this is very encouraging, and the conclusion is that drying is likely to be a long slow process, particularly if the building has been semiderelict for many years. Every effort should be made to promote air flow by whatever compromises and modifications are practical, and restoration should be deferred for as long as possible after the building has been weatherproofed.

12.9 Accelerated drying

Natural air movement may eventually dry the structure, but unfortunately ambient humidities in many parts of the British Isles are normally rather high. The number of days in a year when significant drying could occur may actually be fairly small. It may be useful to consider ways of artificially accelerating the drying process.

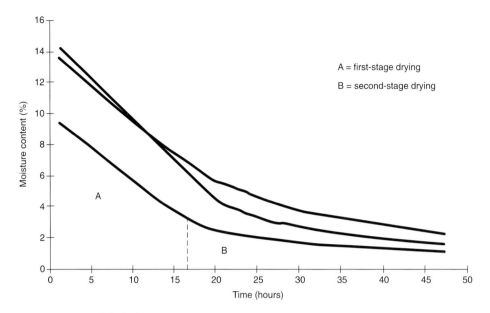

Figure 12.15 Brick drying curves.

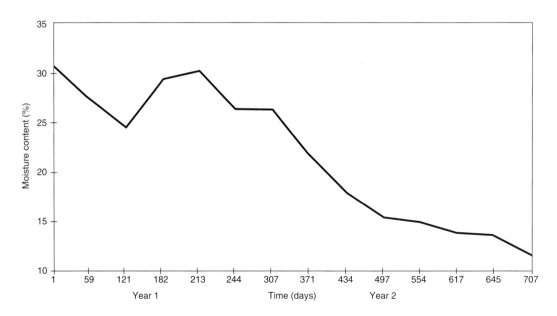

Figure 12.16 Wood equilibrium moisture contents showing gradual drying of timber at a depth of 30 cm in brickwork.

154

Figure 12.17 Quadrupling the air flow across a wall surface doubles the rate of drying.

12.9.1 Air blowers

Drying may be accelerated by forced air movement (Figure 12.17), and blowers directed against wet walls can achieve useful results. Hall *et al.* (1984) showed that quadrupling air speed doubled the rate of drying, as did raising the temperature of the wet material by 10 °C. Any accelerated drying method will, however, be expensive and therefore should be used where it will be most effective. This may be achieved by a preliminary moisture assessment of the building (Browne Morton, 1976). Buildings are rarely uniformly wet, and a planned drying campaign will offer the best value for money.

12.9.2 Dehumidifiers

Rooms which remain intact, particularly on the lower levels of the building, may be dried by dehumidification. This process systematically removes moisture from the air so that a drying gradient is maintained. The following considerations are important if dehumidification is to be effective:

- The room must be sealed to reduce air flow from elsewhere. This may be achieved by covering openings with polythene, and forming doors with polythene fastened with some form of self-adhesive strip (Figure 12.18).
- The room must originally have been dry. There is no point in trying to dry a room that has always had wet walls because of ground water.
- The dehumidifiers must be large enough to produce a significant result. This information can usually be obtained from the suppliers.

Two types of dehumidifier are available, and there are advantages and disadvantages associated with both.

Figure 12.18 If dehumidification is to be attempted then areas should be adequately sealed to reduce air exchange.

Figure 12.19 Refrigerant type dehumidifiers are thought to perform best at temperatures above 10 °C, because at lower temperatures ice accumulates on the coils. Frequent emptying of water containers is essential.

Refrigerant dehumidifiers

These (Figure 12.19) work on the same principle as the domestic refrigerator, except that the coils are rearranged. A refrigerator works by first compressing a suitable gas outside the appliance so that it liquefies and gives out heat as it loses energy in moving from the gaseous to the liquid phase. The phase change is then reversed within the refrigerator by passing the pressurized liquid gas through an expansion valve so that it absorbs energy in the form of heat, thus cooling the storage chamber, and turns back into a gas. In the dehumidification process the air in the room is forced across the low pressure heat-accepting coils so that the air temperature dips below its dew point and water condenses out on the coils. The cold dry air then passes over the heat-generating high pressure coils so that it returns to the temperature of the room having lost most of its moisture loading. Wet air enters the machine and dry air leaves it, while the moisture it contained drips into a tray.

These machines are very effective, but there does need to be some efficient method of emptying the tray. Floors will be flooded by Monday morning if this aspect is neglected over the weekend.

One further problem with refrigerant dehumidifiers is that they do not operate efficiently in cold weather. This is because frost forms too readily on the coils so that their action is effectively blocked (Sanders, 1985). Refrigerant dehumidifiers therefore work best at temperatures above about 10 °C.

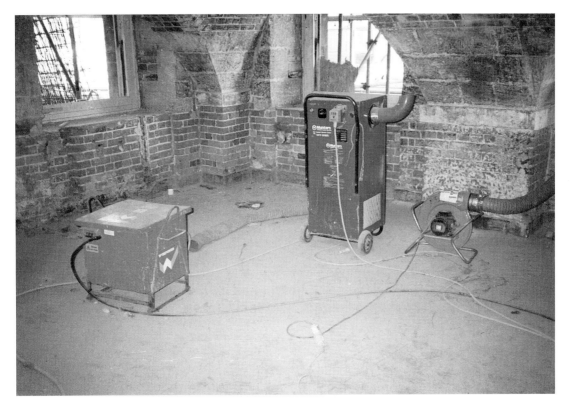

Figure 12.20 Desiccant dehumidifiers are said to perform best at lower temperatures because the desiccant holds more water. Wet air (rather than water) is produced, which relieves the problem of water accumulation, but the outlet hose needs to be vented to the exterior.

Desiccant dehumidifiers

These (Figure 12.20) work on an entirely different principle. Moisture from the air is absorbed by a desiccant contained in a revolving drum. When the desiccant has absorbed as much moisture as it can it is dried by a current of hot air and the hot, moisture-laden air so produced is ducted outside the building.

Desiccant dehumidifiers therefore have three hoses, an inlet and outlet from the room, and a wet air outlet to the exterior. The problem of water trays is thus avoided, but the hoses may themselves be inconvenient. In practice the machine needs to be higher than and near to the wet air exit point, otherwise the water condenses out in the hose and effectively blocks it. Moisture absorption by desiccants decreases as the temperature rises so

that they are rather less efficient in hot weather. Thomson (1986) considered that refrigerant dehumidifiers would be preferable at ambient temperatures above 10 °C, whereas the desiccant type would be preferable at lower temperatures. Choice of machine might therefore depend on the time of year.

12.10 Isolation of timbers and the mobilization of wall salts

It should be clear that even with the best endeavours the building is likely to be damp when restoration is undertaken. Historical timbers may be able to withstand elevated moisture contents provided there is no active fungus within the walls,

Figure 12.21 All replacement timbers should be isolated from damp walls. Vigilance is required to ensure that the barrier is not bridged by debris.

but twentieth-century softwood timbers are likely to be more vulnerable. The problem may be overcome by the pretreatment of all replacement timbers, but they should also be isolated from the walls, either with a damp proof membrane or with an air gap. Attention to detail during the building works will then be vital because detailing will fail if the barrier is bridged by inadequate isolation or debris (Figure 12.21). We have also sometimes seen correctly isolated timbers that have decayed because the carpenter has subsequently used untreated packing pieces or wedges (Figure 12.22). One further problem that should be taken into consideration is the risk of mobilized salt efflorescence as the walls dry. These salts may be in solution during much of the building works, but they will crystallize out on the surface of the walls as they dry. The results can be highly damaging to new finishes, and these may have to be viewed as sacrificial for a few years.

Figure 12.22 In this case the protective wrapping has been enthusiastic, but the joists have been supported with untreated wedges, which will rapidly decay in the wet wall.

CHAPTER THIRTEEN

Monitoring the building environment

13.1 Moisture meters and their accuracy in timber

The most usual non-destructive method of measuring timber moisture content is by the use of a resistance moisture meter. Other types of meter are available, but none has achieved the prominence of the resistance meter, and they will not be discussed further. It is important to remember that these meters do not measure moisture contents directly, but infer them from wood attributes that are affected by moisture change. Many models are available, but all suffer from a variety of limitations.

Oven-dry wood has good insulating properties, and its electrical resistance is similar to that of porcelain (Tsoumis, 1991). At fibre saturation point, however, wood is more than a billion times less resistant. This colossal difference in the electrical resistance of timber is entirely due to its moisture content. Resistance may therefore be used as a measurement of moisture content if a consistent relationship over a useful range of readings for both moisture and resistance can be established (Stamm, 1927). In practice a linear relationship can be derived between the two parameters and moisture meters are effective over a range from about 9% moisture content (below which the resistance is extremely high) to about 25–30% (above which resistance depends on the properties of the free liquids within the wood cells; Chen *et al.*, 1994).

The electrical properties of timber vary from species to species, and even from sample to sample

from the same species, so that some level of basic inaccuracy must be accepted. According to Dean (1972) this would commonly be approximately ±1% moisture content at a reading of 12% rising to about ±2% at a reading of 20%.

Some potential inaccuracies can be corrected to some extent (Vermaas, 1975). For example, to compensate for the effect of the anatomical structure and density of different species on meter readings, the manufacturers of meters usually supply calibration tables. Unfortunately there is no standard according to which these correction factors are derived, so that we do not know how representative of the available timber the samples tested were. Country of growth, speed of growth, sapwood/heartwood differentiation and post-harvest history may all have a significant effect on electrical resistance (Hall, 1994). Correction factors produced by meter manufacturers do not therefore necessarily agree with each other, and timber species may even be grouped in different ways, making it difficult to compare like with like across different sets of tables.

Electrode orientation also needs to be considered. Electrical resistance has been found to be 2–8 times greater across the grain than along the grain (Lin, 1967). Readings taken parallel to the grain have been shown to produce the most accurate assessment of moisture content.

After moisture content, temperature is probably the most important parameter that affects the resistance of wood. The precise effect of temperature varies according to a number of factors, including species, moisture content and the temperature itself. Skaar (1964) reported data from a range of species and moisture contents. He concluded that the average value of the temperature effect would be about 0.15% per degree Centigrade. Most moisture meters are calibrated at a standard temperature, usually 20 °C. Protimeter state that their meters can be corrected approximately by adding 0.5% for every 5 °C below 20 °C or by subtracting 0.5% for every 5 °C above 20 °C.

These inaccuracies are small, but have to be taken into account when considering serial data from remote sensing systems. A cold period in winter can confuse trends, particularly if it is drying that is being monitored.

A more surprising variation in readings occurs when different models of meter are compared. Hall (1994) compared moisture content readings from six readily available European meters when these were connected to seven precision resistors. Readings differed, and the maximum deviation he obtained was 2.5% from one resistor which produced equivalent timber moisture content readings varying from 13.5% to 16%. Ahmet (1994) investigated this phenomenon further by checking the calibration of six different inexpensive multitesters against a commercially obtainable moisture meter calibration block. The deviation in resistance measured between the multitester readings was small. Ahmet therefore concluded that the meters could all accurately measure resistance, but that the calibration of resistance to timber moisture content varied because there were no internationally agreed standards for the conversion. A European Standard for moisture meters produced by the Comité Européen de Normalisation is currently in draft form, but this only states that meters should have an accuracy of ±2% over a range of 8–25% moisture content. No more precise information on calibration is given.

In practice these problems mean that if the meter indicates that the moisture content is 15.8%, for example, then the true value probably lies between 14% and 18% at the position tested. The exact meter reading may, however, be useful for comparison purposes under similar conditions and using the same make of meter.

Timber moisture readings are also liable to vary with depth, particularly where sorption oscillates. In thick timber, the subsurface moisture content may equilibrate to the seasonal average humidity while the surface moisture content fluctuates more freely. This effect is liable to be confused by temperature gradients which may be a significant factor where differences are small. Tsoumis (1991) considers that an average moisture content can only be obtained if the electrodes penetrate to between 20% and 25% of the thickness of the timber.

Sometimes the surface moisture contents are greater than those at depth. This may be the result of the environment, or may be due to some form of surface treatment. Kyte (1972) states that inorganic salts used in water-based preservatives or fire retardants decrease the electrical resistance of the timber and therefore raise the meter reading, whereas 'organic materials such as creosote' increase the resistance and lead to lower readings. Organic solvent preservatives apparently have little effect. These surface phenomena may become more important in the future, as the use of water-based preservatives increases due to the unpopularity of organic solvents.

Some interesting data that illustrate problems with gradients are presented in Table 13.1. Readings were taken by the author in the nave roof of Worcester Cathedral from the surface 5 mm of both the medieval trusses and the adjacent modern softwood walkway, using an uninsulated probe. Readings at depth were made with electrodes that were insulated, except at the tips.

The softwood timbers are air dry according to the meter readings and show a slight gradient from surface to depth. Readings from the adjacent oak, however, show a marked gradient in the reverse direction, so that the surface readings are significantly higher than those deeper within the timber. Both sets of timbers are in an acceptable and stable environment which should produce safe and satisfactory equilibrium moisture contents. The incautious surveyor, however, might conclude from moisture meter readings taken from the surface of the oak that the roof was a damp environment and that decay was inevitable. The

Table 13.1 Resistance moisture meter readings (percentage moisture content) from the nave at Worcester Cathedral at probe depths of 5 mm and 15 mm

Oak trusses (medieval)		Softwood walkway (modern)	
5 mm	15 mm	5 mm	15 mm
22.0	17.1	12.5	13.0
19.2	17.2	12.4	12.7
16.8	15.4	12.5	12.8
20.8	16.0	12.2	12.4
20.7	16.5	11.9	13.2
21.8	17.4	12.3	13.6

reasons for elevated surface readings in ancient timbers with an unknown history are likely to be varied, but what concerns us here is that a few surface readings taken from the oak might be used as the basis for an erroneous prognosis for the roof and its timbers. A comprehensive examination of the roof must be made, including meter readings at depth, before sensible conclusions can be drawn.

Major sources of error encountered with hand-held moisture meters are produced by water-mobilized salts (frequently from brickwork or rising damp), and by insect decay and fungal decay. These can produce very high or variable readings when in fact timber is dry. It should be noted that moisture meters are calibrated against clean samples of fresh sound timber, yet surveyors will use them in roofs constructed from old timbers with an unknown history, frequently coated with an array of surface deposits. They will use meters where damp staining and signs of decay suggest water penetration has occurred, and these are precisely the places where the meter cannot be expected to provide a reliable reading. Decay, in particular, may give elevated readings, as noted in Section 2.3. Moisture meters are a valuable tool for the surveyor, but their limitations must be understood. Frequently the meter will only provide a guide to moisture levels and then only provided that sufficient readings are taken and are intelligently interpreted.

13.1.1 Moisture monitoring by the oven/balance method

If an accurate moisture assessment is required from old and perhaps semidecayed timber, then a destructive test such as the oven/balance method may be required.

Samples can either be removed intact or by means of an auger bit, and these must be placed in airtight containers, or wrapped in polythene bags. Small fragments will rapidly lose moisture after removal. Samples are then removed to the laboratory where they are weighed using a sensitive balance. Alternatively, and more accurately, samples may be weighed on site using a portable balance. The accuracy required from the balance will depend on the size of the specimen, and will vary from 0.1 g in samples above about 10 g in weight to 0.01 g for smaller fragments. Very small samples will need to be weighed in milligrams, and are not recommended, although sometimes they are all that can be removed. Clearly the smaller the sample the less representative of the moisture profile it will be. Small surface fragments are sometimes useful for calibrating moisture meter surveys. After weighing, the wood is placed in an aerated oven and dried at 103±2 °C until a constant weight is achieved. In practice it is generally more convenient to leave it in the oven overnight. The sample should then be placed in a desiccator until cool, and reweighed.

The moisture content is derived from the formula:

$$Y = \frac{(M_x - M_o) \times 100\%}{M_o}$$

where Y is moisture content, M_x is the initial weight and M_o is the oven-dry weight.

The significance of moisture contents in decayed timber may be difficult to evaluate. Hygroscopicity is dependent on hemicellulose and cellulose; if these have been removed by fungi, the sample will be dry. However, any water that is there will be compared with the weight of a light, fragile matrix during the calculation. Obviously, therefore, the moisture content of sound timber cannot be assessed from decayed samples.

13.1.2 Remote moisture monitoring

The frequent monitoring of timber moisture contents is sometimes required in order to assess drying or to detect water penetration. It is difficult to compare data obtained with a hand-held meter for this purpose because timber is never homogeneous, and the comparability of readings will depend on their exact position in the timber and on the depth to which the probes are inserted. Relevant changes in moisture content are therefore difficult to deduce except by comparing the averages from numerous readings. One way of reducing these difficulties is to install permanent sensors and to interrogate these either with a hand-held meter or by some form of automatic interrogation. Remote monitoring has been used for many years to monitor drying within kilns, but it is only recently that the technique has been used in buildings where sensors may need to be installed for decades. These sensors then have to be robust and durable. They are subject to the limitations discussed in Section 13.1, but these need not present a problem if care is taken with siting.

The distance between the two electrodes does not seem to influence the reading greatly over the range supplied by meter manufacturers. Protimeter, for example, supply sensors with electrodes 12 mm and 25 mm apart. These give similar readings.

Permanent probes are commonly constructed from brass or stainless steel (Taylor and West, 1990). The sensors are pins or screws, and these have given satisfactory service. Objections have been made on the grounds that they may corrode or become loosened with time, thus providing inaccurate readings. Neither of these problems is seen as a serious disadvantage if air-dry timber is monitored. Corrosion can be minimized by a careful choice of sensor, and will not occur if the timber remains dry. Similarly there may be an imperfect contact at electrodes if the timber shrinks sufficiently to expand the holes into which they are screwed, but contact will become re-established if the timber is wetted. Duff (1966) developed a sensor which overcame these problems, and has been used extensively by the US Forest Products Laboratory. This consists of a strip 19 mm long of square section (1.8 x 1.8 mm) close-grained hardwood. The opposite electrode surfaces are produced with conductive silver paint. Copper wires are attached to the end with a cellulose acetate glue. These probes seem to have been successful in a wide range of situations. Sell (1985) considered that the Duff probe might have problems in salt-treated wood and described a different system, which had been developed in Switzerland, and had been in use for about 10 years.

The sensor described by Sell was simply a hygrometer inserted into a hole drilled into the timber. Relative humidity was logged, and the equivalent timber moisture content calculated from a formula devised by Simpson (1971). This type of sensor has three main disadvantages.

1. The sensitivity of the probe may drift over a period of time and require recalibration.
2. It is not clear whether the application of Simpson's formula is relevant to old timber.
3. The maximum moisture level that can be recorded equates with 100% humidity, thus making no distinction between wetness and saturation.

Lloyd and Singh (1994) consider that resistance sensors embedded directly into timber are outdated and suffer from several limitations. They state that resistance sensors can only be used for surface readings, and that inaccuracies arise from timber variability, paint treatments and salt contamination. They therefore consider that sensors constructed from hygroscopic polymers are far superior. These criticisms seem unnecessarily harsh and the following points should be noted.

Depth of reading

Moisture meter probes are available with isolated shanks for measuring at depth. A similar technology can also be used for permanent installations; the data presented in Figure 2.2 were obtained with this type of equipment.

Timber variability

The purpose of a sensing system is usually to indicate changes in the moisture content of timbers, which might result in their decay. The properties of timber can certainly be variable, but it is for that reason that direct readings can give more indication of meaningful change than those obtained with surrogate materials. The polymer sensor should presumably be calibrated against timber; what species or age of timber is used? An alternative is to use the sensor merely as a recorder of changes so that an elevated reading is of interest without any need to relate it to timber moisture content. Changes in the polymer moisture content are therefore independent of the timber and a great deal of valuable information is lost.

Modern timbers do not vary greatly within species in their water-absorbing properties, and it was for this reason that it was useful to develop moisture meters. In situations where old timbers give a wide range of readings, confusion can be reduced by the use of blocks of modern timber, placed in various locations in the building under investigation and allowed to equilibrate. These sample blocks can be monitored to establish baseline readings.

Surface coatings and salt contamination

Lloyd and Singh are enthusiastic in their promotion of moisture meters as a diagnostic tool, though not when the same principles are used in automated timber moisture monitoring systems. Meter results are, however, subject to the same potential limitations, because the remote monitoring system is basically an extension of the hand-held instrument.

Salts are moved through a porous material by water in a liquid rather than gaseous phase. It is therefore an easy matter to isolate a timber sensor from timber or wall with a simple barrier, should one be required; it seldom is. The sensor will then equilibrate with the local humidity.

Direct moisture readings from timbers, and from applied timber sensors, have been used for many years and are both simple and reliable if used sensibly. If it is necessary to know whether a wall is wet then the question frequently asked is, 'what effect will this wall have on applied or inserted timber?'. It seems therefore that a timber sensor is likely to provide the most direct answer.

Timber sensors embedded in damp walls may decay, but this can be avoided by dip treatment. Most spirit-based formulations will not affect the readings. Sometimes direct contact between the untreated sensor and the wall is desirable if fungal viability is to be monitored. In this case the sensors are replaced as required.

The present author is not qualified to comment on the long-term stability of hygroscopic polymers in damp conditions, but Lloyd and Singh state that these polymers deteriorate over a long period and become inaccurate.

Sensors are wired back to an interrogation unit. The type of cable used does not seem to matter much because the resistances to be overcome in timber are so high that the resistance of long lengths of cable makes little difference. In practice twisted pair multicore British Telecommunications (BT) cable has proved convenient.

An interrogation unit may, at its simplest, be a switched selector box to be used with a standard moisture meter. Such systems work well, are simple to install and easy to use. They are usually interrogated about every month. Readings are logged and sensors giving unacceptably high readings are investigated. As noted earlier, all timber readings are liable to rise during the winter months as ambient humidities rise and temperatures fall. Individual high sensor readings should only be a problem if they are outside the range shown by other sensors and continue to rise.

Alternatively there is the self-interrogating system, which may incorporate a moisture meter and be fitted with some form of alarm if a preset moisture level is exceeded. Frequent interrogation may be a problem because the wood could theoretically become polarized around the sensors and give erroneous readings. This effect has not caused difficulties with sensors interrogated at intervals of a day or longer. It is possible to remove the chance of error by reversing the direction of current flow at each reading.

Automated self-interrogating systems are discussed in more detail in Section 13.3.

13.2 Brickwork and masonry moisture monitoring

Sometimes, particularly when dry rot activity or the moisture contents at concealed bearings are to be assessed, it is necessary to evaluate or monitor the moisture contents of brickwork and masonry. Moisture meter manufacturers produce probes for this purpose that can be inserted into holes drilled into the wall. In the author's experience these probes are of limited value. The reading obtained from electrodes depends to a large extent on the contact between them and the substrate. Soluble salts may also give inaccurate readings, particularly in damp brickwork – although these readings may be of value in the detection of rising damp. A further, and frequently even more significant problem, is the inherent variability of brickwork. The porosity of bricks, in particular, varies considerably depending on the batch of materials from which they were made, and their position in the kiln.

This variability can be overcome to a large extent by installing timber dowels in the wall to whatever depth is required. A 6–9 mm diameter rod will take about three weeks to equilibrate thoroughly, although it will take up a large proportion of its final moisture content within a few days. These rods provide an assessment of the wetting potential of the wall area in which they are

installed. They do not provide the moisture contents of the various constructional elements except by extrapolation. Formulae can be derived which relate timber to brickwork by installing rods in elements with a variety of known moisture contents, but this operation is tedious and only useful in special circumstances. Attempts to derive useful relationships from dust obtained from drilling the rod holes have so far proved disappointing.

The moisture content of the dowels may be assessed by the oven/balance method, which also provides a moisture profile if the rods are cut into sections, or with a moisture meter. Rods will start to degrade if they are left in a wet wall for more than a few weeks, and this, though sometimes useful for detecting dry rot activity, will eventually invalidate the moisture assessment. If the rods are only required to supply moisture meter readings (and are not to be left in place for the detection of dry rot), then they can be pretreated with a spirit-based preservative.

Rods may have sensors installed, and be wired to a remote interrogation unit. These systems work well in dry walls, but decay and corrosion cause problems in damp walls eventually, even if the rods are pretreated (see Section 13.1.2). Timber sensors may, however, easily be isolated from the masonry and sealed within their holes so that they equilibrate with the relative humidity within the wall.

13.3 Automated remote monitoring

Automated monitoring has developed rapidly during the 1990s and the resulting systems monitor a wide range of situations where the effects of moisture may cause concern. Moisture monitoring now encompasses the logging of air moisture levels (relative humidity–temperature regimes) in order to optimize the environment for the conservation of museum artefacts etc., alarms triggered by an overflowing sump, for example, or the monthly monitoring of the gradual drying-out of timbers following natural disasters such as flood or fire in order to guide a schedule of refurbishment. Monitoring systems currently available generally fall into three broad categories: environmental monitoring, leak detection and timber moisture monitoring. Some systems are able to monitor a combination of these features and are tailored to the needs of each individual building or building contents.

13.3.1 Environmental monitoring

There is a fairly wide range of instrumentation available which will automatically log relative humidity and temperature. Some systems will also monitor wind speed and direction, rainfall, solar radiation etc. Instrumentation varies considerably in its flexibility; some systems require detailed programming, and some are ready-programmed so as to be more user friendly.

Multichannel data loggers are available, to which a variety of sensors can be attached. These generally require a permanent power source, though they usually have a battery back-up. Most sensors are connected to the data logger by cabling, though radio data transmissions are also available. In contrast there are small stand-alone data loggers with 10-year lithium batteries, which record particular parameters such as relative humidity and temperature at programmable frequencies. These loggers are obviously very useful where cabling would be intrusive, or where mains power is unavailable.

13.3.2 Leak detection

There are available several leak-detecting systems based upon an on/off response to the presence/absence of liquid water. They involve significant amounts of hard wiring, and installation may be complex. On flat roofs, for example, sensors should be installed at the time that roof coverings are laid. One moisture detector available at the time of writing is based on a grid of aluminium tape on absorbent fibreglass tissue, linked to a computer. A small electric current is passed through the grid at regular intervals and any drop in electrical resistance at node points where tapes cross is recorded digitally. Such a drop would occur with the presence of moisture.

Other systems are built on pulsed echo radar signals. When such a system is commissioned, it stores the characteristics of the detecting cable in its memory. The control panel transmits a low-voltage pulse echo signal along a continuous length of detecting cable. Water in contact with the detecting cable, damage to or disconnection of any of the cables will result in a change of the cable characteristics stored in the control panel's memory, and hence trigger an alarm. Some such systems can be connected to building management systems, and some may be modem linked.

13.3.3 Multiparameter moisture monitoring

Roof construction in historic buildings is often complex. Subtle, gradual leaks can be difficult to detect visually. A remote moisture sensing system, installed with a knowledge of the history of the building and any past problems, can provide a useful early warning system. Alternatively a moisture monitoring system could be installed in new roofs to act as a safeguard against future water ingress or to monitor drying following neglect, fire or flood.

Timber moisture monitoring, whether using timber sensors or hygroscopic polymers, is based upon electrical resistance. The units are scaled to represent the percentage moisture content as measured between two passive electrodes. Systems are based on out-stations or nodes, each of which receives cable direct from several sensors. They then link to each other and to the main control unit with a single cable, thus minimizing wiring. The system is usually powered from a control unit that uses a standard mains socket, although in some cases batteries can be used as a power source if necessary.

Over 4000 sensors may be interrogated from a single control unit, and data may be downloaded via a portable computer, or by telephone to a site or office anywhere in the world. These systems can also be linked to building management systems.

The most advanced systems are now able to interrogate a wide range of sensors for information, including timber moisture contents, relative humidity, temperature, wind speed and direction, rainfall and solar gain, thus providing valuable information as to how the building responds to its environment. They are also able to provide audio-visual alarms that are triggered when sumps/hoppers become blocked, when condensation occurs or when ground water levels rise to such a point that there is a risk of flooding. In the latter case the control unit could be programmed to activate a pump to remove water until the building is no longer at risk. The control unit may also, for example, be programmed to trigger the opening and closing of vents in order to modify relative humidity–temperature regimes. Limits can be set for individual timber moisture monitoring sensors such that when these are exceeded, an alarm will be activated.

Automated monitoring systems are thus approaching the point where a significant proportion of the complex interactions between the built environment and moisture can be both studied and manipulated.

PART FOUR

Evolving a Philosophy for Timber Treatment

CHAPTER FOURTEEN

Resolving conflicts between treatment and conservation

14.1 Remedial industry

The remedial industry developed from a need to tackle decay caused by two world wars and half a century of construction in poor-quality timber (see Sections 5.1, 9.1 and 11.11). Faith in the newly obtainable biocides and ignorance of their potential effects on health contributed to the rapid post-war expansion of the industry. Large numbers of treatment companies were formed, encompassing a wide range of integrity, knowledge and competence, so that the level of service offered ranged from the conscientious to the 'cowboy'.

There was clearly a need to set standards for companies, and the British Wood Preserving Association (now the British Wood Preserving and Damp-Proofing Association) which had been incorporated on 4 June 1930, assumed this role. The BWPDA is a scientific and advisory organization, but it must be admitted that it is, in its origins and in its membership, closely aligned to the chemical industry, so that a philosophy of minimum intervention would be difficult to assimilate. A great many members undoubtedly do not believe that minimum intervention would work.

Membership of the BWPDA provides a standard by which a treatment firm may be judged. To qualify for membership, a firm must demonstrate a high level of technical competence and organization, together with a sound understanding of health and safety issues and environmental protection. Individual surveyors will probably have passed the Certificated Timber Infestation Surveyors examination or the new Certificated Surveyor in Remedial Treatment examination.

This is all excellent, and misunderstandings only emerge when we confuse roles. Certificated remedial surveyors are qualified technicians. They have been trained in their own practical speciality although they may have wider experience. We should not expect them to have and they normally do not need, the broad overview of knowledge possessed by an architect, or the complementary knowledge expected from a chartered surveyor, building historian, materials scientist or biologist. Thus remedial surveyors faced with dry rot infestation will normally carry out their companies' 'full dry rot treatment' in an efficient, perhaps enthusiastic manner. They cannot be expected to recognize, or be concerned if they do, that it is eighteenth-century joinery they are ripping out, or to assess a dry rot infestation for current activity and decay potential. These architectural conservation issues are only addressed if surveyors, architects and other specialists work in concert, and they may be ignored if architects' concern for their indemnity insurance encourages them to avoid all responsibility. The whole problem is then handed over to the remedial company, which has traditionally only one way of dealing with it. It should also be remembered that free surveys have ultimately to be paid for by work done.

In strict opposition to the remedial industry is the growing number of people who believe that all preservatives are unnecessary, an approach that

171

must be particularly galling for those who have spent their working lives conscientiously saving buildings by excising and treating decay. 'Green' specialists believe that water is the key to decay, and that if the water supply is switched off then the decay will be arrested and can then be largely ignored if the timber remains structurally acceptable. The chemical specialist is largely unconvinced or, accepting the possibility, does not believe that the approach is practical. Where lies the truth?

In 1994 a conference entitled Green Treatment of Timber was held at Taymouth Castle. One of the speakers advocated a return to the use of traditional softwoods without any pretreatment chemicals. The problem is that traditional softwoods that do not need pretreatment are almost unavailable. This type of practical difficulty applies also to dry rot treatment. It is undoubtedly true that dry rot will die if deprived of water. Faults can therefore be remedied so that walls will dry and kill the fungus. Unfortunately, however, walls may take several years to dry, so that the fungus has considerable reserves. One answer to this is to isolate all timbers from the walls as far as is practical. The problem here is that the standard of workmanship on modern building sites is frequently very poor. Isolation alone may not suffice. If an architect wishes to undertake the environmental control of dry rot then attention to detail at the design stage and careful supervision of the work will be vital.

The 'minimum intervention where practical' philosophy is, however, the one we must pursue if we are to formulate a conservation approach. In the author's opinion the answer to the treatment riddle is to use a combined approach, backed by a greater understanding on the part of architects and others involved in the care of buildings. Most eighteenth- or nineteenth-century softwood timbers have a good natural durability and should be retained as far as possible. Most modern plantation-grown softwoods have a lower natural durability and may need to be pretreated, and perhaps also isolated from the walls if the latter are wet or contain fungus.

Preservative treatments may therefore be necessary in order to stabilize infestations or infections while the building dries, and the drying environment brings the decay under control.

14.2 Precautionary treatments

The term 'precautionary treatments' covers a range of tasks and intentions. Some, like the treatment of timber within a zone of dry rot, are normally easy to justify. The application of preservatives in order to avoid some notional future problem, however, may be less acceptable, particularly if it entails loss of historic fabric in order to reach concealed timber.

The concept of the precautionary *in situ* treatment of apparently sound timbers seems to have developed largely from Hickin's work on furniture beetle (see Section 5.1). It was argued then that the absence of emergence holes did not necessarily indicate lack of early infestation, and precautionary treatments were seen as a sensible method of ensuring that the timbers remained free from attack. Many professionals would still agree, and timbers with little or no obvious signs of decay are frequently spray treated during restoration works on the basis that they may never be accessible again, as a routine precaution or because a timber treatment guarantee is required.

To others this is frequently an unacceptable use of chemicals, and if a softwood roof has survived for 100–200 years in spite of all the lapses in maintenance which undoubtedly occurred, then it will last a few more without the need for preservatives. The official guide to government policy and good practice, *Remedial Timber Treatments in Buildings* (see Section 10.4) does not provide much assistance with this controversy as it simply states 'Do not use a wood preservative unless it is judged necessary to halt an attack now or in the future.' Nevertheless, it does compel us to consider the nature of a future attack.

The spray treatment of dry timbers, where there are no signs of current decay or infestation, is known to have little, if any, effect on wood-rotting fungi or death watch beetle. It is not routinely needed for house longhorn beetle because the insect is limited in its distribution, and the use of pretreated timber for structural purposes has been mandatory for several years in localities where the beetle causes a problem. We must therefore conclude that this type of *in situ* treatment is targeted at furniture beetle as in Hickin's day.

The risk of furniture beetle causing significant damage to good-quality historical structural timbers within a dry and well maintained building is non-existent. The risks that are being guarded against in most situations within historic buildings are therefore:

- That poor workmanship or poor maintenance will elevate the timber moisture content to a level favourable to furniture beetle. This would be a long, slow process that would probably not have commenced before the insecticide was lost from the timber.
- That the beetles will cause more damage than they have during previous periods, often probably of extended duration, when conditions favoured attack. This is highly unlikely without substantial water penetration.

It may be argued that the treatment will avoid the continuation of destruction, but few structural timbers are ever destroyed by furniture beetle, and the main reason is that the attack is confined to sapwood. The quantity of sapwood in most historical structural timbers is rather limited, and most has probably been attacked by furniture beetle decades, or perhaps centuries, earlier.

In the author's opinion therefore the precautionary spray treatment with insecticides of dry historical timbers, where there are no significant signs of active infestation, cannot normally be justified.

14.3 Guarantees

In the 1950s a major UK timber treatment company decided voluntarily to extend their company's statutory and common law liability by the issue of a guarantee following timber treatment. This move was a highly successful marketing strategy. All other companies followed suit.

The principle was that treated timbers should be guaranteed against the recurrence of infection or infestation for a period of 20 years. This was later extended to 30 years. The major proviso was that the timber had to be kept dry.

The timbers covered by the guarantee would be likely to be only a small proportion of the timber present within the building, and so a further marketing opportunity was perceived. Thus was born the insurance policy against timber decay. The same proviso was built into the contract, however, that the building had to be well maintained and free from water penetration. One insurance brochure informed us that of over 180 000 houses surveyed, 75% had furniture beetle, while 1 in 3 sheltered some form of fungal decay. The risk of damage was therefore stated to be high and, to give the householder peace of mind, the insurance companies would insure against dry timber decaying.

In the late 1970s James Simpson, an experienced conservation architect practising in Edinburgh, corresponded with a major treatment company regarding some of the philosophical issues involved from an architect's point of view. These arguments are of considerable interest, and it is worth quoting the letter here:

My principal point is that wood-rotting fungi do not develop and thrive unless the conditions are right, and that normally implies some maintenance failure. A great deal of money is wasted every year making good damage which is a direct consequence of inadequate maintenance, and all too often the guarantees and insurances promoted by firms such as yours encourage peace of mind in the building owner which simply makes the real problem worse.

As I said to you I am neither pro nor anti your company or any other specialist firm for that matter, but I believe that building maintenance over the country as a whole could be greatly improved, and that firms such as yours could make a better contribution and improve your public image – which appears to me to be slipping – in the process.

If one takes the cynic's point of view, guarantees and insurances are good selling points for the specialist firms as a group and for individual companies. They help to give you a captive market for eradication work which is paid for on a permanent instalment basis through premiums. This is not a one-sided situation, however, and the success of the system testifies to its attractiveness to the average householder. Nevertheless, in fundamental terms the money spent on premiums would be better spent on a proper maintenance routine which included regular inspections, and which would tackle the causes of, for example fungal attack, rather than waiting for the effects.

Of course, the professions also have a great responsibility for all this and firms such as yours have provided us all with a very convenient escape route. Estate agents and building society surveyors do not, as a rule, go in for very thorough building inspections from the technical point of view, and it is all too easy to demand a specialist report. Surveyors and architects, this firm included, have also found it convenient to transfer responsibility in this area to a specialist firm. I am not necessarily opposed to this because I respect your expertise and would expect somebody whose whole job is to identify and eradicate dry rot, for example, to be good at it, but I do object to the tendency to divorce insect and fungi from the wider question of building maintenance. The specialist firms thrive on mystique and the slight sense of fear which the very words dry rot, furniture beetle, and death watch beetle inspire in the average householder. The possibility of insurance against them suggests that insect and fungal attack are the sort of accidents and unavoidable risks which are best insured against, and this in my view is a widespread and unfortunate misconception which you do little to discourage.

I am sure that firms such as yours and professions such as mine, could actually do a great deal in the way of public education, and that in the broadest possible terms we could better serve the public interest, and our own respective interests, by becoming more involved in the field of preventative maintenance.

This raises some fundamental issues. The marketing incentive has become so firmly established so that anyone wishing to borrow money for the purchase of a property is likely to have to demonstrate that the roof (for example) has been preservative treated, even though there is little wrong with it. Most roof timbers will have a few beetle holes if one searches, and mislaid or unavailable records may result in several timber treatments during the space of a few years. Beetle holes do not disappear after treatment. The peace of mind offered by guarantees and insurance policies discourages worry about timber decay, and this false sense of security leads to neglect of regular maintenance – thus invalidating the guarantees and insurance when these are called upon.

A further problem in the context of conservation is that minimum intervention and treatment guarantees do not fit well together. Few firms will guarantee dry rot treatment, for example, unless they consider that the work has been thorough, and the work is inevitably destructive. Sometimes it is possible to achieve a compromise by approaching a range of companies, because some are now more flexible in their treatment requirements than others.

If minimum intervention is vital then the client may have to forego a guarantee or employ a specialist consultant.

Problems with guarantees have arisen in recent years because numerous companies which issued them are no longer trading. This difficulty was addressed over 10 years ago by the formation of the Guarantee Protection Trust (GPT) which insures guarantees so that valid claims are dealt with by the GPT if the treatment firm which carried out the original work is no longer in business. This insurance is only available for guarantees used by BWPDA members.

14.4 International and national policies on minimal intervention

Conservation of buildings in the UK did not become much of an issue until the middle of the nineteenth century, when concern began to develop regarding the loss of original materials. In 1865 the Royal Institute of British Architects (RIBA) produced a policy statement for its members entitled *General Advice to Promoters of the Restoration of Ancient Buildings*. The views it expressed were subsequently promulgated to a wider audience by William Morris, who founded the Society for the Protection of Ancient Buildings.

During the twentieth century, many international organizations concerned with buildings and monuments set out to define the purpose and parameters of conservation in a series of International Charters. These were an attempt to link ethics with action. The first to provide a systematic code of practice was probably the Athens Charter of 1931 (organized by the International Museums Office). The early charters produced up to and including the 1950s, propounded conservation in terms of art and history, so that only the most important buildings and decorative schemes came within their remit. Appreciation and conservation of great buildings in the post-war years was also seen as a means of promoting international harmony, and these buildings were pronounced to be the heritage of the world, rather than simply that of the country which possessed them. They were to be a symbol of peace and international cooperation.

The 1960s saw a broadening of attitudes. Although the important Venice Charter of 1966 (which superseded the Athens Charter) still approached the conservation of buildings from an academic art history point of view, others perceived a far wider range of qualities. Many buildings became important because of their social or spiritual connotations for example, so that by the 1970s even minor buildings, of no particular age, beauty or history, could nevertheless be seen as expressions of a country's national identity.

The policies indicated in the Athens and Venice Charters are similar, although tailored to the needs of the originating nations. All types of buildings deemed worthy of conservation are encompassed. Charters have no legal status, but they do attempt to set out an international framework for the conservation of the world heritage, and therefore have considerable validity. The Burra Charter adopted by Australia ICOMOS (International Council on Monuments and Sites) in 1981, has proved to be particularly useful, and the Australian government uses it to assess projects before awarding grants. It has thus achieved a more official status than the Venice Charter on which it was based.

Article 3 of the Burra Charter provides clear guidance: 'Conservation is based on a respect for the existing fabric and should involve the least possible physical intervention. It should not distort the evidence provided by the fabric.' 'Fabric' is defined as 'all the physical material of the place'.

This policy seems to provide an excellent basis for a conservation approach to timber and its treatment. The principles outlined are similar to the following English Heritage policy statements:

The purpose of repair
The primary purpose of repair is to restrain the process of decay without damaging the character of buildings or monuments, altering the features which give them their historic or architectural importance, or unnecessarily disturbing or destroying historic fabric.

The need for repair
Intervention through repair must be kept to the minimum required to stabilize and conserve buildings and monuments, with the aim of achieving a sufficiently sound structure to ensure their long-term survival and to meet the requirements of any appropriate use.

Avoiding unnecessary damage
The authenticity of a historic building or monument depends crucially on its design and on the integrity of its fabric. The unnecessary replacement of historic fabric, no matter how carefully the work is carried out, will have an adverse effect on the appearance of a building or monument, will seriously diminish its authenticity, and will significantly reduce its value as a source of historical information.

Adopting proven techniques
In making repairs the aim should be to match existing materials and methods of construction,

in order to preserve the appearance and historical integrity of the building or monument, and to ensure that repairs have an appropriate life. Exceptions should only be considered where the existing fabric has failed because of inherent defects of design or incorrect specifications of materials, rather than from neglect of maintenance or because it has completed its expected life.

(Brereton, 1995)

Historic Scotland's policy is equally succinctly expressed:

Repair Principles
The sound repair of historic buildings requires knowledge, skill and care, which are likely to be based on interest and experience. It is always desirable to keep any intervention to a minimum, to retain maximum original fabric, to know in advance the effect of any work or treatment, to be able to control and wherever possible reverse it if necessary. Simple, direct and straightforward methods, using traditional materials, tools and techniques are almost always the best, though there may be a place for more sophisticated technology, using modern materials and components, where problems are not susceptible to solution by traditional means, or where such methods enable more original fabric to be retained and repairs to be generally more discreet. Substitute materials, chemicals and resins should be avoided where possible.

(Simpson and Brown, 1995, para. 4.4.1)

14.5 Natural control of decay

14.5.1 Natural insect population regulators within the building ecosystem

A wide variety of insects and other creatures may be found within buildings. The majority of these are accidental visitors or species which hibernate through the winter, but some find human's food and furnishings palatable, while a very few attack

the timber from which the building is constructed. Others, and it is this group which interest us in this section, find buildings to be a suitable hunting ground for insect prey.

If building timbers and their environment are suitable for insect infestation, then one might expect the beetles to flourish because competition for the food resource is so limited. In practice, however, the regulating influence of predators and parasites must be taken into consideration. These have been given scant attention, because it has always been accepted that natural predators and parasites will not eradicate their prey population. If, however, a philosophy of minimum intervention and treatment is to become accepted then we cannot ignore them, because in several cases the predator or parasite is easier to kill with insecticide than is the pest species the insecticides are used to control. The effects of the imbalance thus produced have yet to be evaluated.

The major predators and parasites of domestic wood boring beetles are included among the following groups:

Beetles
These comprise several clerid beetles, particularly the little blue coloured *Korynetes caeruleus*, whose larvae pursue the wood borer larvae through their galleries and eat them. *Korynetes* is most commonly associated with death watch beetles.

Parasitic wasps
Hickin (1963a) cites many families of wasp containing species which will prey on death watch beetle, furniture beetle or the house longhorn beetle. The most common species in the UK appears to be the braconid wasp *Spathius exarator*, and the usually wingless pteromalid wasp *Theocolax formiciformis*. These are both very small and inconspicuous insects.

Spathius females have a long ovipositor (4–7 mm) with which they probe the surface of the timber for beetle larvae. Eggs, which hatch within one or two days, are then laid on the beetle larva and the newly emerged wasp larva proceeds to suck the liquids from its host. Parasitism is limited by ovipositor length to larvae in the first few millimetres depth of the timber. Becker and Weber (1952) stated that at least 80% of all the furniture beetle-infested timber in Berlin also included the wasp.

Theocolax has a different approach. The adult wasp, as its specific name suggests, is ant-like in appearance. Occasional specimens have wings but Becker and Weber (1952) could not stimulate flight. The wasp scuttles along beetle burrows and lays its eggs either on the tunnel wall or on the beetle larvae itself. Taylor (1963) also observed the wasps pressing their ovipositors through the surface of the timber when furniture beetle larvae had burrowed close to the surface. Paralysis of the larva by the wasp prior to oviposition seems to be incomplete if it occurs at all. Loss of movement after oviposition does occur, but Becker and Weber record an example where an *Anobium* larva squashed the wasp eggs and ate them. The young wasp grub attaches itself to the surface of a suitable host and slowly destroys it by sucking out internal fluids. Hickin quotes a mean time interval of 18 days for the larva to be fully fed. The adult wasp may bore its own exit tunnel out through the wood and small wasp emergence holes are frequently found in timber where there are well established infestations. The wasps are apparently capable of producing 3–5 generations of adults a year, depending on environmental conditions.

Spiders

Two genera of spider, *Tegenaria* spp. and *Pholcus phalangioides* are probably the commonest spiders found in buildings. Both are opportunist predators, and observations indicate that they capture and devour significant quantities of furniture beetles and death watch beetles (Figure 14.1). *Tegenaria*, the spider frequently found in baths and sinks (Figure 14.2), builds a distinctive web which, when space will allow, consists of a silken platform with a funnel-shaped retreat at one end. In confined spaces it may just spin a tangle of silk. Eggs are normally laid in April, and these hatch in about 21 days. The males when mature will seek out females

Figure 14.1 Spiders are a significant predator of wood-boring insects.

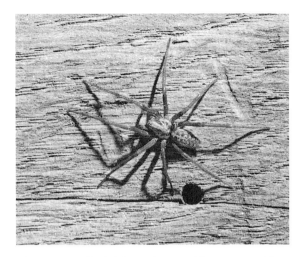

Figure 14.2 Each *Tegenaria* sp. spider may eat 20 or more death watch beetles during the beetle emergence season. A spider colony may therefore regulate a low-density beetle population in a dry building.

The *Pholcus* web is too open to trap many insects, and so when prey shows signs of becoming entangled the spider vibrates the web rapidly so that the prey is firmly enmeshed. It is then twisted around, swathed in silk and left suspended as a food resource (Foelix, 1982).

Mites

The mite *Pyemotes ventricosus* is a parasite on the larvae of wood-boring insects, particularly furniture beetle, in damp timber. The life cycle of this creature is rather peculiar. The eggs hatch before they are laid, and the larvae develop inside the abdomen of the female. When the mites emerge they are sexually mature. Males emerge first and these suck the body fluids of the parent while awaiting the females. Females then drop off the parent after fertilization has occurred and await a passing host. Many mites may subsequently suck the body fluids of one beetle larva.

Pyemotes mites represent a minor health hazard to man because their bites, though trivial, can provoke dermatological allergic reaction. Other species within the genus cause a condition sometimes known as 'grain itch' because skin irritation results from contact with infected grain, hay or straw. The mite we are concerned with, *P. ventricosus*, does not normally cause a problem although Rook (1985) quotes a case in Singapore where an outbreak of grain itch affected 17 workers in a child health clinic. The cause was finally traced to *P. ventricosus* preying on furniture beetle in the clinic furniture.

and may live together in harmony with them in the web for several weeks. Males, however, die in the autumn whereas the females may continue to live for several years. The female survives the winter period when prey is scarce by storing fats, with some carbohydrates and proteins, in the autumn. Some at least of this food reserve comes from the corpse of her partner (Foelix, 1982).

Tegenaria webs in roofs may contain considerable quantities of wood-boring beetle fragments. The preferred method of feeding appears to be to kill by puncturing the abdomen through the elytra and then to dissect the insect into its component skeletal parts. Small heaps of beetle wingcases (Figure 14.3) and other fragments are also found, and examination of these shows that they have been assembled by spiders (Uetz, 1992).

Pholcus is a strange and rather more primitive creature with a cylindrical body and long spindly legs (Figure 14.4). The web when fully developed is a tangled maze of wandering threads usually woven near the ceiling or in roofs. Mature males and females frequently share a web during the summer months, and the eggs, which are laid in the autumn, are carried around by the female (Savory, 1928).

All of these predators and parasites (with the possible exception of *Pyemotes*) have little interaction with man, but they do significantly limit beetle populations. Observations and mark/release experiments with death watch beetle in cathedral roofs indicate that a significant proportion of these insects are destroyed by spiders (see Section 4.4.5). Wise (1993) concludes that although spiders do not eradicate insect populations they do set an upper limit to their numerical increase. Bats may also eat any beetles they encounter and Hickin (1953) believed that he had found fragments of *Korynetes* in bat droppings. If Hickin was correct

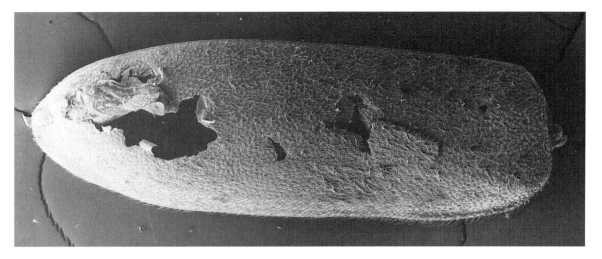

Figure 14.3 The common house spider *Tegenaria* sp. punches holes through beetles' wingcases with its fangs.

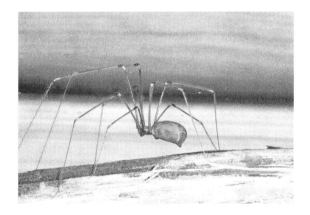

Figure 14.4 The spider *Pholcus* sp. entangles its prey in a cocoon of threads and leaves it as a future food source. Death watch beetles are frequently found in this condition.

then presumably the bats would also eat death watch beetle and furniture beetle. Fragments would, however, be very small and therefore rather more difficult to identify.

These discussions lead us to postulate a model for the interactions between pest species, predators/parasites and preservative treatments in buildings. This model (Figure 14.5) describes three habitats which may represent roof spaces or any other relevant areas in buildings. Clearly a building may contain more than one of these

habitats. Moisture content assessments should be based on numerous readings obtained with a moisture meter and preferably taken at depth with insulated probes. The locations from which readings are taken should be carefully chosen to avoid factors that might artificially elevate or depress readings (see Chapter 13). Nineteenth-century repairs will often give truer readings than medieval timbers (see Section 13.1). If more modern timbers are not present within the structure, and time allows, some modern pieces of wood should be distributed around the site and left for two or three weeks to equilibrate with the environment before readings are taken.

Habitat A – Moisture content less than 15% (all the year round) and free from active infestation.
Dry and well maintained buildings, or parts of buildings, do not allow decay organisms to thrive, and do not require preservative treatments. This is particularly true in older buildings, where timber may have a high natural durability, or in subfloor spaces where heating pipes produce an environment lethal to the insects.

Habitat B – Moisture content between about 15% and 18% and/or with some possible indications of limited decay and insect activity.

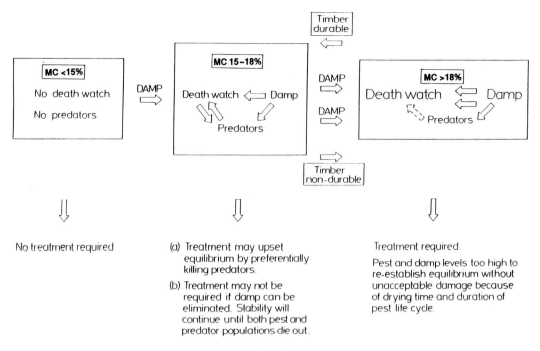

Figure 14.5 Pest and predator habitat diagram based on timber moisture contents (MC).

Most old buildings will have damp areas. Some decay may be occurring but it should be restricted to zones of sapwood and limited by the natural balance of the environment. General treatments in this habitat may kill a few pest insects during the few years that the chemicals remain effective, but they will also destroy large quantities of natural predators, particularly spiders (see Section 4.4.5). However, limited and targeted treatments may be required for some timbers. Improved maintenance and minor building works may be all that is required to upgrade the habitat to A.

Habitat C – Moisture content greater than 18% and with evidence of widespread active insect infestation.

General preservative treatments may be justified in this situation in order to reduce the pest population and limit further damage. Building and maintenance works will be required to dry the timbers but control of active infestations by this method alone is slow, although it is sometimes acceptable if the timber is of good quality and/or of generous dimension.

Applied treatments must take account of the identity, biology and decay potential of the pest insects. It is now therefore necessary to discuss environmental control of these wood-boring insects in some detail.

14.5.2 Environmental control of death watch beetle: Westminster Hall

Chapter 4 explained how treatments to eradicate death watch beetle were rarely entirely successful, and how this was related to the insect's biology. If an appropriate insecticide does not reach the targeted pest in sufficient quantity the insects will not be killed.

A high proportion of the buildings containing timbers that have been damaged by death watch beetle do not contain active infestation, and it is a common mistake to assume that damage is evidence that beetles are present. Extensive treatments in these cases result from a lack of understanding of the insects' population dynamics. The beetle is frequently one of the easiest timber pests to control (though not, perhaps, to eliminate) by environmental modification, and this will be illustrated by returning to the problems of Westminster Hall (see Section 4.1).

Westminster Hall, a building central to the history of England, provides what is probably a uniquely documented history of death watch beetle damage and its treatment which spans several centuries. The current roof, which was erected for Richard II between 1394 and 1400, is 72.5 m (238 ft) long, 20.6 m (67 ft 6 in) wide, and rises to a height of over 27.4 m (90 ft) from the floor. Baines (1914) calculated that it contained about 40 000 cubic feet (1132 m^3) of timber, exclusive of roof boarding.

The earliest accounts of repairs date to 1663 when limited restoration works were undertaken, but a good picture of the condition of the roof is not given until two skylights were installed in 1746 to provide light for the trial of Lord Lovat. An account in the *General Advertiser* for 8 October 1746 states: 'Divers plumbers are now repairing Westminster Hall which is very much decayed in the Upper Part and the wood which has been for such a number of years standing is so rotten that it may be compared to touchwood.' The extent to which the roof was repaired is unknown, but a note in the same journal for 5 August 1748 states that several new 'spars' were required, and bolts were driven into the 'arches'. Lead was removed and the roof was slated to make it lighter. During preparations for the coronation of George IV in 1821 the roof timbers were drilled for chandeliers. The timbers involved were so decayed that substantial repairs had to be made. Over 60 years later, on 24 January 1885, the Irish Republican Brotherhood (Fenians) damaged the roof with a nearby dynamite explosion and it had to be reslated.

In 1909 the two ex-sailors employed to dust the roof timbers reported a number of defects and this eventually led to a full structural inspection of the roof. Many of the timbers were found to be severely decayed and a major restoration was undertaken between 1914 and 1923. In order to minimize the loss of original material the roof was resupported with a lightweight steel structure so that only about 10% of the timber had to be replaced, and

an insecticide treatment was sought to kill the death watch beetle (Ridout, 1999).

The story of the search for an effective treatment is beyond the scope of this study, but what is important is that only a very few beetles could be found for the 1914–23 research into insecticide. The damage was severe, but the actual number of the beetle population was small.

Treatment was completed, and nothing further is recorded about the beetles until 1935 when the Hall was prepared for the Silver Jubilee celebrations of George V. The Forest Products Research Laboratory were then asked to make an inspection from movable scaffolding and this was undertaken during March and April. The impression gained by the surveyor was that there were some signs of recent activity, but there was no conclusive evidence.

Between 1951 and 1971 beetles that fell to the floor were collected on a daily basis and their positions marked on charts. During this period 43 770 beetles were recorded. What had happened to cause this increase?

In order to answer this question we must examine the distribution of the beetles that were collected. The chart for 1965 is shown in Figure 14.6. Beetles were collected in the early morning before the floor was swept and so the majority probably did not move far. Most of the beetles emerged at the south end of the roof and in the north-west corner.

Figure 14.7 shows areas of damage caused by three fire bombs that fell through the roof during the war years. The similarity between beetle distribution and fire damage is marked. The 1941 fire took 8 hours to extinguish, and the safety margin of damping down would have been extensive. The incendiary bombs in 1944 produced a much smaller fire which also would have required damping down. Temporary roof coverings were placed over the holes, but repairs could not be commenced until 1947, and were not completed until 1950. Thus for 9 years the dampened roof timbers had only a temporary covering and drying would have been severely impaired (see Section 12.2).

A wide array of treatments were tried over the years but none of them can be shown to have had

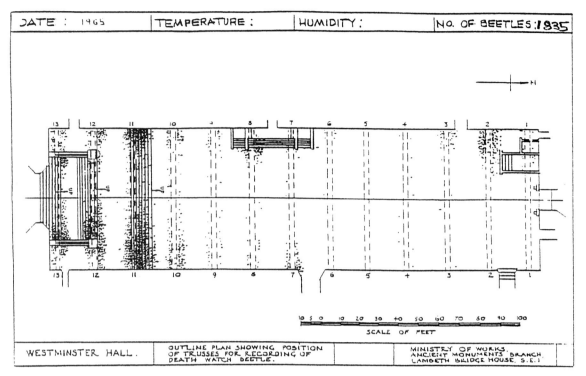

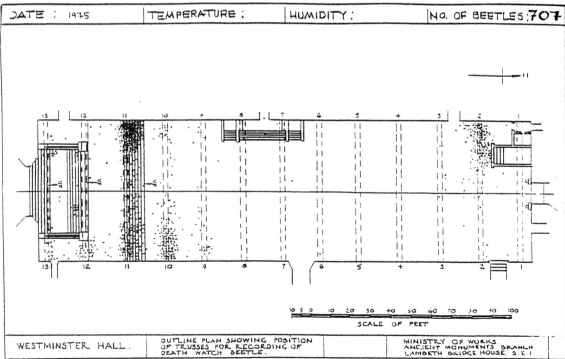

Figure 14.6 Westminster Hall: death watch beetle collection records for 1965 and 1975.

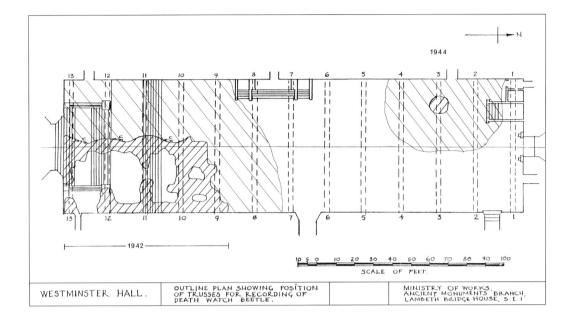

Figure 14.7 Westminster Hall: zones of fire damage (///) and probable damping-down (\\\).

much effect upon the beetle population. However, beetle numbers did decline markedly during the late 1960s and, although this has been said to be due to the annual smoke treatments initiated in 1968, it can be demonstrated that the decline had already commenced. A small residual population remains, and in the 1996 emergence season 126 beetles were collected.

The conclusions to be derived from this story may ultimately be applicable to most buildings where there is death watch beetle damage. A likely hypothesis that fits the known facts from the Westminster Hall history is that beetle numbers were at a low level during the early decades of the twentieth century, in spite of considerable historical damage. The probable reason for this was that the roof had been kept in good repair and therefore dry during the nineteenth century. The war years caused a rapid rise in timber moisture content and humidity, which was accompanied by an expansion of the beetle population. During the period 1950–70 there was a time lag during which the timber dried and the beetle population declined erratically to its normal level within the building.

Beetle population explosions are easily understood if, as seems likely, death watch beetles respond in the same way to moisture changes as furniture beetle (see Section 5.2). With the latter insect, increasing the moisture content decreases the larval growth period and produces larger adults which lay more eggs. The survival rate is also enhanced. The potential result of a prolonged moisture increase may be simplistically illustrated by assuming a base-line population of 100 male and 100 female beetles. If each female beetle lays 50 eggs and the larvae take 10 years to develop then at the end of that period 5000 beetles could emerge. If, however, we wet-up timbers and reduce the larval growth period to 5 years, and if we assume the same sex ratio as before, then after 10 years the number of beetles emerging could be 125 000.

Beetles are rarely eradicated in buildings because many are not accessible to insecticides, but the population remains at a low level provided that the building is dry and well maintained. The numbers may slowly increase but will tend to be controlled by low population viability and predation. Any events that allow the timber moisture content to rise locally for an extended period of time will cause a rapid increase in beetle numbers, and the population will then take several years to decline when dry conditions are restored. Targeted treatments should therefore be reserved for the period when the beetle population is at a high level, unless there are obvious pockets of activity.

14.5.3 Environmental control of furniture beetle

Furniture beetle should not cause a problem in a dry and well maintained building. If the building is unavoidably damp, as sometimes it is in the basement for example, then furniture should be kept away from the walls in order to keep the timber as dry as possible. If damp is suspected inspect all timber items regularly for insect activity by checking the undersides, especially joints and fixing blocks which may have been fastened with animal glues. If active infestation is found the item should be moved to a drier environment and the limited application of an insecticide should be considered.

Some useful guidelines for treatments based on timber quality have been suggested (Baker, 1972) and these are summarized in Table 14.1.

14.5.4 Environmental control of dry rot

The suggestion that dry rot can frequently be eliminated with little or no recourse to chemicals sometimes causes trepidation, even though wall sterilization and *in situ* timber treatments are largely twentieth-century inventions. In earlier times decayed timbers were removed and fungus

within walls was destroyed by drying. A clear appraisal of the decay and its control was given in the late eighteenth century, in what appears to be the first book on dry rot published in the English language. *Some Observations on That Distemper in Timber Called Dry Rot* was published by J. Johnson in 1795. Johnson was living in a 50-year-old house on Sunbury Common, which had been 'grievously neglected'. There was considerable dry rot in plates, bressumers, wainscots and beam ends. Johnson attributed the problem to ground water, augmented by high ground levels and blocked downpipes. If this wasn't clear-sighted enough, considering the beliefs held by his contemporaries, he also decided that the decay was caused by 'a perverted vegetation' – a wonderful description of a fungus. Two paragraphs in particular are worth quoting for the information they provide on the problems of the day:

Rot depends on the looseness or closeness of the timber quality. Fir [pine] is least eligible but now almost the only timber used in buildings, because oak cannot be obtained in sufficient quantity.

For the purpose of working more easily and perhaps of measuring better, the fir beams stored by the timber merchants are generally kept soaked in water till they are sawed and prepared for their specific uses; and they are forthwith fixed in buildings long before the moisture they had acquired can be exhaled.

(Johnson, 1795, p. 34)

Johnson's method of dealing with the problem was to remove the source of moisture wherever

Table 14.1 Furniture beetle treatment determined by the age of the structural timber (based on Baker, 1972)

Age of timber	Treatment
Pre-1900	None should be required. *Anobium* attack is probably diminishing or extinct.
1900–1939	Treat on merit. Widespread active infestation may require whole-space treatment, but small attacks could be individually treated.
Post-1939	Treatment usually required.

possible. He avoided the use of replacement timber whenever practical, and cautioned against the application of paint before the timber was dry because it trapped moisture. He notes that dry rot did not reappear above ground floor level, which would be in the areas where water ingress could be controlled.

Dry rot in ground floor timbers was more difficult to deal with, but methods did emerge in response to a protracted campaign launched by the Royal Society of Arts (RSA), following a letter on the subject sent to their London headquarters by Robert Baldwin:

If the following subject has not already been agitated in the Society of Arts. A premium may be well bestowed for the discovery of the various causes of the Dry Rot in timber, and of the certain method of prevention.
(RSA, 1783: letter book 27 December)

and with the postscript:

The large new building in Chancery Lane for the Offices of this Court is said to be greatly decayed by a dry rot in the timber.

Baldwin's letter was referred to the Committee of Chemistry and it was resolved at the next meeting (7 January 1784) to place an advertisement in the Society's journal offering a gold medal or 30 guineas 'to the person who shall discover to the Society the Causes of the Dry Rot in timber and disclose a certain Method of Prevention superior to any hitherto known'.

This advertisement continued to be inserted until the issue of the journal for 1841–43. In 1824 the premium was raised to 50 guineas and in 1832 a Gold Isis Medal was also offered for 'the best account illustrated by microscopic and other drawings'. There is no evidence that either was ever awarded.

Two medals were, however, given by the RSA for the control of dry rot in ships. The first was a gold medal awarded to Bowden in 1818 for the total immersion of the Navy's ships in sea water. The second was a silver medal awarded to Mr

Edward Carey in 1829. He had built a 200-ton brig for a Mr Williams, and this brig had been found to be still sound after 30 years. Lack of decay was attributed to the fact that Carey bored a hole into the centre of each timber head and filled it with cod or seal oil, salt and charcoal mixed to a thick consistency. Unfortunately Mr Williams had died and so the story could not be verified – hence, perhaps, the silver medal rather than a gold.

Contenders did emerge for the original medal, two letters being reported at a Committee meeting on 17 December 1785. The first suggested that dry rot was caused by felling timber out of season and recommended the use of oil of turpentine as a preservative. The second correspondent suggested that dry rot was caused by stagnant air and was frequently accompanied by fungi that enjoyed those conditions. He therefore suggested a free circulation of air and cautioned the workman against leaving sawdust or shavings. He also recommended the use of 'Lime core and dry stuff' to fill the spaces within the ground floor. Charring was considered to be a good protection for timbers, but the correspondent conceded that this presented difficulties on a large scale, and pinned his faith on the application of green vitriol (copper sulphate).

Mr Batson of Limehouse wrote to the Committee seeking the medal in 1793 after discovering and treating dry rot in a closet at his home. Some recent authors have stated that Batson was awarded the medal but this is incorrect, although his method certainly aroused a great deal of interest. It did not, however, differ greatly from the method described in 1785. The committee noted the following procedure:

In 1787 it was determined that a closet lining and floor should be taken out 'leaving not a particle of wood, and dig and take away about 2 feet of earth in depth', the whole being then well dried and cleansed was filled to a sufficient height for the joists with Anchor Smith's ash and the joists and plates well charred, and directions given that the Boards and Scantlings were not cut or planed lest any dirt or shavings might fall amongst the ashes.

The Committee inspected this work 6 years after its completion and declared the area to be free from dry rot or damp. Further enquiries were also made in 1803 with the same results but no award was made.

The literature on dry rot throughout the nineteenth century is mostly concerned with the pretreatment of timber, and decayed wood was invariably replaced if it was located. The association of damp with dry rot had now been firmly made, and recommendations for the prevention and control centred on the removal of the infected timber and on drying. Much blame for dry rot was placed on poor-quality speculative buildings which frequently remained half completed and saturated by rain for long periods awaiting the funds to complete. Britton (1875) believed that a 'considerable period of time' should elapse between building and plastering to allow the structure to dry before timber, and particularly joinery, was installed.

Eighteenth- and nineteenth-century buildings provide us with the best evidence that dry rot can frequently be destroyed by environmental modification alone. Many large buildings contain fungus which developed because of a fault which allowed water into the building and died when that fault was remedied, without the occupants being aware of the dry rot. When this fungus is now revealed the worried architect calls in the uncritical remedial specialist and expensive preservative treatment ensues, yet the fungus is long dead and not a threat to the building. This was demonstrated to the author some years ago when he was asked to undertake a fibre optic inspection for dry rot behind ornamental plaster in one of London's more important buildings. Extensive wall irrigation costing about £10 000 had been used the year before to flood the walls at roof level with preservatives, and the remedial company now wished to dismantle the plasterwork in order to complete the treatment. Suspicions were aroused when it was found that the wall and studwork were dry, and that the fungus remnants were brittle. It transpired that the roof had been altered at the end of the eighteenth century to destroy the dry rot that had now been treated some 200 years later. This is not an uncommon situation. The various methods by which wall moisture contents may be assessed, and this problem avoided, are discussed in the case histories in Appendix B.

Dry rot will die if the walls and timber dry out. It is the building that presents the problem, not the fungus. Thick saturated walls may take many years to dry, and decay will continue during that period. Preservative treatments may be essential in some situations if the spread of the fungus is to be restricted, and critical timbers are to be protected, while the structure dries.

The retention of partially decayed timber would rarely, if ever, have been contemplated in the past because it was considered to be of little importance. Nowadays we place a far higher value on the preservation of original finishes and materials. However, it is important to remember that partially decayed wood does not have the same properties as sound. This may not matter if we consider damaged beam ends or other timbers which can be resupported, but it becomes critical when joinery and sometimes fragile studwork or laths are to be conserved. Further water penetration must clearly be avoided but abnormally dry conditions will be equally damaging.

Timber is stable within a range of relative humidity between about 45% and 65% (at 18–20 °C). At lower humidities joints and splits may open in sound timber, but partially decayed timber may seriously buckle and deform. Low humidities generally occur in buildings where temperatures are elevated, and in many situations these can be offset by humidification. One example of a potentially damaging environment might be an office where desk work and little physical activity produce the requirement for a hot atmosphere in order to keep warm. A less obvious and more localized problem occurs in the vicinity of radiators and heating pipes. Cracked dado panels are frequently observed behind radiators in window recesses because the timber has desiccated. This must be taken into account if dry rot or other fungal decay is also present because of the excessive deformation which may occur, and it may be necessary to keep the adjacent radiator turned off.

14.6 Holistic approach to dry rot treatment

Damage, cost and volume of preservatives can all usually be reduced, sometimes dramatically, if each situation is carefully evaluated (Ridout, 1987, 1989a, 1989b). This assessment should include the following tasks.

14.6.1 Evaluate the cause and level of fungal activity

This measure is fundamental, but its significance is frequently ignored. An active dry rot infestation has to have a current or recent source of moisture, which may be concealed or obvious, but it must be or have been there. Once the fungus has been located then the cause must be carefully ascertained. Decay in a wall plate, for example, may not need treatment if it can be related to faulty gutters which were adequately repaired several years previously. In this case it will only be necessary (provided there are no structural implications) to record the decay so that it is not rediscovered by the next architect or surveyor, and to check it periodically. Photography may be useful for future comparison. A remote moisture-sensing system might be appropriate in this situation (see Chapter 13) and be better value for money than destructive treatments.

Simple timber sensors can also be useful in assessing fungal activity. These consist of timber rods inserted into the wall so that they can be removed without having to expose or remove structural timbers. If the infestation is active, the rods will be affected. This technique is only useful if the rods are used in the right place, that is, along the active front of the fungus.

If a current source of damp is located, it must be remedied in an appropriate and thorough fashion. It should be noted that the major cause of water penetration may not be the only one and that all causes must be located.

14.6.2 Evaluate moisture levels and distribution

The assessment of cause and activity outlined above will provide valuable information on the likely moisture distribution. Further data will probably be obtained with a hand-held moisture meter, and the limitations of these instruments must be thoroughly understood (see Section 13.1). Timber sensors may again be appropriate.

14.6.3 Locate and assess all timbers at risk

This means all timbers within about 2 m of the last signs of decay. An assessment of timbers should take account of concealed bearings and the backs of wall plates, but as little damage as possible should be done to the timbers in the course of inspection. A close inspection is essential; little is gained by shining a torch from the centre of a roof space. Cavities at junctions of plates and joints in brickwork should be carefully examined for fungus.

Inspection of cavities with fibre optics may be useful if boards, for example, cannot be lifted, but direct observation is preferable because dry rot around a joist bearing, for example, may be visible from one side yet not from the other.

The various parameters to be taken into consideration may be assessed in the form of a key and this is given in Appendix A. Appropriate case studies are discussed in Appendix B.

14.7 Conclusions

The policy statements discussed in Section 14.4 are a requirement when dealing with listed buildings, but there seems little reason why the philosophy expressed should not be more widely prescribed. The current situation is unlikely to change, however, until and unless architects and their clients lose their old prejudices and gain a greater knowledge of decay organisms and their potential. For example, it is still common practice for many architects to strip historic plaster finishes in order to expose interior partition wall studs for inspection, when there is unlikely to be very much wrong with them.

It must be appreciated that the quest for decay is not the only reason for exposure work. Change of usage may require structural inspection and resupport of floors, for example; the upgrading of services may be equally disruptive. However, there is no reason why this exposure work should be carried out unnecessarily, and a general stripping-out policy has little to recommend it except convenience – indeed, the stripping may be illegal if the appropriate consents have not been obtained.

Once studwork and floor timbers have all been exposed then it is traditional (see Section 14.2) to argue in favour of precautionary preservative treatment. It is generally considered a wise precaution because the timbers will never be exposed again. The argument that timbers are unlikely to decay in the few years the treatment will last if they have not decayed over decades or centuries is not considered. In fact, the treatment means that the architect either does not understand the process of decay, has no faith that his repair works will keep water out, or fears the accusation of negligence. Whatever the reason, the remedial company will be happy to oblige, and to issue their guarantee: a guarantee that dry timber will not decay.

The discovery of decay, particularly dry rot, exacerbates the problem because the architect,

worried about the client's interests and his or her own insurance, relies on the specialist contractor. The specialist contractor, with a far narrower field of expertise, worries in turn about guarantees, and perhaps also about low income due to free surveys and competitive tenders. The consequences of this unfortunate alliance are, inevitably, destructive and expensive. They frequently do not benefit either the client or the building.

If those concerned with historic buildings have more understanding of timber decay and more faith in their own judgement, then loss of historical materials can be minimized. Timber should only be exposed and removed if there is good reason to suppose that significant decay may have occurred. This information may be obtained with a variety of techniques, but mostly from a close inspection of the building itself. The identification of faults that have allowed water penetration and an assessment of water distribution, together with a knowledge of the construction, will usually indicate timbers at risk.

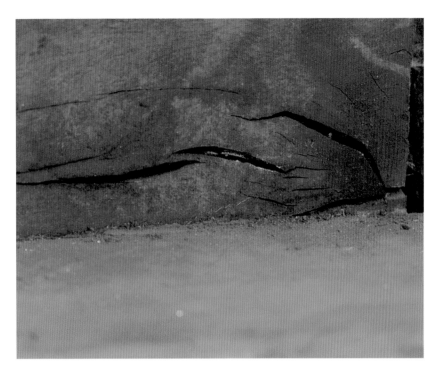

Colour Plate 1 A photograph taken under ultraviolet light to show fluorescent dust from a labelled death watch beetle that re-entered the timber via a shake.

Colour Plate 2 A photograph taken under ultraviolet light to show a fluorescent dust trail left by a labelled death watch beetle entering an old emergence hole.

Colour Plate 3 Fresh dry rot fruits are orange, usually with a white margin. The fruit turns black and dries up after the spores are released.

Colour Plate 4 Some dry rot fruits are bracket-shaped. Note the red spore dust below the fruit.

Colour Plate 5 Considerable amounts of mycelium may be produced if humidities are high.

Colour Plate 6 Dry rot in ground-floor timbers may grow through into cellars below. Note the fungus growing along the metal tie rod.

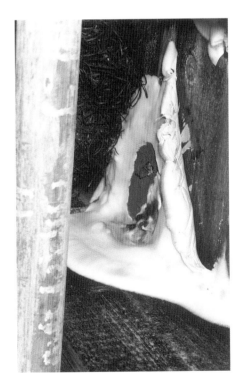

Colour Plate 7 Dry rot frequently produces denser surface growth which is easily peeled from the wall or timber. Note the fruit forming at the centre.

Colour Plate 8 Dry rot growing in a cupboard. All such spaces need to be investigated. Note the strands formed by the fungus.

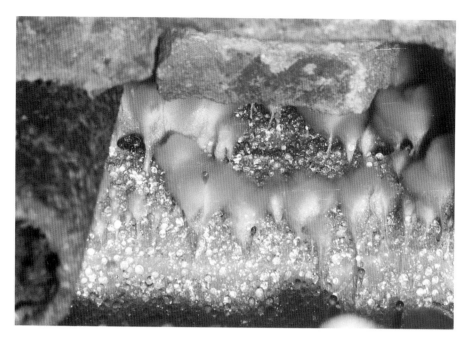

Colour Plate 9 If conditions are very humid, excessive moisture weeps from the fungus.

Colour Plate 10 Dry rot in a subfloor void grows in an arc around the source of moisture, which was an external downpipe.

Colour Plate 11 An ornate and heavy plaster ceiling collapses because dry rot has destroyed joist bearings and ceiling laths.

Colour Plate 12 Fruits of the slime mould *Reticularia lycoperdon*. The lower specimen has burst to reveal brown spores. These fruits can be 6 cm across and can cause concern, but the fungi feeds on bacteria and organic debris. They do not damage timber.

Colour Plate 13 The fruits of the elf cap fungi are firm and brittle. They may be several centimetres in diameter. These fungi do not damage timber.

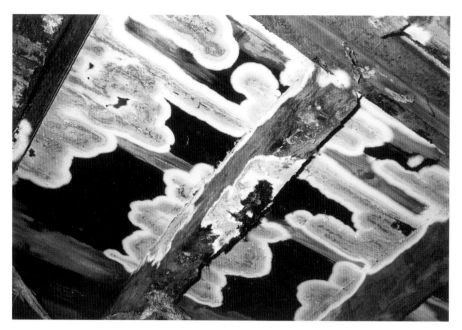

Colour Plate 14 Fruits of the cellar rot fungus (*Coniophora puteana*) growing on the underside of floor boards (first-floor level). These fruits are fairly common in buildings but tend to be called dry rot. Note the beads of moisture glistening on the fungus. This is one of the phenomena that are said to be characteristics of dry rot.

Colour Plate 15 Black strands of cellar rot (*Coniophora puteana*) growing in a subfloor void. These strands frequently grow through walls and are mistaken for dry rot.

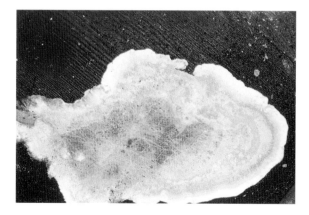

Colour Plate 16 A fruit of the wet rot fungus *Asterostroma cervicolor*. This fungus produces large quantities of buff-coloured strands and is frequently found attacking softwoods.

Colour Plate 17 The wet rot fungus *Gleophyllum sepiarum* has elongated pores like thick gills. It occasionally occurs in buildings and may easily be mistaken for dry rot. (See also Table 8.2.)

Colour Plate 18 *Gleophyllum sepiarium* is one of a wide range of fungi that may produce large amounts of visible mycelium. (See also Table 8.2.)

Colour Plate 20 A different species of *Coprinus* producing chocolate-coloured mycelium.

Colour Plate 19 A gilled wet rot fungus (*Coprinus* sp) fruiting out of a wall. This fungus causes a slow decay in hardwoods.

Colour Plate 21 Ginger *Coprinus* mycelium with the shrivelled remains of fruits.

Analytical approach to preservative treatment

A.1 Introduction to the use of analytical keys

If treatments are to be based on conservation principles, a wide range of factors must be taken into account. The following analytical keys are intended to help specifiers decide what course of action is most appropriate and to aid the decision-making process by assessing those considerations that the author has found to be significant. This approach has been used successfully for many years. The keys are, however, only offered as those the author would use, and it is accepted that individual problems may require the specifier to consider factors that are not included here. No responsibility can be assumed by the author for problems arising from following the keys.

Keys are suggested for the appraisal of death watch beetle, woodworm and decay fungi, because these are the decay organisms that cause most concern. Treatment of the other problems is included in the relevant chapters.

A.2 Key to the treatment of death watch beetle

Look for evidence of death watch beetle infestation: check window sills, floors and surfaces below and between building timber. If the floors are regularly swept, check crevices and ledges or ask for sweepings to be retained during the beetle emergence season.

To use key start at couplet 1. Choose the most appropriate from 'a' or 'b' and proceed to the next couplet indicated (e.g. if 1b was chosen then proceed to couplet 2). Continue until a treatment policy is established.

1a	Holes have sharp edges, light interiors and bore dust (frass) trickling from them. Beetle may be present in accumulated bore dust.	proceed to 7	
1b	Holes have rounded (blunt) edges and dark interiors. Any bore dust present may be due to dislodgement through floor or building vibration (e.g. recent building works).	proceed to 2	
2a	Death watch beetles or fragments of beetles are plentiful even though holes look old.	proceed to 7	
2b	Beetles absent or a few beetles or beetle fragments found.	proceed to 3	
3a	No beetles, fragments of beetles or frass located after a careful search.	proceed to 4	
3b	A few beetles or beetle fragments found.	proceed to 5	
4a	Active decay still suspected in some localized timbers.	Treatment A	Securely and closely fasten (using water-soluble glue) tissue paper or similar to small areas where activity is expected and leave over the months April–June. If beetle emergence holes appear through the papers or beetles are trapped behind the papers then return to 7 in the key.
4b	No activity suspected.	No treatment necessary	
5a	Building works have been undertaken during the last decade to halt water penetration or condensation. Structure drying.	Treatment B	Monitor beetle emergence annually. Ensure good ongoing maintenance. If beetle numbers increase then return to 6 in the key.
5b	No building works undertaken during last decade or water penetration/condensation may still be occurring.	proceed to 6	*key continued . . .*

6a	Beetle or beetle fragments appear randomly scattered. No obvious focus of infestation.	Treatment C	Seek out and rectify any sources of water penetration. Increase ventilation if practicable and acceptable. Monitor beetle numbers annually and try to identify foci of infestation from beetle distribution and sources of damp. If beetle numbers increase then proceed to 7 in the key.
6b	Distribution of beetles or beetle fragments allows them to be associated with individual timbers.	proceed to 8	
7a	Current activity widespread in the sapwood edges of timbers.	Treatment D	Ensure that all possible sources of water penetration have been halted. Spray or brush treat the infested surfaces with a spirit-based insecticide. Whole space treatments may have to be repeated twice at 3-yearly intervals in order to maximize depletion of the beetle population.
7b	Current activity in small localized areas or timber bearings and plates associated with walls.	proceed to 8	
8a	Timbers are adjacent to or in contact with important plasterwork/decorative finishes so that staining could result from treatment.	Treatment E	Cautiously coat the top or accessible surfaces of the timbers with preservative paste. Ensure that there is no spillage or run-off. The minimum safe distance between the pasted surfaces and plaster will vary in different situations and has not therefore been established. Experience suggests that about 225 mm will provide a good safety margin.
8b	Timbers are remote from important plasterwork/decorative finishes and maximum penetration is required.	Treatment F	Coat accessible surface of the timbers with a paste preservative. Aid penetration where practicable and acceptable by drilling holes at about 100 mm centres to about three-quarters of the depth of the timber.

A.3 Key to the treatment of furniture beetle

1a	Beetles present on floors, window sills, in spiders' webs etc. and/or bore dust trickling from flight holes in timber and/or beetle larvae in decayed wood.	proceed to 11	
1b	None of the above present, unequivocal indications of current insect activity.	proceed to 2	
2a	Beetle emergence holes with dark interiors and blunted edges. Damage clearly old.	No treatment necessary	
2b	All or some emergence holes with light interiors and sharp edges. May be limited recent activity.	proceed to 3	
3a	Timber is oak, some other durable hardwood or softwood dating to pre-1900.	proceed to 4	
3b	Timber is softwood dating to post-1900.	proceed to 9	
4a	Building is dry and well maintained (timber moisture content < 12–14%)	proceed to 5	
4b	Building is damp and neglected, or has been difficult to keep dry.	proceed to 6	
5a	Components large and sapwood content low. Damage not significant.	No action required	
5b	Components large and damage critical.	Repair as necessary	
6a	Building repaired, occupied and probably heated. Humidity usually below 65%.	proceed to 7	
6b	Building to remain empty and unheated for the foreseeable future, or conditions are difficult to improve. Humidity frequently above 65%.	proceed to 8	
7a	A small possibility of minor further damage while the building dries is acceptable.	No treatment necessary	
7b	All further damage must be avoided because of decorative finishes or fragile, historically important timber etc.	proceed to 11	
8a	Sapwood content in timber low. Localized signs of past or current infestation.	Treatment A	Brush treat localized areas of decay with a spirit-based or paste preservative.
8b	Sapwood content high. Signs of past or current infestation widespread.	proceed to 9	
9a	Beetle activity can be monitored by tightly fastening tissue paper or similar to a representative selection of surfaces where beetle activity is suspected. Leave fastened	proceed to 10	*key continued . . .*

192

(9a)	for at least 12 months. Alternatively, clog holes with wax polish.		
9b	Beetle activity monitoring not possible.	proceed to 11	
10a	Holes punched though paper by emerging beetles.	proceed to 11	
10b	No holes punched through paper.	No action required unless/until beetle activity confirmed	
11a	Infested items transportable.	proceed to 12	
11b	Infested items not transportable.	proceed to 13	
12a	Fumigation or freezing facilities available and affordable.	Treatments B or C	B: Fumigation facilities using hazardous gases are commercially available. A mobile chamber system has now been introduced which utilizes carbon dioxide or nitrogen (see Section 5.4.5). This overcomes many of the problems encountered with other gases. C: The deep freezing of furniture and other artefacts in order to destroy infestations is worth consideration. Either a commercial freezer or a temperature/ humidity controlled freezer (Florian, 1997) is normally used; the freezer should be capable for reaching a temperature of –20 °C. The items are kept at room temperature prior to treatment so that the woodworm are active. They are then placed in polythene bags containing a little silica gel to absorb excess moisture and positioned in the freezer so that air can circulate around them. A temperature of –20 °C or lower should be maintained for 48 h and it would be usual to monitor with surface-temperature probes to ensure that the correct temperature has been reached. The temperature after removal should be allowed to rise slowly over about an 8 h period while the item remains in the polythene bag. Some authorities suggest that the freeze–thaw cycle should be immediately repeated.
12b	Fumigation or freezing facilities not available and affordable.	proceed to 13	
13a	Finishes can be stripped from the timber, or component less than about 25 mm with unfinished surfaces accessible.	Treatment D	Spray or brush treat all accessible surfaces with a spirit based preservative containing a contact insecticide.
13b	Finishes cannot be removed, component thick or unfinished surfaces not accessible.	Treatment E	Carefully inject the spirit-based preservative into flight holes using either a hypodermic syringe, or a can fitted with a suitably constructed nozzle.

A.4 Key to the treatment of decay caused by fungi, including dry rot

1a	Fungus restricted to the decayed timbers or only decayed timber visible. No signs of strand formation on the timber, on the wall surface or within the wall. No signs of fine red spore dust or dry rot fruits.	proceed to 2
1b	Fungus producing surface growth and strands that extend on to the wall surface and within the wall, or red spore dust, or dry rot fruit.	proceed to 4
2a	Damage minor, or of little consequence.	proceed to 3
2b	Structural integrity of timber impaired or damage severe.	Promote drying; cut back decayed wood to sound timber and/or consult a structural engineer
3a	Damage to hardwoods in a building which contains signs of death watch beetle activity.	Promote drying; coat damage with a paste preservative
3b	Damage to hardwoods or softwoods, no death watch beetle activity present.	Promote drying; no further action
4a	strands appear dead/inactive (grey-brown and brittle) and do not produce condensation when left in a warm place in a polythene bag.	proceed to 5
4b	Strand appears active (white-grey and flexible) and produce condensation when left in a warm place in a polythene bag.	proceed to 6
5a	Building structure dry. Source of moisture cured in the past, e.g. masonry < 2%, timber < 20%.	No treatment (see Case study 2)
5b	Building structure damp.	proceed to 6
6a	All sources of water located and easily rectified, e.g. faulty downpipe replaced, or little chance that wetting will recur.	proceed to 7
6b	Sources of moisture not obvious or not easily rectifiable. Decay caused by widespread water penetration. Only temporary or emergency elimination of damp source possible. Possibility of damp penetration recurring.	proceed to 8	*key continued . . .*

7a	Structure could be left exposed for an appropriate time in order to dry.	No treatment (see Case study 3)	
7b	Significant time constraints. No time to dry out.	proceed to 8	
8a	Cost constraints, or treatment possible only on a temporary or emergency basis; quality of structure or finishes important and/or no opportunity for opening up and reinstating conservatively.	proceed to 9	
8b	Structure and finishes apparently less important, or no cost constraints, or structure saturated.	Treatment A (see Case study 4)	1. Remove all sources of water penetration. 2. Remove plaster to expose full extent of fungus. Start from centre of infection and work outwards to edge, but not beyond. 3. Expose any concealed bearings – on one side if joists, on both sides if thick beams. 4. Cut back decayed timbers to sound wood or coat the exposed bearings with a paste preservative to 0.5 m past the last signs of decay. Preservative may need to be caulked into predrilled holes if the timber is thick. If the timber is wet, a preservative formulation based on ethylene glycol and boron will give the best penetration. 5. Remove timber lintels within the zone of decay and replace with an inorganic material. (It may be possible to retain hard old oak if fungus is a superficial growth, but effective treatment of the oak will not be practicable). 6. Remove bonding timbers, grounds and other embedded timbers within zone of decay. Brick up cavities left by timber removal. 7. Resupport structural timbers as necessary using an inorganic material or timber pretreated to BS4072 part 2. The cut ends of pretreated timber should be brush treated or dip treated in an end treatment fluid as supplied by the treatment company. All new timber should be isolated from the walls with an impervious membrane. 8. Remove window and door joinery within the zone of decay; discard, or strip off paint and repair as appropriate. Apply two brush coats of a spirit-based preservative to the edges or backs and replace, isolated from the wall as far as is practicable. 9. Spray treat exposed brickwork and stonework with a water-based fungicide.
9a	Client prepared to accept small risk of further damage as structure dries. Particularly if timbers are good-quality historical softwood or a hardwood.	Treatment B; monitor	1. Remove all sources of water penetration. 2. Expose cavities as far as practicable by lifting floorboards etc. and leave exposed for as long as possible. 3. Thoroughly clean out all debris and loose

key continued . . .

(9a)		(Treatment B)	or unimportant decayed material from the zone of decay. 4. Consider the installation of a remote moisture-sensing system to detect any further wetting of the structure. The following additional measures may be relevant if the structure is softwood: 5. Paste treat accessible softwood timber to within 100 mm of decorated surfaces. 6. Treat embedded timbers by partial exposure and paste application or by localized wall irrigation.
9b	No risks acceptable; guaranteed treatments required.	Treatment A	(see above)

196

Dry rot case studies

B.1 Case study 1: Arniston House, Midlothian

Arniston House was constructed between 1720 and 1730 to a design by William Adam. Additions were subsequently made in 1755. Two of the most splendidly decorated rooms in the building were the dining room and the drawing room (Figure B.1).

In 1957 dry rot was uncovered during rewiring works, and one of the major remedial firms of the time was asked to investigate the situation. The result was almost total destruction of the two principal rooms, and of the rooms above. Because of the cost, it is only now, 40 years later, that repairs can be contemplated.

In 1995 it was estimated by the architect that the damage wrought in the president's drawing room alone would cost about £150 000 to repair.

Arniston was visited in 1995 in order to try to ascertain the true extent of the fungus and thus to assess the effectiveness of the treatment that had been carried out. This is usually possible even after many years because strands of fungus will still be present within the walls. These are inevitably visible within joints and behind loose stones because they are not removed by the treatment process even if the walls are brushed down. It was found that walls, ceilings and floors had all been partially or totally stripped out (Figure B.2). Joists and floor beams had been cut back and the thick, rubble-filled stone walls had been irrigated as part of the work carried out in 1957. There were, however, no indications of dry rot.

It must be assumed that some dry rot had been present, probably in the joist and rafter bearings at roof level. One beam bearing which still remains buried in the wall does have some unidentified brown rot damage on one edge. These timbers were, however, constructed from excellent quality slow-grown imported softwood, and it is unlikely that they really needed to be cut back, as they had been, to about 1 m from the wall.

The first-floor walls had all been irrigated, probably with considerable difficulty because many of the holes penetrate stone blocks. The irrigation of thick, rubble-filled stone walls is a pointless procedure because the fluid finds its own route through the wall and much of the fungus will remain untouched by the fungicide.

There is little doubt that if dry rot at roof level had been sufficiently extensive to require such drastic exposure work at principal floor level then the walls of the first floor (in between the two zones) would have been thoroughly coated with fungus. Remaining window linings are, however, unaffected and, as noted above, there were no signs of fungus within the walls.

This problem could have been dealt with by making whatever roof repairs were necessary. Exposure work need not have been continued down to the principal floor; it may not even have been necessary to the extent that it was undertaken on the first floor. Any fungus that was present behind the plaster would have died through lack of water, and would in any case have found it difficult to attack the high-quality timbers. Any strengthening of the drawing room ceiling joist

Figure B.1 The drawing room at Arniston House before dry rot treatment.

bearings that was required could have been undertaken from above without destroying the ceiling.

It would be pleasant to be able to say that the needless destruction carried out here was typical of past practices now superseded, but we cannot. The attitude of the immediate post-war period, that dry rot was a 'cancer of buildings' which could only be cured by ruthless treatments, remains prevalent. The legacy of this period is continuing destruction of historic fabric, which may be unintentional, but which is certainly unnecessarily carried out in the name of exposure work or treatment.

B.2 Case study 2: Bute Hall, University of Glasgow

Bute Hall was built in the 1860s to a design by Sir George Gilbert Scott, and altered between 1878 and 1884 by J. Oldrid Scott. The roof (Figure B.3) is constructed from Baltic redwood with a high natural durability. There are ample signs in many places that water penetration has occurred over long periods of time, but few signs of decay. Insect damage is minimal because the timber sapwood content is low. Some decay is, however, present at the eaves.

Rafters bear onto a quartered 225 mm^2 softwood plate. This, in the sections which could be closely examined because of earlier exposure work, had been laid so that the less durable core was in the lower outer quadrant. This would have been a usual method of positioning, but the juvenile wood was thus in the dampest position when water penetration occurred and has decayed along much of its length. The plate was probed in 42 places using a Sibert decay drill. In most of these samples the decay zone was only a small percentage (perhaps 5%) of the cross-sectional area.

Figure B.2 The drawing room at Arniston House after dry rot treatment.

Figure B.3 Bute Hall, University of Glasgow, showing the boarded ceiling timbers in contact with a damp wall.

The plate carrying the timber ceiling of the hall is secured to the wall by timber fixing blocks. At least four of these blocks, which measure about 275 mm · 150 mm · 375 mm, have been destroyed by dry rot. The blocks have decayed because they were built into damp masonry, but a 37 mm (approximate) gap between the wall and the ceiling timbers has largely protected the latter from decay (Figure B.4). The causes of the decay have been faults in the leadwork of the parapet gutter, exacerbated by frequent blockages in gutters and outlet boxes.

Orthodox treatment would require substantial timber loss and preservative treatment both in the roof and in the decorative interior of the hall. The decay that has been located is largely historical and there are no indications of current activity.

We do not believe that the use of preservatives is necessary or justifiable in this case. Decayed timber may safely remain *in situ*, provided that the roof and ceiling can be made structurally sound, and further slow deterioration will not occur as long as future water penetration is avoided. The gutters should be releaded and a moisture monitoring system would be useful as a back-up to routine maintenance.

B.3 Case study 3: Walsworth Hall, Gloucestershire

Walsworth Hall (Figure B.5) is a fine, brick-built house that dates from the early eighteenth century. Its recent history, as far as it concerns this case

Figure B.4 Bute Hall, University of Glasgow: the ceiling trimmer was attached to the wall by fixing blocks. Dry rot has destroyed a fixing block and the surface growth on the trimmer is now isolated from a moisture source and will die.

study, commences in 1953 when, having been a nursing home for many years, it was purchased with 20 acres of land by a neighbouring farmer. The farmer wanted the land to expand his farm and had no interest in the house, which was by that time rather dilapidated. A minimal expenditure was made in order to partition it into eight flats, and the building was then totally neglected until 1979, when the farmer died having bequeathed the house to his grandchildren. They obtained estimates for repairs, but found that it would cost £30 000 just to make the roof weathertight and so, in 1983, the house was sold at auction with no reserve.

The new owner decided to restore the property for resale, and accordingly, over the next few years, embarked upon what is picturesquely, though perhaps vulgarly, termed a 'tart-up job'. That is to say that only obvious faults were remedied and the rest were concealed. The house was then sold again. This concealment of decay was not spotted by the prospective purchaser's surveyor, so that the new owners, who knew nothing of the building's history, found extensive dry rot within a few months. The legal wrangle that ensued need not concern us, but the causes and consequences of the dry rot are of considerable interest.

Four remedial firms were invited to make a survey and provide a report with estimates for treatment and repair. The following quotations were received: £2 220 (for exposure work only), £3 200, £6 900 and £20 500 – a wide but not unusual spread of estimates, which demonstrates the advantage of obtaining several quotations.

Figure B.6 shows the spread of fungus along the front wall and there are three observations of interest to be made at first-floor level:

1. Two rainwater pipes were replaced during the refurbishment works.
2. There are irrigation holes for dry rot treatment along the front wall of room 2.
3. The fungus spreads along most of the front wall of room 3 behind a new skirting (Figures B.7 and B.8).

Observation 1 suggests that the previous down-pipes were in poor condition, whereas observation 2 indicates that there had been a problem which was identified and treated as dry rot. The water which caused the latter had probably come from faults in the parapet gutter above. The dry rot should have been killed by the releading of gutters and the replacement of rainwater goods during the

Figure B.5 Walsworth Hall, Gloucestershire.

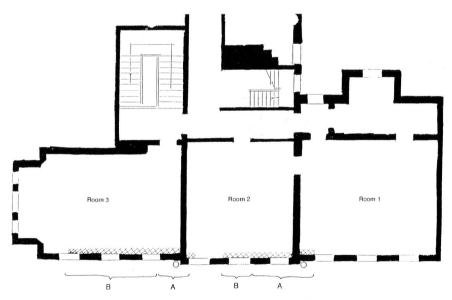

Figure B.6 The spread of dry rot at first-floor level, Walsworth Hall, Gloucestershire: (A) = fungus present before the restoration; (B) = fungus spread by wall washing; cross-hatched area = dry rot.

Figure B.7 Dry rot in room 3 at Walsworth Hall was able to spread along skirtings from a faulty downpipe because of exterior wall washing.

refurbishment works; it should not have spread along the walls behind the skirtings.

The key to this anomaly, and therefore to the treatment required, was found when the refurbishment works were re-examined. The developer, anxious to present the building as attractively as possible, had thoroughly washed down the exterior. Water had percolated into the brickwork and reactivated the fungus, which found the new skirting to be an easily exploited source of food and therefore spread along the front wall.

Reactivation of the fungus was caused by an event which would not recur, provided that the gutter and downpipes did not allow more water into the walls. Some structural damage which had been concealed had to be repaired, but most of the remedial works entailed removing the decayed timber and lifting floorboards along the walls to encourage drying. The wall plaster was not damp-stained or detached and so it was left on the walls even though this probably retarded drying.

B.4 Case study 4: Sea Captain's House and Calendering Works, Dundee

The Sea Captain's House (Figure B.9) dates from about 1770 and is one of the oldest buildings in Dundee. Behind it is a Calendering Works dating from 1822, and the two buildings were linked in about 1890. The buildings continued in use processing jute until the early 1970s, when they were taken over by a carpet company and used as a store. What maintenance there had been ceased; water poured into the walls from blocked/faulty rainwater goods and from the disrepair of the link roof, that joined both buildings at first-floor

Figure B.8 Detail of Figure B.7, showing dry rot on the wall behind the skirting.

Figure B.9 The Sea Captain's House, Dundee, before restoration.

window sill height (Figure B.10). This resulted in extensive decay by wet rots and dry rot.

In recent years a building company acquired the site and applied for permission to demolish the Sea Captain's House. This proposal was out-manoeuvred by the Dundee Building Preservation Trust, which successfully applied for the buildings to be listed, purchased both for 50 pence each and initiated a feasibility study for re-use.

The control of the dry rot was an initial consideration, and a reputable local timber treatment firm was asked to produce a report. This was a very cautious document because exposure work might uncover more decay. Extensive stripping out and chemical sterilization was recommended, and the likely cost of treatment and timber repair was provisionally set at £23 000. This represented

a considerable initial investment, and a more detailed survey of the building was therefore undertaken. The results are discussed below.

The building is constructed from thick, random-bedded stonework walls with rubble cores. The early nineteenth-century dates of both buildings, taken in conjunction with Dundee's importance as a port, strongly suggest that the original timbers would have been imported. The close grain of the roof timbers, their rich red colour and the lack of much insect activity despite years of neglect, all suggest that the timber is slow-grown north European redwood, probably shipped from the Baltic. Decay is thus likely to be restricted to embedded sections of structural timbers except where excessively high humidities have maintained timber moisture contents that approach fibre

Figure B.10 Many sources of water penetration at the rear of the building. Note the roof that connects the Sea Captain's House to the Calendering Works.

saturation. Each floor of the Sea Captain's House provides some useful information, and will be discussed in turn.

Attic
It was immediately obvious that decay was restricted to the periphery of the building where faulty or damaged rainwater goods had channelled water into the walls (Figure B.11). Walls hold the moisture, and the timber therefore remains wet for an extended period of time. Two or three types of fungi had caused the damage, and the risk of dry rot or wet rot attack was controlled by the probability of spore germination and growth rather than by variations in local moisture content. Insect damage also occurred in the vicinity of the walls because the elevated humidities and

consequent timber equilibrium moisture contents were advantageous to larval development.

The decay in the two east truss bearings along the front wall made it advisable to expose the two west bearings.

First floor
The dry rot in the roof above Room 4 spread out and extended down the walls because considerable volumes of water had entered the walls at gutter level. This water was augmented by the damaged link roof, which drained into the same wall at sill level. The latter encouraged dry rot in the north-east corner rooms (Figure B.12).

The dry rot above Room 7, however, had no additional supply of water, and the water from the original fault was not sufficient to carry the fungus down past window head level.

Ground floor
An additional complication occurred at this level (Figure B.13). Whereas the dry rot in Room 1 was simply the result of the fungus spreading down the saturated wall, the dry rot in Room 3 was less easy to understand. This fungus extended up the wall to dado height and appeared therefore to have been caused by rising damp. It was, however, in an internal wall.

The answer became apparent when the construction of the floors was considered. The suspended floor in Room 3 is surrounded on three sides by solid floors (concrete slabs replacing the original, suspended timber floors) and the floors of the link space and Calendering Works were also solid. The water that poured down through the rear wall of the building saturated the ground below the solid floors. This trapped water tended to rise to the surface in the first available positions, which were the north and west walls of Room 3. The result was dry rot in the floor and joinery. Rooms 1 and 2 also have suspended floors surrounded by solid floors, but a cellar extends beneath them, giving a far greater surface area for evaporation.

Treatment
Environmental control by leaving all sound timber and plaster alone and relying on drying was not an

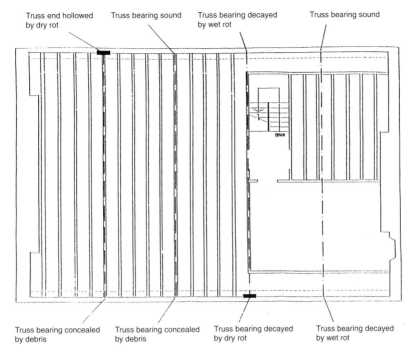

Figure B.11 Sea Captain's House, Dundee: attic floor. Thick lines show the extent of dry rot.

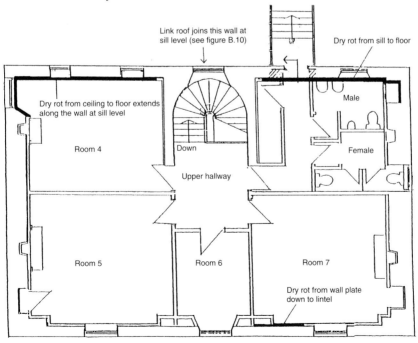

Figure B.12 Sea Captain's House, Dundee: first floor. Thick lines show dry rot extent.

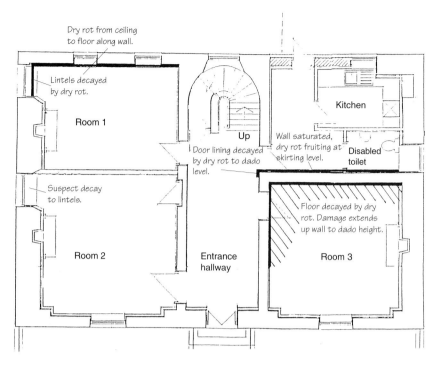

Figure B.13 Sea Captain's House, Dundee: ground floor. Thick lines show the extent of dry rot.

appropriate option, except perhaps in Room 7. Structural timbers were repaired and the water penetration was halted, but the walls would still take many months to dry. The fungus would be liable to spread and fruit through the walls until significant drying had been achieved.

Damaged and saturated plaster was removed from within the zones of dry rot to accelerate drying. This inevitably led to the loss of original materials (although much of these were in any case damaged by damp), but their retention would have significantly complicated the proceedings, and the results might not have been entirely satisfactory for the client. Dry rot can occasionally be surprisingly persistent, and a non-destructive approach with saturated walls is not a commercial proposition.

In the case of the Sea Captain's House and Calendering Works the careful survey and limited treatment advocated enabled a cost saving of about one-third to be made on remedial works and timber replacement (Figure B.14). A local remedial

company treated the building in accordance with the new specification, and issued their guarantee.

B.5 Case study 5: Lees Court, Kent

This building was constructed during the mid-seventeenth century by a local builder, in the style of Inigo Jones. In about 1913, the building was substantially damaged by fire, and required considerable reconstruction.

Of particular interest here is the roof truss bearing shown in Figure B.15. There would seem to have been dry rot in the vicinity, because both the wall and the timber have irrigation holes drilled in them. The wall plate has been coated with a paste preservative, which was held against the timber with polythene. There are two interesting lessons to be learnt from this treatment.

First, the treatment suggests the presence of dry rot, but the brickwork around the truss bearing had

Figure B.14 The Sea Captain's House after restoration.

not been disturbed. There was no sign that any effort had been made to investigate the structural integrity of the tie beam and there may have been significant concealed decay.

Second, the cause of the problem had apparently been a blocked or faulty parapet gutter. This gutter had not been repaired by the time of our inspection, and there was a fine growth of dry rot in the irrigation holes (Figure B.16). This confirms the fact that most treatments with biocides are likely to fail unless the source of moisture is removed. Fungicidal treatments should be seen as a stabilizing measure as the structure dries, rather than as a solution to the problem on their own.

The remedial works specified were to relead the gullies and to investigate the condition of the concealed bearings.

B.6 Case study 6: Christchurch, Waterloo, Merseyside

Designed by Paley, Austin and Paley of Lancaster, Christchurch was started in 1891. It is built with sandstone which has been selected and laid so that natural bonding produces a highly decorative interior (Figure B.17). The church has been redundant for about 10 years and has suffered from severe vandalism. At the time of writing it seems likely that it will be taken over by the Churches Conservation Trust, who have initiated current repair works.

Vandalism and lack of maintenance had resulted in extensive water penetration and decay by dry rot and the obscure wet rot fungus *Schizoporus flavipora*, but two factors have restricted the damage and treatment required.

First, the walls do not contain any bonding or levelling timbers below plate level, so that there are

Figure B.15
Partial dry rot
treatment at
Lees Court,
Kent. Note the
irrigation holes
in the wall at
the tie beam.

Figure B.16
Dry rot
growing in an
irrigation hole
at Lees Court,
Kent, because
the source of
moisture was
not removed.

Figure B.17 The interior of Christchurch, Waterloo.

Figure B.18 A section of wild-grown Baltic pine with 209 growth rings. Most of the timber is mature heartwood with a good resistance to decay. Dry rot has attacked the timber where it was in contact with a wet wall.

no further food sources that might allow dry rot to spread down the wall. Dry rot is of no consequence in a wall, provided that there is nothing for it to attack. Wall irrigation would be meaningless as a treatment, but it would disfigure the surface and might promote salt efflorescence as the wall dried.

Second, the timber was wild-grown Baltic pine, and the section shown in Figure B.18 had 209 growth rings. It was therefore mostly mature heartwood with a good natural durability. The fungus had considerable difficulty in decaying the timber, and damage was restricted to zones where there was substantial water penetration. Cutting back the timbers to a safety-margin past the decay would have been an unjustifiable waste of an irreplaceable material.

The repair policy chosen has been to eliminate water penetration and to clear all accumulated debris from around the timbers to allow drying. Decayed bearings have been cut back to sound. Smaller section replacement components were pretreated with copper–chromium–arsenic to BS 4072. Larger section timbers were not pretreated. All replacement timber was isolated from the walls with a membrane because the walls would take many months to dry. Original timber which was judged to be sound enough to retain was treated *in situ* with a paste preservative containing boron in order to obtain a good depth of biocide penetration in the damp timber.

References and bibliography

Aaron, J. and Richards, E. (1990) *British Woodland Produce*, Stobart Davies, London.

Adler, E. (1977) Lignin chemistry – past, present and future, *Wood Science and Technology*, **11**, 169–218.

Ahmet, K. (1994) A note on the discrepancy between various moisture meters, in *ASTM Hand-Held Moisture Meter Workshop*, **49**, Forest Products Society, Madison, USA.

Anderson, M.L. (1967) *A History of Scottish Forestry*, C.J. Taylor (ed.), Thomas Nelson, London.

Bagchee, K. (1954) *Merulius lacrymans* (Wulf) Fr. in India, *Sydowia*, **8**, 80–85.

Baines, F. (1914) *Report to the First Commissioner of H.M. Works on the Condition of the Roof Timbers of Westminster Hall, with Suggestions for Maintaining the Stability of the Roof*, HMSO, London.

Baker, A.J. (1974) *Degradation of Wood by Products of Metal Corrosion*, Forest Services Research Paper FPL229, United States Department of Agriculture, Madison, USA.

Baker, G. (1967) Estimating specific gravity of plantation-grown red pine, *Forest Products Journal*, **17** (8), 21–24.

Baker, J.J. (1988) Corrosion of metals in preservative treated wood, *Wood Protection Techniques and the Use of Treated Wood in Construction*, Forest Products Research Society Proceedings 47358, Forest Products Research Society, Madison, USA.

Baker, J.M. (1956) Investigations on the oak pinhole borer *Platypus cylindrus* Fab., a progress report, *Record of the 1956 Annual Convention of the British Wood Preserving Association*, 92–102.

Baker, J.M. (1964) Flight behaviour in some Anobiid beetles, *Proceedings of the 12th International Congress in Entomology*, London, 319–320.

Baker, J.M. (1969) Digestion of wood by *Anobium punctatum* de Geer and comparison with some other wood-boring beetles, *Proceedings of the Royal Entomological Society of London. Series C Journal of Meetings*, **33** (8), 31–33.

Baker, J.M. (1970) Wood boring weevils in buildings, *Timberlab News*, **4**, 6–7.

Baker, J.M. (1972) The pest status of British wood-boring insects, *Record of the 1972 Annual Convention of the British Wood Preserving Association*, 3–16.

Barber, N.F. (1968) A theoretical model of shrinking wood, *Holzforschung*, **22**, 99–103.

Barber, N.F. and Meylan, B.A. (1964) The anisotropic shrinkage of wood. A theoretical model, *Holzforschung*, **18**, 146–156.

Bariska, M., Pizzi, A. and Conradie, W. (1988) Structural weakening of CCA treated timber, *Holzforschung*, **42** (5), 339–345.

Barrett, J. and Kellogg, R.M. (1984) *Strength and Stiffness of Second-growth Douglas Fir Dimension Lumber*. Paper prepared for the Science Council of British Columbia by Forintek Canada Corp., Vancouver, BC.

Bayley Butler, J. (1951) Dry rot Part III: The technique of examining buildings in order to locate dry rot fungi and a description of methods of eradication and reinstatement, *Architects Journal*, Feb, 252–259.

Beall, F.C. (1982) Effect of temperature on the structural uses of wood and wood products, in R.W. Meyer and R.M. Kellogg (eds) *Structural Use of Wood in Adverse Environments*, Society of Wood Science and Technology, Van Nostrand Reinhold Company, New York, 9–19.

Beaver, R.A. (1989) *Insect Fungus Relationships in the Bark and Ambrosia Beetle, Insect-Fungus Interactions*, Academic Press, London, 121–143.

Bech Anderson, J. (1991) *The Dry Rot Fungus and Other Fungi in Houses*, International Research Group on

Wood Preservation document IRG/WP/2389, Hussvamp Laboratoriet Aps, Denmark.

Becker, G. (1942) Ökologische und physiologische Untersuchungen über die holzzerstörenden Larven von *Anobium punctatum* Deg., *Zeitschrift für Morphologie und Ökologie Tiere*, **39**, 98–151.

Becker, G. (1943) Zur Ökologie und Physiologie holzzerstörender Käfer, *Zeitschrift für angewante Entomologie*, **30**, 104–118.

Becker, G. (1977) Ecology and physiology of wood destroying Coleoptera in structural timber, *Material und Organismen*, **12** (3), 141–160.

Becker, G. (1976) Some effects on decay of wood caused by redistribution of nutrients during drying, in T.A. Oxley, B. King and K.D. Long (eds) *Record of the 1976 Annual Convention of the British Wood Preserving Association*, 87–99.

Becker, G. and Weber, W. (1952) *Theocolax formiciformis* Westwood (Hym. Chalcid.) Ein Anobienparasit, *Zeitschrift für Parasitenkunde*, **15**, 339–352.

Behrenz, W. and Technau, G. (1959) Versuche zur Bekämpfung von *Anobium punctatum* mit Symbionticiden, *Zeitschrift für angewante Entomologie*, **44** (1), 22–28.

Belmain, S., Simmonds, M. and Blaney, W. (1999) Life cycle and feeding habits of the Deathwatch beetle (*Xestobium rufovillosum De Geer*), *English Heritage Research Transactions*, Volume 5, in press.

Berry, W.R. and Orsler, R.J. (1985) *Timbers, Their Natural Durability and Resistance to Preservative Treatment*, Building Research Establishment Digest 296, Building Research Establishment, Watford.

Birch, M.C. and Keenlyside, J.J. (1991) Tapping behaviour is a rhythmic communication in the death watch beetle (*Xestobium rufovillosum*), *Journal of Insect Behaviour*, **4** (2), 257–263.

Blake, E.G. (1925) *Enemies of Timber, Dry Rot and Deathwatch Beetle*, Chapman & Hall, London.

Blanchette, R.A., Nilsson, T., Daniel, G. and Abad, A. (1990) Biological degradation of wood in archeological wood: properties, chemistry and preservation, in R.M. Rowell and R.J. Barbour (eds) *Advances in Chemistry Series 225*, American Chemical Society, Washington, USA, 141–174.

Bletchley, J.D. (1952) A summary of some recent work on the factors affecting egg laying and hatching in *Anobium punctatum* de Geer, *Transactions of the 9th International Congress of Entomology*, **1**, 728–734.

Bletchley, J.D. (1957) The biological work of the Forest Products Research Laboratory, Princes Risborough, III: the work of the entomology section with particular reference to the common furniture beetle *Anobium punctatum* de Geer, *Proceedings of the Linnaean Society*, **168**, 111–115.

Bletchley, J.D. (1966) Aspects of the habits and nutrition of the Anobiidae with special reference to *Anobium punctatum* de Geer, *Beihefte zu Material und Organismen (Internationales Symposium Berlin-Dahelm 1965)*, supplement to *Material und Organismen*, 371–381.

Bletchley, J.D. (1969) Seasonal differences in nitrogen content of Scots pine (*Pinus sylvestris*) sapwood and their effects on development of the larvae of the common furniture beetle (*Anobium punctatum* de Geer), *Journal of the Institute of Wood Science*, **4** (22), 43–47.

Bletchley, J.D. and Farmer, R.H. (1959) Some investigations into the susceptibility of Corsican and Scots pines and of European oak to attack by the common furniture beetle *Anobium punctatum* de Geer (Col. Anobiidae), *Journal of the Institute of Wood Science*, **3**, 2–20.

Bordass, W. (1997) The underside corrosion of lead roofs and its prevention, *English Heritage Research Transactions*, **1**, 1–52.

Bowden, A. (1815) *A Treatise on the Dry Rot*, Burton & Briggs, London.

Bravery, A.F. (1991) The strategy for eradication of *Serpula lacrymans*, in D.H. Jennings and A.F. Bravery (eds), *Serpula lacrymans: Fundamental Biology and Control Strategies*, John Wiley & Sons, Chichester.

Bravery, A.F. (1992) *Wood Preservation in Europe: Development of Standards for Preservatives and Treated Wood*, Building Research Establishment, Watford.

Bravery, A.F., Berry, R.W., Carey, J.K. and Cooper, D.E. (1992) *Recognising Wood Rot and Insect Damage in Buildings*, Building Research Establishment, Watford.

Brereton, C. (1995) *The Repair of Historic Buildings: Advice on Principles and Methods*, English Heritage, London.

British Wood Preserving and Damp Proofing Association (December 1952) *Guidance Notes on the Construction (Design and Management) Regulations*, 2nd issue.

Britton, T.A. (1875) *A Treatise on the Origin, Progress, Prevention and Cure of Dry Rot in Timber*, E. & F.N. Spon, London.

Broese Van Groenou, H., Rischen, H. and Van den Berge, J. (1951) *Wood Preservation during the Last 50 Years*, A.W. Sijthoff's Uitgeversmaatschappij N.V., Leiden, Holland.

Brown, J., Fahim, M.M. and Hutchinson, S.A. (1968) Some effects of atmospheric humidity on the growth of *Serpula lacrymans*, *Transactions of the British Mycological Society*, 77, 33–40.

Browne, F.L. (1960) Wood sidings left to weather naturally, *Southern Lumberman*, **201** (2513), 141–143.

Browne Morton, W. (1976) Field procedures for examining humidity in masonry buildings, *Association for Preservation Technology Bulletin*, **8** (2), 2–19.

Browning, B. (1963) *The Chemistry of Wood*, Interscience, New York and London.

Bruun, H. and Wilberg, J. (1964) The heartwood contents of pine (*Pinus silvestris*) and spruce (*Picea abies*), *Paperi ja Puu*, **46** (4), 221–227.

Bryant, P. (1984) The impact of fast growth on wood quality and utilisation, *Proceedings of Symposium on Site and Productivity of Fast Growing Plantations*, IUFRO, Pretoria.

Buchwald, G. (1986) *On Donkioporia expansa (Desm.) Kotl and Pouzer*, International Research Group on Wood Preservation, Document No. IRG/WP/1285.

Building Research Establishment (1983) *Emulsion-based Formulations for Remedial Treatments against Woodworm*, Information Paper 15/83, Building Research Establishment, Watford.

Building Research Establishment (1986a) *Controlling Death Watch Beetle*, Information Paper 19/86, Building Research Establishment, Watford.

Building Research Establishment (1986b) *Identifying Damage by Wood Boring Insects*, Digest 307, Building Research Establishment, Watford.

Building Research Establishment (1987) *Insecticidal Treatments against Wood-Boring Insects*, Digest 327, Building Research Establishment, Watford.

Building Research Establishment (1989) *Wet Rots: Recognition and Control*, Digest 345, Building Research Establishment, Watford.

Building Research Establishment (1993) *Dry Rot: Its Recognition and Control*, Digest 299, Building Research Establishment, Watford.

Burkholder, W.E. and Phillips, J.K. (1988) Trapping techniques for Dermestid and Anobiid beetles, in L.A. Zacherman and J.R. Schrock (eds) *A Guide to Museum Pest Control*, Foundation of the American Institute for Conservation of Historical and Artistic Works and the Association of Systematic Collections, USA.

Burnell, F.G.S. (1860) On building woods: the causes of their decay and the means of preventing it, *Journal of the Society of Arts*, 554–567.

Campbell, W.G. and Bryant, S.A. (1940) A chemical study of the bearing of decay by *Phellinus cryptarum* Karst. and other fungi on the destruction of wood by the death watch beetle (*Xestobium rufovillosum* de Geer), *The Biochemical Journal*, **34** (10/11), 1404–1414.

Carey, J., Savory, J., Mendes, F. and Bravery, A. (undated) Unpublished poster abstract. Building Research Establishment, Watford.

Cartwright, K. St. G. and Findlay, W.P.K. (1933) Dry rot in wood, *Bulletin of the Forest Products Research Laboratory*, **1** (2nd edn).

Cartwright, K. St. G. and Findlay, W.P.K. (1936) *The Principal Rots of English Oak*, HMSO, London.

Cartwright, K. St. G. and Findlay, W.P.K. (1946) *Decay of Timber and its Prevention*, HMSO, London.

Cartwright, K. St. G. and Findlay, W.P.K. (1952) Dry rot in wood, *Forest Products Research Bulletin*, **1** (5th edn), HMSO, London.

Catt, R. (1991) Timber repairs and treatment, *The Building Surveyor*, **2**, 10.

Chalk, L. (1963) Variation in density in stems of Douglas fir, *Forestry*, **26** (1), 33–36.

Chapman, R.F. (1971) *The Insects, Structure and Function* (2nd edn), English Universities Press, London.

Charles, F.W.B. (1984) *Conservation of Timber Buildings*, Donhead, London.

Chattaway, M.M. (1949) The development of tyloses and secretion of gum in heartwood formation, *Australian Journal of Scientific Research (B)*, **2**, 227–240.

Chen, Z., Wengert, M. and Lamb, F.M. (1994) A technique to electrically measure the moisture content of wood above fibre saturation, *Forest Products Journal*, **44** (9), 57–62.

Coggins, C.R. (1977) *Aspects of the Growth of Serpula lacrymans the Dry Rot Fungus*, Ph.D. Thesis, University of Liverpool.

Coggins, C.R. (1991) Growth characteristics in a building, in D.H. Jennings and A.F. Bravery (eds) *Serpula lacrymans. Fundamental Biology and Control Strategies*, John Wiley & Sons, Chichester.

Coleman, R.F. (1977) Toxicity of permethrin smoke to adult deathwatch beetle *Xestobium rufovillosum*, *International Biodeterioration Bulletin*, **13** (2), 49–50.

Coleman, R.F. (1978) A laboratory evaluation of the effectiveness of Gamma-HCH smoke deposits against deathwatch beetle, *Xestobium rufovillosum* de Geer, *International Pest Control*, **20** (2), 16–18.

Coleman, R.F. (1999) The chemical control of death watch beetle, *English Heritage and Research Transactions*, 5, in press.

Connell, M. (1991) Industrial wood preservatives: their history, development, uses, advantages and future trends, in R. Thompson (ed.) *The Chemistry of Wood Preservation*, The Royal Society of Chemistry, London, 16–33.

Cope, B., Garringon, N., Mathews, A. and Watt, D. (1995) Biocide residues as a hazard in a building under conservation: pentachlorophenol at Melton Constable Hall, *Journal of Architectural Conservation*, 1 (2), 36–44.

Corona, E. (1966) Variations and disagreements in series of annual growth rings, *Monti e Boschi*, 17 (2), 27–34 (Ref. Forestry Abstracts 1966: 6527).

Cowling, E.B. and Merrill, W. (1966) Nitrogen in wood and its role in wood deterioration, *Canadian Journal of Botany*, 44, 1533–1544.

Cox, R.N. and Laidlaw, R.A. (1984) The effect of preservatives on the corrosion of galvanised metal plate fasteners in timber, Part 2, the relative corrosivity of 'salt' and 'oxide' formulations of copper-chrome-arsenic (CCA), *The Journal of the Institute of Wood Science*, 10 (2), 87–90.

Cross, N.J., Bailey, G., Sussen, G. and Schofield, A. (1989) Performance of metal fasteners in CCA treated timber, *Record of the 1989 Annual Convention of the British Wood Preserving Association*, 3–5.

Cymorek, S. (1965) Verfahren zur beschleunigten Züchtung des *Anobium punctatum* und Laboratorium, *Proceedings of the 12th International Congress of Entomology* (1964), London, 687–689.

Cymorek, S. (1968) *Hylotrupes bajulus* – Verpuppung und Flug, deren Klimaabhängigkeit und Beziehung zur Artverbreitung, *Zeitschrift für angewandte Entomologie*, 62, 316–344.

Dawson, H.B. and Czipri, J.J. (1991) Microemulsions – A new development for the wood preservation industry, *Wood Protection*, 1 (2), 55–60.

Dean, A.R. (1972) A practical comparison of moisture determination by means of the oven drying method and the use of electrical moisture meters, in *Report of a Seminar on Moisture Content Determination of Wood*, Timberlab Papers 24-1970, 21–25 (reprinted 1972), Building Research Establishment/Princes Risborough Laboratory.

Decock, C. and Hennbest, G.L. (1994) *Wood-decaying Fungi in Belgian Buildings: 4 Years of Investigations*, Fifth International Mycological Congress, Poster Abstracts, Vancouver.

Desch, H.E. and Dinwoodie, J.M. (1981) *Timber, its Structure, Properties and Utilisation* (6th edn of Desch, H.E., 1968), Macmillan Education, London.

Dewar, A.H. (1933) Some experiments in the control of dry-rot in floors, *Journal of the British Wood Preserving Association*, 3, 33–45.

Dickinson, D.J. and Murphy, R.J. (1991) The cause and control of pre-treatment decay in home-grown poles, in *Record of the 1991 Annual Convention of the British Wood Preserving and Damp-Proofing Association*, 41–50.

Docks, E.L. (1991) Developing quality control procedures and standards for diffusible preservatives, in R.Thompson (ed.) *The Chemistry of Wood Preservation*, The Royal Society of Chemistry, London, 177–191.

Dodd, R. (1815) *Practical Observations on the Dry Rot in Timber*, Hatchard, London.

Drow, J. (1957) *Relations of Locality and Rate of Growth to Density and Strength of Douglas Fir*, Forest Service, Forest Products Laboratory Report 2078, United States Department of Agriculture.

Duff, J.E. (1966) *A Probe for Accurate Determination of Moisture Content of Wood Products in Use*, Forest Service, Forest Products Laboratory Research Note 0142, United States Department of Agriculture.

Duffy, E.A.J. (1954) Research on long-horned timber beetles and its relationship to timber preservation, *Record of the 1954 Annual Convention of the British Wood Preserving Association*, 80–90.

Ealand, C.A. (1916) *Insect Enemies*, Grant Richards, London.

Edwards, R. and Mill, A.E. (1986) *Termites in Buildings: Their Biology and Control*, The Rentokil Library, East Grinstead.

Elliot, G. (1970) *Wood Density in Conifers*, Commonwealth Forestry Bureau Technical Communications, 8.

Encyclopaedia Britannica (4th edn) (1824) Dry-rot: 677–684.

Erikson, H. and Harrison, A. (1974) Effects of age and stimulated growth on wood density and anatomy, *Wood Science and Technology*, 8 (3), 207–226.

Esser, P. and Tas, A. (1999) The roles of location, age and fungal decay in the chemical composition of oak, *English Heritage Research Transactions*, Volume 5, in press.

Falck, R. (1912) *Die Merulius-fäule des Bauholzes*, in A. Möller (ed.) *Hausschwammforschungen*, Jena: Fischer, 6, 1–405.

Faraday, M. (1836) *On the Practical Prevention of Dry Rot in Timber*, Lecture given at the Royal Institution, 22 February 1833, Adlard, London.

Feist, W.C. (1982) Weathering of wood in structural uses, in R.W. Meyer and R.M. Kellog (eds) *Structural Use of Wood in Adverse Environments*, Society of Wood Science and Technology, London, and Van Nostrand Reinhold, New York, 156–178.

Feist, W.C. and Mraz, E.A. (1978) Comparison of outdoor and accelerated weathering of unprotected softwoods, *Forest Products Journal*, **28** (3), 38–43.

Fengel, D. and Wegener, G. (1989) *Wood Chemistry, Ultrastructure, Reactions*, Walter de Gruyter, Berlin.

Findlay, W.P.K. (1953) *Dry Rot and Other Timber Troubles*, Hutchinsons Scientific and Technical Publications, London.

Findlay, W.P.K. and Badcock, E.C. (1954) Survival of dry rot fungi in air dry wood, *Timber Technology*, **62**, 137–138.

Fisher, R.C. (1937) Studies of the biology of the death watch beetle *Xestobium rufovillosum* de Geer I: A summary of the past work and a brief account of the developmental stages, *Annnals of Applied Biology*, **24**, 600–613.

Fisher, R.C. (1938) Studies of the biology of the death watch beetle *Xestobium rufovillosum* de Geer II: The habits of the adult with special reference to the factors affecting oviposition, *Annals of Applied Biology*, **25** (1), 155–180.

Fisher, R.C. (1940) Studies of the biology of the death watch beetle *Xestobium rufovillosum* de Geer III: Fungal decay in timber in relation to the occurrence and rate of development of the insect, *Annals of Applied Biology*, **27**, 545.

Fisher, R.C. (1941) Studies of the biology of the death watch beetle *Xestobium rufovillosum* de Geer IV: The effect of type and extent of fungal decay on the rate of development of the insect, *Annals of Applied Biology*, **28**, 244–260.

Florian, M.L. (1997) *Heritage Eaters: Insects and fungi in heritage collections*, James and James, London.

Foelix, R. (1982) *Biology of Spiders*, Harvard University Press.

Food and Agriculture Organisation of the United Nations (1986) *Wood Preservation Manual 1*, Forestry Paper 76, Rome.

Forest Products Research Laboratory (1947) *Dry Rot in Buildings, Recognition and Care*, Leaflet 6 (revised).

Forest Products Research Laboratory (1962) *The Kiln Sterilization of Lyctus Infested Timber*, Leaflet 13 (revised).

Frankland, A.W., and Hay, M.J. (1951) Dry rot as a cause of allergic complaints, *Acta Allergologica*, **4** (2), 186–200.

Fuller, H. and Moore, C. (1999) Recent studies on the oak rot fungus *Donkioporia expansa*, *English Heritage Research Transactions*, Volume 5, in press.

Gahan, C.J. (1925) *Furniture Beetles, their Life History and How to Check or Prevent the Damage Caused by the Worm*, Economic Series, Natural History 11 (2nd edn), British Museum, London.

Gay, F.J. (1953) Observations on the biology of *Lyctus brunneus* (Step.), *Australian Journal of Zoology*, **1**, 102–110.

George, J. (1829) *The Cause of Dry Rot Discovered*, Longman, London.

Girdwood, J. (1927) *Worms in Furniture and Structural Timber*, Oxford University Press.

Goodburn, D. (1995) Early carpenters and treewrights. An underground view, *The Mortise and Tenon: UK Journal for Traditional Timber Framers, Carpenters and Conservators*, **1**.

Goring, D.A.I. and Timell, T.A. (1962) Molecular weight of native celluloses, *TAPPI*, **40**, 454–460.

Goulson, D., Birch, M.C. and Wyatt, T.D. (1993) Paternal investment in relation to size in the death-watch beetle, *Xestobium rufovillosum* (Coleoptera: Anobiidae), and evidence for female selection for large males, *Journal of Insect Behaviour*, **6** (5), 539–547.

Gray, V.R. (1958) The acidity of timber, *Journal of the Institute of Wood Science*, **1**, 58–64.

Hägglund, E. (1935) Undersükningar üver redbeskäffenhetens inflytande pâ utbyte och kvalitet av sulfit och sulfatmassa 2, Undersükning ar tallved, *Svensk Papperstidning*, **38**, 454–463.

Hakkila, P. (1967) On wood quality in sulphate pulping of Scots pine, *Paperi ja Puu*, **49** (7), 461–464.

Hakkila, P. (1968) Geographic variation of some properties of pine and spruce pulpwood in Finland, *Matsätieteellisen tutkimuslaitoksen julkaisuja*, **66**, 8.

Hall, C., Hoff, W. and Nixon, M. (1984) Water movement in porous building materials – VI, evaporation and drying in brick and block materials, *Building and Environment*, **19** (1), 13–24.

Hall, G.S. (1994) A perspective on wood moisture content and its measurement in Europe, in *ASTM Hand-Held Moisture Meter Workshop*, Forest Products Society, Madison, USA, 33–36.

Hallenberg, N. (1985) *The Lachnocladiaceae and Coniophoraceae of North Europe*, Fungiflora A/S, Oslo.

Hammad, S.M. (1955) The immature stages of *Pentarthrum huttoni* Woll. (Coleoptera: Curculionidae), *Proceedings of the Royal Entomological Society of London (A)*, **30**, 33–39.

Hansen, L.S. (1992) *Use of Freeze Disinfestation for the Control of the Common Furniture Beetle* Anobium punctatum, International Research Group on Wood Preservation, IRG/WP/1528-92.

Harris, E.C. (1969) Assessment of insecticidal smokes for the control of wood-boring insects, *Record of the 1969 Annual Convention of the British Wood Preserving Association*, 5–23.

Harris, E.C. (1977) A long term field trial of Gamma-HCH/dieldrin smoke against death watch beetle (*Xestobium rufovillosum*) in an ancient oak roof, *International Biodeterioration Bulletin*, **13** (3), 61–65.

Harris, J.M. and Meylan, B.A. (1965) The influence of microfibril angle on longitudinal and tangential shrinkage in *Pinus radiata*, *Holzforschung*, **19**, 144–153.

Hart, G. (1990) Economics of softwood lumber drying: cost of degrade, in M.P. Hamel and D. Robertson (eds) *Drying Softwood and Hardwood Lumber for Quality and Profit*, Forest Products Research Society Proceedings 47356, Forest Products Research Society, Madison, USA, 9–12.

Hartig, R. (1874) *Wichtige Krankheiten der Waldbäume*, Julius Springer, Berlin.

Health and Safety Commission (1991) *The Safe Use of Pesticides for Non-agricultural Purposes*, HMSO, London.

Health and Safety Executive and Department of the Environment (1991) *Remedial Timber Treatment in Buildings: A Guide to Good Practice and the Safe Use of Wood Preservatives*, HSE, London.

Henderson, F.Y. (1939) *Timber, Its Properties and Preservation*, Crosby Lockwood & Son, London.

Hickin, N.E. (1945) *Lyctus*: the enemy of home-grown oak, *The Cabinet Maker and Complete House Furnisher*, 25 August, 193–194.

Hickin, N.E. (1949) Woodworm in structural timbers, *The Illustrated Carpenter and Builder*, 10 June.

Hickin, N.E. (1952) *Nacerdes melanura* L. (Col. Oedomeridae) at a considerable height above ground, *Entomologists Monthly Magazine*, **88** (May), 107.

Hickin, N.E. (1953) Bats and the death watch beetle, *The National Builder* (June).

Hickin, N.E. (1957) House longhorn beetle (*Hylotrupes bajulus* L.) in Ireland, *Entomologists Monthly Magazine*, **93** (May), 96.

Hickin, N.E. (1960) An Introduction to the Study of the British *Lyctidae*, *Record of the 1960 Annual Convention of the British Wood Preserving Association*, 57–83.

Hickin, N.E. (1963a) *The Woodworm Problem*, The Rentokil Library, Rentokil Ltd, East Grinstead.

Hickin, N.E. (1963b) *The Dry Rot Problem*, The Rentokil Library, Hutchinson & Co., London.

Hickin, N.E. (1966) *Woodworm, Dry Rot and the Law*, British Wood Preserving Association, News Sheet No. 61.

Hickin, N.E. (1971) *Termites: A World Problem*, The Rentokil Library, Hutchinson & Co., London.

Hickin, N.E. (1975) *The Insect Factor in Wood Decay* (3rd edn) The Rentokil Library, Associated Business Programmes, London.

Highley, T.L. and Scheffer, T.C. (1970) A need for modifying the soil block test for testing natural resistance to white rot, *Mater. Org. Beich*, 5, 281–292.

Hilditch, E.A. (1991) Organic solvent preservatives: application and composition, in R. Thompson (ed.) *The Chemistry of Wood Preservation*, The Royal Society of Chemistry, London.

Holland, G.E. and Orsler, R.J. (1992) *A Preliminary Assessment of the Penetration into Wood Achieved by Bodied Mayonnaise Emulsion Wood Preservatives*, The International Research Group on Wood Preservation, IRG/WP/3725-92.

Hon, D.N.S., Clamson, F. and Feist, W. (1986) Weathering characteristics of hardwood surfaces, *Wood Science and Technology*, **20**, 169–183.

House, F.H. (1965) *Timber at War, an Account of the Organisation and Activities of the Timber Control 1939–1945*, Ernest Benn, London.

Hudson, H.J. (1986) *Fungal Biology*, Edward Arnold, London.

Hum, M., *et al.* (1980) Wood boring weevils of economic importance in Britain, *Journal of the Institute of Wood Science*, **8** (5), 201–207.

Hutson, A.M. (1987) *Bats in Houses*, Fauna and Flora Preservation Society, London.

Ifju, G. (1964) Tensile strength behaviour as a function of cellulose in wood, *Forest Products Journal*, **14**, 366–372.

Jackman, P.E. (1981) The fire behaviour of timber and wood based products, *Journal of the Institute of Wood Science*, **9** (1), 38–45.

Jalava, M. (1952) *Puun rakenne ja ominaisuudet*, Helsinki.

Jane, F.W. (1970) *The Structure of Wood*, A & C Black, London.

Johnson, D. (1981) *The Effect of Forest Stand Thinning on Selected Strength and Pulping Characteristics of Douglas Fir*, M.Sc. Thesis, Oregon State University.

Johnson, J. (1795) *Some Observations on That Distemper in Timber Called Dry Rot*, London.

Kennedy, R. and Jeffries, M.G. (1975) *The Two-Toothed Longhorn* Ambeodontus tristis *(F) (Col. cerambycidae)*

Breeding in Leicestershire, British Wood Preserving Association, News Sheet No. 138.

Klem, G. (1969) The influence of increased growth rate in some wood properties of *P. abies* and *P. sylvestris*, *Medd frå det norske Skogforsekvesen*, **27**, 63–90.

Klem, G. (1970) The effect of a rapid increase in growth rate of Scots pine on drying effects, bending strength and shear strength of wood, *Norsk Skogindustri*, **24** (2), 43–48.

Kobylinski, F. (1969) Macrostructure, density and main mechanical properties of Scots pine wood, *Prace Instytutu Technologie Drewna*, **16** (3), 63–68 (ref. Forestry Abstracts 1970: 7092).

Koch, A.P. (1991) The current status of dry rot in Denmark and control strategies, in D.H. Jenning and A.F. Bravery (eds) *Serpula lacrymans, Fundamental Biology and Control Strategies*, John Wiley & Sons, Chichester.

Koenigs, J.W. (1974) Hydrogen peroxide and iron: a proposed system for decomposition of wood by brown rot Basidiomycetes, *Wood and Fibre*, **6** (1), 66–80.

Koltzenburg, C. (1954) Untersuchung einer auf einem haubholtzstandort erwashsenun Wertholzkeife, *Archiv für Forstwesen*, **3** (5/6), 503–517.

Körting, A. (1975) Hausbockbefall und jahreszeitliche Schwankungen der Holzfeuchtigteit, *Dachstuhl. Prakt. Schädlingsbekämpf*, **27**, 137–138.

Krahmer, R. (1986) Fundamental anatomy of juvenile and mature wood in *Juvenile Wood, What Does it Mean to Forest Management and Forest Products?* Forest Products Research Society, Madison, USA.

Kühne, H., *et al.* (1972) Outdoor weathering tests on wood and exterior wood finishes, *Eidgenossische Materialprüfungs- und Versuchsanstalt* (EMPA) Dübendorf, Bericht, **198**, 1–51.

Kyte, C.T. (1972) Resistance type moisture meters, in *Report of a Seminar on Moisture Content Determination of Wood*, Timberlab Papers, No. 24 (1970, reprinted 1972), Building Research Establishment, Watford and Forest Products Research Laboratory, Princes Risborough, 5–7.

Label, R.A. and Morrell, J.J. (1992) *Wood Microbiology, Decay and its Prevention*, Academic Press, New York and London.

Lamb, F.M. (1990) Reducing stresses and moisture content variation when drying hardwood lumber, in M.P. Hamel and D. Robertson (eds) *Drying Softwood and Hardwood Lumber for Quality and Profit*, Forest Products Research Society Proceedings 47356, Madison, USA, 76–78.

Larson, P. (1957) *Effect of environment on the percentage of summer wood and specific gravity*, Yale School Forestry Bulletin 63.

Lea, R.G. (1994) *House Longhorn Beetle: Geographical Distribution and Pest Status in the UK*, Building Research Establishment Information Paper IP/8/94.

Liese, W. and Bauch, J. (1967) On anatomical causes of the refractory behaviour of spruce and Douglas fir, *Journal of the Institute of Wood Science*, **19**, 3–14.

Lin, R.T. (1967) Review of the electrical properties of wood and cellulose, *Forest Products Journal*, **17** (7), 154–61.

Lingard, J. (1819) *A Philosophic and Practical Inquiry into the Nature and Constitution of Timber*, Evans & Ruffy, London.

Linscott, D. (1967) Wood-boring weevils in Great Britain, *Proceedings of the 2nd International Pest Control Association Conference*, 42–47.

Linscott, D. (1970) *The Amount of Sapwood Now Present in Pinus sylvestris Timber in Building Construction*, British Wood Preserving Association News Sheet 107.

Little, R.L. and Moschler, W.W. (1993) Dry kiln corrosion: a survey of the wood drying industry, *Forest Products Journal*, **43** (2), 6–10.

Little, R.L. and Moschler, W.W. (1994) Controlling corrosion in lumber dry kiln buildings, in *Profitable Solutions for Quality Drying of Softwoods and Hardwoods*, Forest Products Society, Madison, USA, 90–97.

Lloyd, H. and Singh, J. (1994) Inspection, monitoring and environmental control of timber decay, in J. Singh (ed.) *Building Mycology*, E. & F.N. Spon, London, 159–186.

Lloyd, J.D. (1995) *Leaching of Boron Wood Preservatives – A Reappraisal Record of the 1995 Annual Convention of the British Wood Preserving and Damp-Proofing Association*, 52–58.

Locke, P. (1986) *Timber Treatment, a Warning About the Defrassing of Timbers*, Information Sheet 2, Society for the Protection of Ancient Buildings, London.

McBurney, L.F. (1954) Hydrolytic degradation, in E. Ott and H. Sparlin (eds) *Cellulose and Cellulose Derivatives, Part 1*, Interscience, New York.

McConnell, C.T. (1990) Upgrading older high-temperature dry kilns, in M.P. Hamel and D. Robertson (eds) *Drying Softwood and Hardwood Lumber for Quality and Profit*, Forest Products Research Society, Proceedings 47356, Madison, USA, 31–39.

McCoy-Hill, M. (1967) *An Account of Deathwatch Beetle in Softwood*, The British Wood Preserving Association, News Sheet 71, 7–8.

McKimmey, M. (1966) A variation and heritability study of wood specific gravity in 46-year-old Douglas fir from known seed sources, *TAPPI*, **49** (12), 542–549.

McKimmey, M. (1971) Genetic differences in wood traits among half-century-old families of Douglas fir, *Wood and Fiber*, **2** (4), 247–355.

McKimmey, M. (1985) Stand management for the future, *Proceedings of Symposium on Douglas Fir*, University of Washington, Seattle, USA.

Mack, G.W. and Savory, J.G. (1952) A new treatment for walls infected with dry rot, *The Builder*, **182** (5706), 975–977.

Mangin, L. and Patouillard, N. (1922) Sur la déstruction des charpentes au Château de Versailles par le *Phellinus cryptarum* Karst., *Compte Rendu de l'Académie des Sciences*, **175** (9), 389.

Maxwell Lefroy, H. (1924) The treatment of the death watch beetle in timber roofs, *Journal of the Royal Society of Arts*, **52**, 260–266.

Meyer, O.E. (1970) On adult weight, oviposition preference and adult longevity in *Anobium punctatum* (Col. Anobiidae), *Zeitschrift für angewandte Entomologie, Sounderdruck aus Bd.*, **66**, 103–112.

Miller, U.V. (1932) *Points in the Biology and Diagnosis of House Fungi*, State Forestal Technical Publishing Office, Leningrad (Summary in 1933 *Review of Applied Mycology*, **12**, 257–259).

Milota, M.R. and Wengert, E.M. (1995) Applied drying technology 1988 to 1993, *Forest Products Journal*, **45** (5), 33–41.

Moore, G.L. (1983) The effect of long term temperature cycling on the strength of wood, *Journal of the Institute of Wood Science*, **9** (6), 264–267.

Mühlethaler, K. (1960) Die Feinstruktur der Zellulosemikrofibrillen, *Scheitzerische Zeitschrift für das Forstwesen*, Beihefte 30, 55–64.

Nature Conservancy Council (1991) *Bats in Roofs, a Guide for Surveyors*, Peterborough.

Nault, J. (1988), Radial distribution of thujaplicins in old growth and second growth Western red cedar, *Wood Science and Technology*, **22** (1), 73–80.

Nicol, W. (1820) in E. Sang (ed.) *The Planter's Kalender*, Edinburgh.

Nilsson, T. and Daniel, G. (1990) Structure and the ageing process of dry archaeological wood, in R.M. Rowell and R.J. Barbour (eds) *Archaeological Wood: Properties, Chemistry, and Preservation*, Advances in Chemistry Series 225, American Chemical Society, Washington, DC, 67–86.

Nisbet, J. (1905) *The Forester, a Practical Treatise on British Forestry and Arboriculture for Landowners, Land Agents and Foresters*, Volume 1, Blackwood, Edinburgh and London.

Orsler, R.J. (1983) A method for the consolidation of degraded wooden carvings from the ceiling of the House of Lords, Palace of Westminster, *Journal of the Institute of Wood Science*, **9** (6), 246–253.

Orton, P.D. and Watling, R. (1979) Coprinaceae Part 1: Coprinus. Part 2 of D.M. Henderson, P.D. Orton and R. Watling (eds) *British Fungus Flora Agarics and Boleti*, HMSO, Edinburgh.

Paine, S. (1998) *Bats in Churches, Guidelines for the Identification, Assessment and Management of Bat-related Damage to Church Contents*, English Heritage and English Nature, London.

Panshin, A.J. and DeZeew, C. (1980) *Textbook of Wood Technology*, 4th edn, McGraw-Hill, New York.

Parker, M., Hunt, K., Warren, W. and Kennedy, R. (1976) Effect of thinning and fertilisation on intra-ring characteristics and Kraft pulp yield of Douglas fir, *Applied Polymer Symposium*, **28**, 1075–1086.

Parkin, E.A. (1934) Observations on the biology of *Lyctus* powder-post beetles, with special reference to oviposition and the egg, *Annals of Applied Biology*, **21**, 495–518.

Parkin, E.A. (1940) The digestive enzymes of some wood-boring beetle larvae, *Journal of Experimental Biology*, **17**, 364–377.

Parkin, E.A. (1943) The moisture content of timber in relation to attack by *Lyctus* powder-post beetles, *Annals of Applied Biology*, **30**, 130–142.

Paton, R. and Creffield, J.W. (1987) The tolerance of some timber pests to atmospheres of carbon dioxide and carbon dioxide in air, *International Pest Control*, **29**, 10–12.

Paul, B. (1950) Wood quality in relation to site quality of second-growth Douglas fir, *Journal of Forestry*, **48** (3), 175–179.

Pegler, D.N. (1996) Hyphal analysis of Basidiomata, *Mycological Research*, **100** (2), 129–142.

Pillow, M. (1952) Some characteristics of young plantation-grown red pine in relation to properties of the wood, *Forest Products Journal*, **2** (1), 25–31.

Pinniger, D.B. and Child, R.E. (1996) Woodworm – a necessary case for treatment? New techniques for the detection and control of furniture beetle, *Proceedings of the International Conference on Insect Pests in the Urban Environment*, Edinburgh, 353–359.

Pitman, A., Jones, A. and Gareth Jones, E. (1993) The wharf borer *Nacerdes melanura* L: a threat to stored archaeological timber, *Studies in Conservation*, **38** (4), 274–285.

Pitman, A.J., Cragg, S.M. and Sawyer, G. (1994) *An Investigation of the Nutritional Physiology of the Wood Boring Weevil* Euophryum confine Brown, The International Research Group on Wood Preservation, Document No. IRG/WP 94-10082.

Plenderleith, H.J. and Werner, A.E.A. (1971) *The Conservation of Antiquities and Works of Art*, 2nd edn, Oxford University Press, London.

Price, T.J. (1952) Where should timber preservation start? *Record of the 1952 Annual Convention of the British Wood Preserving Association*, 37–57.

Rackham, O. (1986) *The History of the Countryside*, Dent, London.

Rackham, O. (1990) Medieval timber supply, *Understanding Timber Framed Buildings: Archaeology, Recording and Repair*, ICOMOS UK Wood Seminar, 27 October 1990, 1–9.

Raczkowski, J. (1963) The toughness of earlywood and latewood from Douglas fir of Polish origin, *Holzforschung*, **17** (6), 189–190.

Ramsay Smith, W. and Briggs, D.G. (1986) Juvenile wood: has it come of age? *Juvenile Wood: What Does it Mean to Forest Management and Forest Products?* Forest Products Research Society, Society of American Foresters, 5–11.

Ramsbottom, J. (1937) Dry rot in ships, *Essex Naturalist*, **25**, 231–267.

Rennerfelt, E. (1945) The influence of the phenolic compounds in the heartwood of Scots pine (*Pinus sylvestris*) on the growth of decay fungi in nutrient solution, *Svensk botanisk tidskrift*, **39**, (4), 311–318.

Richardson, B.A. (1993) *Wood Preservation*, 2nd edn, E. & F.N. Spon, London.

Richardson, S.A. (1977) *Protecting Buildings: How to Combat Dry Rot, Woodworm and Damp*, David & Charles, London.

Ridout, B.V. (1987) A revolutionary palace: its authentic restoration, *Architects Journal* (November), 59–67.

Ridout, B.V. (1989a) Dry rot and destruction, *Architects Journal: Renovation Supplement* (October), 28–33.

Ridout, B.V. (1989b) A tale of two castles, *Construction Repair*, **3**, (4), 10–12.

Ridout, B.V. (1999) The population dynamics of the deathwatch beetle, and how their mode of attack influences surface treatments, as demonstrated by Westminster Hall, London, *English Heritage Research Transactions*, Volume 5, in press.

Ridout, B. and Ridout, E. (1999) The effect of fungi on the growth of deathwatch beetle larvae and their ability to attack oak, Part 1: The concentration of available nitrogen, *English Heritage Research Transactions*, Volume 5, in press.

Rietz, R.C. and Page, R.H. (1975) Summarized guide for air-drying practices in *Lumber Drying Sourcebook, 40 Years of Practical Experience*, Forest Products Society, Madison, USA, 113–116.

Rook, A. (1985) *Arthropod Bites*, Marcel Dekker, New York.

Rosel, A. (1952) *The Breeding of Anobium. Preliminary Observations in Oviposition*, Commonwealth Scientific and Industrial Research Organisation, Progress Report 1.

Royal Institute of British Architects (1865) General advice to promoters on the restoration of ancient buildings, *Sessional Papers of the RIBA, 1864–1865*, London.

Royal Society of Arts (1783) Letter book: 27 December.

Rudman, P. and Da Costa, E.W.B. (1959) Variation in extractive content and decay resistance in the heartwood of *Tectona grandis* L.f, *Journal of the Institute of Wood Science*, **3**, 33–42.

Rundel, P.W. and Yoder, B.J. (1998) Ecophysiology of *Pinus*, in D.M. Richardson (ed.) *Ecology and Biogeography of* Pinus, Cambridge University Press, 296–323.

Saiki, H. (1970) Proportion of component layers in the tracheid wall of earlywood and latewood of some conifers, *Mokuzai Gakkaishi*, **16**, 244–249.

Samuels, R. and Prasad, D.K. (eds) (1994) *Global Warming and the Built Environment*, E. & F.N. Spon, London.

Sanders, C. (1985) Domestic dehumidifiers, *Building Services* (September), 93.

Sandwith, H. and Stainton, S. (1984) *The National Trust Manual of Housekeeping*, Allen Lane, London.

Sang, E. (ed.) (1820) *The Planter's Kalender* (by W. Nicol), Edinburgh.

Savory, J.G. (1954) Breakdown of timber by Ascomycetes and fungi imperfecti, *Annals of Applied Biology*, **41** (2), 236–247.

Savory, J.G. (1955) The role of microfungi in the decomposition of wood, *Record of the 1955 Annual Convention of the British Wood Preserving Association*, 3–35.

Savory, J.G. (1964) Dry rot: a reappraisal, *Record of the 1964 Annual Convention of the British Wood Preserving Association*, 69–76.

Savory, J.G. (1971) *Dry Rot – Causes and Remedies*, Timberlab Paper 44, Forest Products Research Laboratory, Princes Risborough.

Savory, J.G. (1980) *Treatment of Outbreaks of Dry Rot*

Serpula lacrymans, British Wood Preserving Association, News Sheet 160 (May).

Savory, T.H. (1928) *The Biology of Spiders*, Sidgwick & Jackson, London.

Schmidt, E.L. and Amburgey, T.L. (1994) Prevention of enzyme stain of hardwoods by log fumigation, *Forest Products Journal*, **44** (5), 32–34.

Schmidt, E.L. and French, D.W. (1976) *Aureobasidium pullulans* on wood shingles, *Forest Products Journal*, **26** (7), 34–37.

Schuch, K. (1937) Beiträge zur Ernährungsphysiologie der Larvae des Hausbockkäfers (*Hylotrupes bajulus* L.), *Zeitschrift für angewante Entomologie*, **23**, 547–548.

Schultze-Dewitz, G. (1958) Einfluss der soziologischen Stellung auf den Jahrringbau sowie auf die Hölzernte bei Kiefern, Birken und Lärchen eines Naturwaldes, *Holzzentralblatt*, **84** (65), 849–851.

Schweinfurth, J. and Ventur, D. (1991) TBTO and TBTN – safe and effective biocides for wood preservation, in R. Thompson (ed.) *The Chemistry of Wood Preservation*, The Royal Society of Chemistry, London, 192–223.

Seco, O.J. and Barra, M. (1996) Growth rate as a predictor of density and mechanical quality of sawn timber from fast-growing species', *Holz als Roh- und Werkstoff*, **54** (3), 171–174.

Sell, J. (1985) Long term measurements of wood moisture content in structural members, *Forest Products Journal*, **35** (11/12), 27–29.

Senft, J., Quanci, M. and Alan Beudtsen, B. (1986) *Property Profile of 60-year-old Douglas Fir in Juvenile Wood, What Does it Mean to Forest Management and Forest Products?* Forest Products Research Society, Madison, USA.

Serdjukova, I.R. (1993) Investigation of digestive enzymes of some wood-boring beetle larvae (*Coleoptera, Anobiidae*), *Zoologicheeky Zhurnal*, **72** (6), 43–51.

Serment, M.M. and Pruvost, A.M. (1991) Les Termites en France: Répartition Géographique, Propagation, Prophylaxie, Centre Technique du Bois et de l'Ameublement, *CTBA Info.*, **36**, 35–38.

Shain, L. (1979) Dynamic responses of differential sapwood to injury and infection, *Phytopathology*, **69**, 1143–1147.

Shigo, A.L. (1983) *Tree Defects: A Photo Guide*, United States Department of Agriculture, General Technical Report NE-82.

Siau, J.F. (1984) *Transport Processes in Wood*, Springer, New York.

Siau, J.F. (1995) *Wood: Influence of Moisture on Physical Properties*, Department of Wood Science and Forest Products, Virginia Polytechnic Institute and State University.

Simmonds, M., Belmain, S. and Blaney, W. (1999) Integrated pest management for the control of deathwatch beetles (*Xestobium rufovillosum De Geer*): trapping, *English Heritage Research Transactions*, Volume 5, in press.

Simonsen, J.L. (1954) Timber extractives, *Record of the 1954 Annual Convention of the British Wood Preserving Association*, 3–22.

Simpson, W.T. (1971) Equilibrium moisture content prediction for wood, *Forest Products Journal*, **21** (5), 48–49.

Simpson and Brown Architects (1995) *The Care of Historic Buildings and Ancient Monuments by Government Departments in Scotland*, Historic Scotland in consultation with the Conservation Unit of the Department of National Heritage, Edinburgh, 86.

Singer, J.T., Jackson, J.A. and Rice, R.W. (1995) Investigation of potential toxicity and mutagenicity of distillates from the drying of five species of wood, *Forest Products Journal*, **45** (5), 45–50.

Singh, J., Bech-Anderson, J., Elborne, A.S., Singh, S., Walker, B. and Goldie, F. (1994) The search for the wild dry rot fungus (*Serpula lacrymans*) in the Himalayas, *Journal of the Institute of Wood Science*, **13** (3), 411–413.

Skaar, C. (1964) Some factors involved in the electrical determination of moisture gradients in wood, *Forest Products Journal*, **84** (6), 239–243.

Skaar, C. (1988) *Wood–water Relations*, Springer, New York.

Slaytor, M. (1992) Cellulose digestion in termites and cockroaches: what role do symbionts play? *Comparative Biochemistry and Physiology*, **103b** (4), 775–784.

Smith, J. (1980) Influences of spacing in radial growth and percentage latewood of Douglas fir, Western hemlock and Western red cedar, *Canadian Journal of Forest Research*, **10** (2), 169–175.

Spalt, H.A. (1958) The fundamentals of water vapour sorption by wood, *Forest Products Journal*, **8**, 288–295.

Spiller, D. (1948a) Effect of humidity on hatching eggs of the common house borer *Anobium punctatum* de Geer, *New Zealand Journal of Science and Technology (Section B)*, **30** (3), 163–165.

Spiller, D. (1948b) An investigation into numbers of

eggs laid by field collected *Anobium punctatum* de Geer, *New Zealand Journal of Science and Technology (Section B)*, **30** (3), 153–162.

Spiller, D. (1964) Numbers of eggs laid by *Anobium punctatum* de Geer, *Bulletin of Entomological Research*, **55** (2), 305–311.

Sporne, K.R. (1965) *The Morphology of Gymnosperms*, Hutchinson University Library, London.

Sporne, K.R. (1974) *The Morphology of Angiosperms*, Hutchinson University Library, London.

Stamm, A.J. (1927) The electrical resistance of wood as a measurement of its moisture content, *Industrial Engineering and Chemistry*, **19** (9), 1021–1025.

Staniforth, S., Hayes, B. and Bullock, L. (1994) Appropriate technologies for relative humidity control for museum collections based in historic buildings, in A. Roy and P. Smith (eds) *Preventative Conservation Practice, Theory and Research*, The International Institute for Conservation of Historic and Artistic Works, London.

Stebbings, R.E. and Jefferies, D.J. (1982) *Focus on Bats, their Conservation and the Law*, Nature Conservancy Council, Peterborough.

Stephens, J.F. (1839) *A Manual of British Coleoptera*, Orme Brown, Green & Longmans, London.

Stobart, T.J. (1927) *The Timber Trade of the United Kingdom*, Crosby Lockwood & Son, London.

Stumbo, D.A. (1990) How and why stresses occur during wood drying, in M.P. Hamel and D. Robertson (eds) *Drying Softwood and Hardwood Lumber for Quality and Profit*, Forest Products Research Society, Proceedings 47356, Madison, USA, 69–73.

Synder, T.E. (1961) *Supplement to the Annotated Subject Heading Bibliography of the Termites 1955–1960*, Smithsonian Miscellaneous Collections, Washington DC, **143** (3).

Szabo, I. and Varga, F. (1995) Additional data on the occurence and biology of *Donkioporia expansa* (Desmaz) Kotl and Puzer, *Mikologiai Kozlemengek*, **34** (1), 53–58.

Taylor, F.W. (1994) An overview of wood moisture relations, *Profitable Solutions for Quality Drying of Softwoods and Hardwoods*, Forest Products Society, Madison, USA, 29–30.

Taylor, G.D. and West, D.J. (1990) Use of stainless steel pins for in-situ measurements of moisture contents in the structural members of a glulam-framed church, *Journal of the Institute of Wood Science*, **12** (2), 71–76.

Taylor, J.M. (1963) Studies on *Theocolax formiciformis* Westw. (Hym. Pteromalidae) a parasite of *Anobium punctatum* (Deg.), (Col. Anobiidae), *Bulletin of Entomological Research*, **54** (4), 797–803.

Thomson, G. (1986) *The Museum Environment*, 2nd edn, Butterworths, London.

Thompson, W.S. (1982) Adverse environments and related design considerations: chemical effects, in R.W. Meyer and R.M. Kellogg (eds) *Structural Use of Wood in Adverse Environments*, Van Nostrand Reinhold, New York, 117–130.

Tiemann, H.D. (1906) *Effect of Moisture upon the Strength and Stiffness of Wood*, United States Department of Agriculture Forest Services, Bulletin 70.

Toth, L. (1952) The role of nitrogen-active micro-organisms in the nitrogen metabolism of insects, *Tijdschrift voor Entomologie*, **95**, 43–59.

Tsoumis, G. (1991) *Science and Technology of Wood: Structure, Properties, Utilization*, Van Nostrand Reinhold, New York.

Uetz, G.W. (1992) Foraging strategies of spiders, *Trends in Ecology and Evolution*, **7** (5), 155–159.

United Nations Environment Programme, Industry and Environment/Programme Activity Centre (1994) *Environmental Aspects of Industrial Wood Preservation, a Technical Guide*, United Nations, France.

Uusvaara, O. (1974) Wood quality in plantation-grown Scots pine, *Metsantutkimuslaitoksen Julkaisuja*, **80** (2), 1–109.

Venebles, R. (1993) The supply of timber for repair, in *The Timber Frame from Preservation to Reconstruction*, ICOMOS UK Timber Seminar, Haydock Park.

Vermaas, H.F. (1975) A summary of literature references of factors affecting moisture content determination with DC resistance measurements, *South African Forestry Journal*, **95** (December), 35–36.

Viitanen, H. and Paajanen, L. (1988) *The Critical Moisture and Temperature Conditions for the Growth of Some Mould Fungi and the Brown Rot Fungus Coniophora puteana on Wood*, The International Research Group on Wood Preservation, Document No. IRG/WP/1369.

Viitanen, H. and Ritschkoff, A-C. (1991a) *Brown Rot Decay in Wooden Constructions, Effect of Temperature, Humidity and Moisture*, Swedish University of Agricultural Sciences, Department of Forest Products, Report No. 222.

Viitanen, H. and Ritschkoff, A-C. (1991b) *Mould Growth in Pine and Spruce Sapwood in Relation to Air Humidity and Temperature*, Swedish University of Agricultural Sciences, Department of Forest Products Report, No. 221.

Vinden, P. and Butcher, J.A. (1991) Wood preservation: strategies for the future, in R. Thompson (ed.) *The Chemistry of Wood Preservation*, The Royal Society of Chemistry, London.

Wade, T. (1815) *A Treatise on the Dry Rot in Timber*, Cadell & Davies, London.

Wangaard, F.F. and Granados, L.A. (1967) The effect of extractives on water vapour sorption by wood, *Wood Science and Technology*, **1**, 253–277.

Waangart, F. and Lumwalt, E. (1949) Some strength properties of second-growth Douglas fir, *Journal of Forestry*, **47** (1), 18–24.

Wengert, E.M. (1990) Chemical stain and stain control in hardwood lumber drying, in M.P. Hamel and D. Robertson (eds) *Drying Softwood and Hardwood Lumber for Quality and Profit*, Forest Products Research Society, Proceedings 47356, Madison, USA, 81–84.

Wengert, G. and Denig, J. (1995) Lumber drying today and tomorrow, *Forest Products Journal*, **45** (5), 22–30.

White, P.R. and Birch, M.C. (1987) Female sex pheromone of the common furniture beetle *Anobium punctatum* (Coleoptera: Anobiidae), *Journal of Chemical Ecology*, **13** (7), 1695–1706.

Williams, L.H. (1977) Responses of *Xyletinus peltatus* (Harris) (Coleoptera: Anobiidae) larvae to favourable and unfavourable temperatures, *Material und Organismen*, **12** (1), 59–67.

Williams, L.H. (1983) Wood moisture levels affect *Xyletinus peltatus* infestations, *Environmental Entomology*, **12** (1), 135–140.

Williams, L.H. (1997) Laboratory and field testing of borades used as pesticides, *Second International Conference on Wood Protection with Diffusible Preservatives*, Forest Products Society, Madison, USA.

Wimmer, R. (1995) Intra-annular cellular characteristics and their implications for modelling softwood density, *Wood and Fiber Science*, **27** (4), 413–420.

Wise, D.H. (1993) *Spiders in Ecological Webs*, Cambridge Studies in Ecology, Cambridge University Press.

Wise, L.E. and John, E.C. (1952) *Wood Chemistry*, 2nd edn, Vol. 2, Reinhold, New York.

Wyman, R.L. ed. (1991) *Global Climate Change and Life on Earth*, Routledge, Chapman & Hall, New York.

Yli Vakkuri: (1955) Moose damage in seedling stands of pine in Osthrobothnia, *Silva Fennica*, **88**, 3.

Zabel, R.A. and Morrell, J.J. (1992) *Wood Mycology*, Academic Press, London.

Zobel, B., Kellison, R. and Kirk, D. (1972) Wood properties of young loblolly and slash pines, *Proceedings of the Symposium on the Effect of Growth Acceleration on the Properties of Wood*, Forest Products Research Laboratory, Madison, USA.

Index

contact 38, 49, 50, 70, 103
crystalline 53
cyclodiene 38
development of 38–9
health risk from 57
paste with 53
smoke generated 53–4
solvent-based 70
unnecessary treatment with 72
Insects 24, 30, 31, 89, 105
bats' diet of 112
damage caused by 25–7
growth regulators 75
minor decay 65–75
specialized 23
substances toxic to 101
see also Beetles; Larvae
Insulation 147
Invertebrates 30
Ireland 37
Irish Republican Brotherhood 181
Iron fastenings 34–5
Iron tannate 35
Irrigation 87, 88, 186
Isobutane 104
Isolation of timbers 157–8
Isopropyl 104

Jackson (London chemist) 100
Japan 69
Johnson, J. 184–5
Joinery 17, 125, 138, 146, 147, 186
dismantling 149
little point in salvaging 148
new 86, 88, 89
pretreatment of 104–5
softwood 93
Joints 17, 31, 41, 50, 186
burnt 89
loose 131
Joists 61, 77, 129, 133, 140, 147
Juvenile wood 13–14, 15, 137, 138
fungal attack 23, 24

Kamesan, Sonti 102
Keenlyside, J. J. 47
'Kenford-Death-watch-Beetle
Fluid' 38
Kent 65
Lees Court 206–7
Kerosene 103
Kiln drying 36, 69–70, 75, 103,
121–5
Kilns 78–9
Körting, A. 66
Kyan (pretreatment expert) 100–1

Kyte, C. T. 161

Lamellae 6, 7, 8
Landfill sites 109
Larch 135
Larvae 25–6, 27
clerid beetle 176
death watch beetle 39, 43, 50,
53, 183
furniture beetle 41–2, 51, 58–9,
60, 64, 177
house longhorn beetle 65, 66
pinhole and shothole borer 72
powder post beetle 70
termite 74
wasp 176
weevil 71
wharf borer 72
Lateral restraint 17
Latewood 10, 14, 15, 32, 106, 132,
137
orientation 17
Lavatory pans 72
Lead 48
roofing 36
salt deposition 34
Leak detection 166
Leaves 10, 76
Legislation *see* Regulations
Leningrad 84
Life cycles 27, 49, 71
Light
absorption 8
attraction to 54, 70
dead weevils found around 71
visible and UV 32
Lignin 5, 6, 7, 10, 12, 59, 102
decreased production 15
degradation of 32, 33
excreted in frass 71
fire damage and 31
fungi unable to break down
29–30
photo-degradation of 18
substantially modified 29
thermal softening of 32
Lime 56, 100
Lindane 39, 49, 53, 54, 70, 105
Lingard, J. 77
Linings 17, 148
Linscott, D. 70
Linseed oil 56
Lintels 37, 86, 140
Lisburn, Co. Antrim 65
Lloyd, H. 89, 163–4
Lloyd, J. D. 105

Locke, P. 50
Logs 72, 122
air-seasoned 70
decomposing 27
felled 23, 119, 120
narrow 138
squaring 131
London 53, 65, 71, 77, 100, 186
Chancery Lane 185
Deptford 72, 76
House of Lords 32
Imperial College 56
Limehouse 185
Milestone Hotel 142
St Pancras Chambers 33
St Pancras Parish Church 72
Westminster Hall 38, 52, 56,
180–4
Woolwich Dockyard 78–9, 101,
102
Longhorn beetles
forest 66, 67
two-toothed 67
see also House longhorn beetle
Longitudinal shrinkage/changes 14,
16
Lowry process 103
Lukin (kiln constructor) 78–9, 100
Lumen 29
Lures 62

Magnesium silica fluoride 89
Mammals 49, 105
Mangin, L. 96
Margary. 101
Margo 8
Marine environments 30
Masonry 92, 104, 129, 135
biocides 88
damp 83, 86
drying of 151, 153
moisture monitoring 165
saturated 80
Mature wood 13, 14–15
longitudinal changes 16
Maxwell Lefroy, H. 38, 45, 52, 56,
59
Medieval timbers 17, 54
Mediterranean 73, 74
Melanin 92
Membranes 89, 158
pit 19, 28
Mercuric chloride 38, 100, 101
Metabolic products 14
Metabolism 41, 120
Metabolites 12